Practicing Perfection
Memory and Piano Performance

Expertise: Research and Applications
*Robert R. Hoffman, Nanacy J. Cooke, K. Anders Ericsson, Gary
Klein, Eduardo Salas, Dean K. Simonton, Robert J. Sternberg,
and Christopher D. Wickens,* Series Editors

Practicing Perfection
Memory and Piano Performance

Roger Chaffin
University of Connecticut

Gabriela Imreh

Mary Crawford
University of Connecticut

Psychology Press
Taylor & Francis Group

New York London

Copyright © 2002 by Lawrence Erlbaum Associates, Inc.

Lawrence Erlbaum Associates, Inc., Publishers
10 Industrial Avenue
Mahwah, NJ 07430

Library of Congress Cataloging-in-Publication Data

Chaffin, Roger.
Practicing perfection : memory and piano performance / Roger Chaffin, Gabriela Imreh, Mary Crawford.
    p. cm.
Includes bibliographical references (p.), discography (p.), and index.
ISBN 0-8058-2610-6 (cloth : alk. paper)
1. Piano–Instruction and study. 2. Music–Memorizing. 3. Piano—Performance. 4. Piano—Performance—Psychological aspects.
I. Imreh, Gabriela. II. Crawford, Mary (Mary E.) III. Title.
MT220 .C473 2002
786.2'143—dc21   2001053240
                                                        CIP

10 9 8 7 6 5 4 3 2 1

In memory of John Stephen Chaffin,
who loved the piano
—R.C. & M.C.

❧ ❧ ❧ ❧

To my husband Dan,
who provided continuous inspiration and support
for the writing of this book
—G.I.

Contents

Series Editor's Foreword

The initial motivation for Roger Chaffin, Gabriela Imreh, and Mary Crawford's project came when Imreh—a professional musician—recognized that ideas in the cognitive psychology of expertise were not just pertinent to her work as a musician, but were actually helpful in her practice. What ensued was a collaboration among a cognitive psychologist, a concert pianist, and a social psychologist. Both the methods the researchers adopted, and the way they present the material are innovative. This makes for a creative case study in cognitive field research. Not just for individuals interested in musical expertise, or even the broader relations between memory and performance, this book could have a substantial impact, both on expertise studies and piano pedagogy.

—*Robert R. Hoffman*
Pensacola, FL
December 2001

Preface

We have all experienced the fascination and awe of witnessing a world class performance, whether a musician in a virtuoso rendition, an ice skater making triple axel leaps, or a kayaker hurtling down a class six rapid. Most of us have also marveled at the skill that makes such feats possible. For example, the performance of even a moderately complex piano piece places incredible demands on memory and physical dexterity, requiring the execution of between 10 and 20 notes a second for minutes on end. How does a performer remember it all, hitting every note, and at the same time give an aesthetically satisfying performance? Practice, of course, is part of the answer—to make the performance automatic. Still, how can a performance that is totally automatic be aesthetically satisfying? What does the performer think about as the fingers fly across the keyboard? What happens if something goes wrong?

To answer these questions, we convened an unlikely trio: a concert pianist and two psychologists. The pianist, Gabriela Imreh, videotaped her practice as she learned the third movement, *Presto*, of the *Italian Concerto* for a CD of works by J. S. Bach (Imreh, 1996). The CD that accompanies this book contains the performance that marked the end point of the learning process. (The CD includes the entire concerto, although our study was confined to the learning of the third movement, *Presto*.) The *Presto* is not unusually difficult, but it is hard to memorize. Its rapid tempo provides little opportunity for the performer to think ahead, while its recurring themes require close tracking of what comes next. Retrieval from long-term memory must be rapid and automatic. This made it the perfect choice for our study, since it turned out that the answers to all our questions were to be found in the process of memorization.

The initial impetus for the study came when Roger Chaffin, a cognitive psychologist, offered to talk to Gabriela's students about memory. Gabriela was struck by how well cognitive psychology's understanding of expert memory meshed with her own experience of memorizing and preparing for performance. As the conversations that followed grew into collaboration, Mary Crawford, a social psychologist, joined the team in order to record how two people from such different backgrounds could work out the differences between their viewpoints to arrive at a common understanding. We have tried to make the resulting story accessible to both psychologists and musicians. For psychologists, the tale is one of how principles of memorization developed in the laboratory apply in a real-world domain where people make a living performing from memory. For musicians, the story is how these principles can shed new light on the mysterious process of memorizing for performance and so help make practice more effective.

We begin by reminding the reader of the bottom line in a performer's life—the numbing fear and the adrenaline rush of stepping onto the concert stage in front of an audience. Chapter 1 describes a day-in-the-life of a concert pianist—the day of a recital. Performance is the crucible in which the hours of preparation and practice are put to the test, and we want you, the reader, to have this clearly in mind as you learn, in later chapters, what goes into that preparation. Chapter 2 tells how our collaboration came about and the issues it raised. Whose viewpoint would our description of the learning process represent? Performer and scientist speak to different audiences, with different goals, rhetorical strategies, and ideas of what counts as evidence. To the extent that we have succeeded in providing insights into the creation of a performance, it is because we were able to harness the creative tension inherent in these differences.

Given the difficulty of playing long, complicated programs flawlessly from memory, and the public humiliation that attends memory lapses, it might be expected that the pedagogical traditions in music schools and conservatories would include detailed strategies for addressing the problems involved. This proves not to be so. Conservatory training provides plenty of experience with performance, but memorization is seen as a largely idiosyncratic matter. Chapter 3 makes this point by analyzing interviews with well known pianists in which they talk about memory and performance. Their comments reveal widespread agreement about the primacy of auditory and motor memory and a consensus that there are large individual differences in the use of visual memory. In contrast, the form of memory most studied by psychologists, conceptual or declarative memory, is scarcely mentioned. There is plenty of discussion of particular manifestations of conceptual memory, e.g., the importance of architecture or musical form, but rarely in the context of memorization. The pianists seem to think of memorizing as something quite distinct from the study of musical form or harmonic structure. If true, this would mean that musical memory is different from other types of expert memory.

One of the hallmarks of expertise is an ability to memorize with a facility that often seems superhuman. Musicians are no exception. The biographies of famous performers are full of tales of amazing memory feats, and Gabriela has some of her own to tell. Psychologists have been able to explain the memory abilities of other kinds of experts in terms of general principles of memory. Their research has, however, focused on domains like memory for chess games and digit strings in which the memory is largely conceptual (or declarative). It is not immediately obvious that the same principles would account for the memory feats of musicians. Conceptual memory may be much less important in music, because motor and auditory memory are so much more central.

We suggest in chapter 4 that, contrary to what many pianists appear to think, conceptual memory is important in musical performance. Gabriela reported that one of her main challenges in learning the *Presto* was integrating "hands and head." Her fingers were playing the notes just fine. It was her mind (conceptual memory) that needed the practice, to keep up with the rapid pace of the performance. The solution was the practice of *performance cues*, or features of the music selected for attention during performance. During practice, a pianist must make many decisions about basic issues, e.g., fingering, and interpretation , e.g., phrasing, whose implementation becomes automatic. This allows the pianist to select particular features or aspects of the music to pay attention to in performance, e.g., a tricky fingering or critical phrasing. Gabriela reported that she selects particular features to attend to and practices thinking of them as she plays so that they come to mind automatically during performance, along with the associated motor responses. These performance cues become the retrieval cues that automatically elicit the music from conceptual memory as the performance unfolds.

During practice, attention is directed mainly toward problems. In performance, however, problems must recede into the background so that musical expressiveness can take center stage, both in the mind of the performer and, as a result, in the aesthetic experience of the audience. This transformation does not happen by magic, but requires preparation.

Gabriela reports that, in the weeks before a performance, she practices attending to a new kind of performance cue, *expressive cues*, which represent the feelings she wants to convey to the audience, e.g., surprise, gaiety, or excitement. Expressive goals are identified earlier, but in this final phase of practice their use as memory retrieval cues is deliberately rehearsed. The result is a reorganization of the retrieval hierarchy, adding a new level of expressive cues at the top. This "re-chunking" allows the performer to play while focusing on expressive goals, that automatically elicit from memory all the detailed decisions and complex motor responses built up over the weeks and months of practice.

It was these ideas about the role of performance cues in memorization that we set out to examine in the tapes of the practice sessions. The tapes also provided, as an incidental benefit, the opportunity to see how a concert pianist practices. Psychologists have been interested in discovering how much and what kinds of practice are necessary to reach and maintain high levels of skill. For example, it requires an absolute minimum of ten years to reach a professional level of competence in any field, and continued practice is needed to maintain and develop these skills over the course of a career. Little is known, however, about how experts practice. In chapter 5, we describe the few studies of skilled musicians' practice, with an eye to identifying characteristics that might distinguish the practice of experts from that of less experienced musicians. If the route to expertise involves thousands of hours of practice, then even small increases in efficiency may yield large savings in time or improvements in performance.

The studies of music practice described in chapter 5 provide a wealth of empirical detail, but few tools for testing theoretical claims about memorization. Could our tapes of Gabriela's practice sessions provide evidence to support her claims about practicing and "re-chunking" performance cues? In the remainder of the book, we describe how we developed the necessary tools and used them to answer our questions. Chapter 6 describes the milestones of the learning process, dividing the preparation of the *Presto* into six stages and showing how quantitative measures of practice changed from one stage to the next. This outsider's perspective on the learning process is complemented in chapter 7 with an inside story. As she practiced, Gabriela often paused to comment on what she was doing. Her comments show how the problems she worked on changed as learning progressed.

Chapter 8 brings the insider and outsider perspectives together, linking the practice of particular passages to the problems they contain. Three months after recording the *Presto*, Gabriela sat down with copies of the score and noted every decision she had made in learning the piece, every feature she had paid attention to, and every cue she had used in performance. When these features were laid alongside the detailed records of practice, they provided the key that unlocked the secrets of the practice records. We were able to see how some kinds of features dominated practice more than others, and how these changed over time. Gabriela was astonished at how her innermost thoughts were revealed. In particular, we could point to sessions, early on, in which expressive goals first began to shape her practice and then the re-emergence of these goals during the final polishing of the piece.

At this point, we return to the question of memorization. Do the principles of expert memory, developed to account for memory for chess games and digit strings, apply to concert pianists? Did the pianist use a retrieval organization and practice the use of retrieval cues? The answer is a resounding, "Yes!" Gabriela went to great lengths to ensure that she could rely on conceptual as well as motor and auditory memory, engaging in prolonged practice so that her conceptual representation of the piece could keep up with the tempo of the performance. These efforts left their mark on practice, affecting where playing started and stopped, where hesitations occurred when Gabriela began to play from memory, and how well the music was recalled when she wrote out part of the score from memory two years later.

The final two chapters integrate our conclusions. Chapter 10 returns to the stages of the learning process introduced in chapter 6, filling out the description with insights gained from the in-depth analyses of practice and comments. Chapter 11 summarizes what we learned about memorization and about the characteristics of expert practice. We conclude by considering what we each learned from our collaboration and how it changed us as scientists, musicians, and friends.

ACKNOWLEDGMENTS

Many people have contributed to the work described in this book. First, we thank the undergraduate students who collectively put in thousands of hours of work transcribing the practice and compiling the data. Ellie Corbett, Jennifer Culler, and Elizabeth Dohm at Furman University were the first to take on this enormous task and helped develop the methods we used. Aaron Williamon and Helene Govin at the University of South Carolina continued the work and brought order to the huge data base that was developing. The division of practice into work and runs (chap. 6), done by Aaron, formed the basis of his undergraduate honors thesis at the University of South Carolina. Ben Chaffin provided critical technical help by writing the program that converted practice records into the elegant graphs and quantitative measures reported in chapter 6. Amelia McCloskey and Sandra Paez at The College of New Jersey compiled the practice records for input to this program. Together with Alethea Pape, they also transcribed the comments Gabriela made during practice. Julie Konik at West Chester University undertook the content analysis of these comments (chap. 7). Helma de Vries at The College of New Jersey developed the measurements of bar duration reported in chapter 9. Michelle Moore, at the University of Connecticut prepared the bar graphs in chapters 6 and 7, and Helen Morales typed the interview excerpts reproduced in chapter 3. The index was prepared, with great attention to detail, by Barbara Stroup.

This book would not have been completed without the advice and encouragement of many colleagues and friends. In particular we thank Daniel Spalding, who provided help and assistance at every stage. He was the audience for Gabriela's first practice performances, and provided her with advice and discussion of interpretive decisions, in addition to setting up and maintaining the video camera used to record practice. As we wrote, Dan read and commented on successive drafts, making helpful suggestions and encouraging us to write for musicians as well as for psychologists. Dan also compiled the bibliography of sources used in selecting the excerpts from interviews with pianists in chapter 3.

We are indebted to Carola Grindea, whose invitation to give a workshop on memorization at the London meeting of the European Piano Teachers Association (EPTA) provided the stimulus that first began our collaboration. Judi Amsel, our first editor at Lawrence Erlbaum Associates, encouraged us as we struggled to shape our ideas into book form, and Bill Webber, who took over as our editor, saw the process through and saved us from making the book too long. Bruno Repp and Andreas Lehmann read the entire manuscript, making many helpful suggestions and saving us from inaccuracies. Rita Aiello and Blair Johnson provided helpful comments on chapters 3 through 5. Dan Phillips provided statistical advice about the interpretation of the regression analyses. Finally, thanks to the many others who encouraged us along the way by their interest in our work.

I also want to thank the departments of psychology at Furman University, the University of South Carolina, The College of New Jersey, and the University of Connecticut that provided me with congenial places to work, colleagues to share ideas with, and laboratory space and equipment, while this work was in progress. The compilation and analysis of the practice records were supported by faculty research grants from The College of New Jersey, and the final preparation of the book manuscript was supported by a Chancellor's Fellowship from the University of Connecticut.

—Roger Chaffin
December 2001

ONE

In the Green Room

Mary Crawford

Take the deepest of breaths and watch for a tremble; the recital is about to begin.
—Noah Adams, *Piano Lessons*

T he green room is a lonely place, however crowded it may be. In the green room—performing artists' generic name for the place they wait before going on stage—the laser focus of a great performance must gather its intensity.

It is Sunday, October 12, 1997, two-thirty in the afternoon, and I am in the green room with Gabriela Imreh. This particular green room, at Trinity Cathedral, Trenton, New Jersey, is less than luxurious. It seems to be a dressing room for clergy and a catchall for church equipment. The room is quite cold with a high ceiling. Vestment cupboards line the wall. Tables scattered around the room are crowded with flower vases, brass candlesticks, hymnals, and old programs from services.

Still it is better than some. Another time, I accompanied Gabriela to a recital at a well-known college of the performing arts, where the green room, a basement with dripping pipes, was also a thoroughfare for custodial staff. I improvised a screen from my coat while she slipped into her gown for the performance. Rather than be dripped on, she did her hair while standing in the wings. I remember watching her fasten the tiny clasp of a necklace, her hands steady and quick, minutes before stepping on stage to play the gigantic Bach–Busoni Chaconne.

When a live performance works—when the technical proficiency, the aesthetic sensibility, the rapport between the audience and performer come together—beauty is created. When it doesn't work—when there is memory failure, technical or aesthetic limitation, debilitating performance anxiety, or a mismatch between audience and performer—the result is painful to all. Live performance persists in an age of technically perfect recording precisely because of the tension, uncertainty, and excitement of real-time music making. Literally, anything can happen.

Gabriela, still in her street clothes, hangs her stage dress from a doorjamb and goes on stage to try the piano. Her program today is demanding:

Chromatic Fantasy and Fugue in D minor (BVW 903), J.S. Bach

Sonata No. 14 in C-sharp minor, Op. 27, No. 2 (Moonlight), L. van Beethoven

Etude, Op. 12, No. 12, "Revolutionary," Frederic Chopin

Nocturne, Op. 27, No. 2 Preludes, Op. 28, Nos. 22, 23, 24, Frederic Chopin

Intermission

Two Valses-Caprices from "Soirées de Vienne," Franz Liszt

Aprés une lecture de Dante "Dante Sonata," Franz Liszt

We have an hour before the performance. The cathedral is empty, the Baldwin grand standing ready at the front outside the altar rail. Gabriela begins her warmup with the slow movement of the *Moonlight Sonata*, then runs through one of the waltzes from *"Soirées de Vienne."* A big, powerful passage from the *Dante Sonata* is next, followed—incongruously—by *"Flight of the Bumblebee,"* a much played encore this season. Next she takes on some fast runs from the third movement of the *Moonlight*, more bits from the *Dante Sonata*, another waltz. After 20 minutes of concentrated work, she stands up, stretches, and returns to the piano to try a particularly difficult passage from the *Dante Sonata*. She fumbles, takes a wrong turn, and loses her direction. She plays it again and then a third time before getting through the passage without a mistake.

It is now after 3:00 p.m., less than half an hour before the performance. She has not played a single note of the difficult opening piece, the *Chromatic*

Fantasy and Fugue. Unlike many pianists, who open recitals with a warmup piece that is not particularly difficult for them, Gabriela almost always chooses a big, demanding work. She says that she prefers to do the hardest thing first, rather than have it "hanging over" her throughout the first half of the performance. (Typically, she has chosen to make huge demands on herself at both ends of the performance, ending today's recital with the virtuoso *Dante Sonata*.) I know that the Bach fantasy and fugue, with its difficult polyphonic structure, has given her memory problems in the past. I am starting to get very nervous. My hands and feet are cold, and the muscles in my shoulders and back are tense. At 3:05, she stands again, stretches, and walks to the back of the cathedral. She talks about the piano. "It's good," she says, though a bit "flimsy" in the touch. "It can run away from you if you're not careful." Back at the instrument, she riffs through a few short passages from the *Chromatic Fantasy*. To me, they seem like random bits, her practice without focus. By now I can hardly write my notes; my hands are shaking and my movements clumsy. My breath is shallow, my chest constricted. Empathy—and memories of my days in music school—make the waiting and watching almost unbearable.

Much of Gabriela's practice in the hour before the performance seems aimed at getting to know the instrument. Only a few artists can afford to have their own piano shipped with them on tour. The rest are at the mercy of out-of-shape, unreliable instruments (not to mention equally out-of-shape and unreliable technicians and tuners). Gabriela often plays in small towns where the community's sole concert piano may not have been played or tuned for months at a time. Tales of performances sabotaged by the piano-from-Hell are a fixture of pianists' lives. Perhaps none surpasses this one, seen through the eyes of a music critic:[1]

A Humid Recital Stirs Bangkok

A hush fell over the room as Mr. Kropp appeared from the right of the stage, bowed to the audience and placed himself upon the stool.

As I have mentioned on several occasions, the Baldwin Concert Grand, while basically a fine instrument, needs constant attention, particularly in a climate such as Bangkok. . . . In this humidity, the felts which separate the white keys from the black tend to swell, causing an occasional key to stick, which apparently was the case last evening with the D in the second octave.

During the "raging storm" section of the D minor Toccata and Fugue, Mr. Kropp must be complimented for putting up with the awkward D. However, by the time the "storm" was past and he had gotten into the Prelude and Fugue in D Major, in which the second octave D plays a major role, Mr. Kropp's patience was wearing thin.

Some who attended the performance later questioned whether the awkward key justified some of the language, which was heard coming from the stage during softer passages of the fugue. . . . [O]ne member of the audience had a valid point when he commented over the music and extemporaneous remarks of Mr. Kropp that the workman who had greased the stool might have done better to use some of the grease on the second octave D. Indeed, Mr. Kropp's stool had more than enough grease and during one passage in which the music and lyrics were both particularly violent, Mr. Kropp was turned completely around. Whereas before his remarks had been aimed largely at the piano and were therefore somewhat muted, to his surprise and that of those in the chamber music room he found himself addressing himself directly to the audience. . . .

Mr. Kropp appeared somewhat shaken. Nevertheless, he swiveled himself back into position facing the piano, and leaving the D Major fugue unfinished, commenced on the Fantasia and Fugue in G Minor.

Why the concert grand piano's G key in the third octave chose that particular time to be sticking I hesitate to guess. However, it is certainly safe to say that Mr. Kropp himself did nothing to help matters when he began using his feet to kick the lower portion of the piano instead of operating the pedals as is generally done.

Possibly it was this jarring or un-Bach-like hammering to which the sticking keyboard was being subjected. Something caused the right front leg of the piano to buckle slightly inward; leaving the entire instrument listing at approximately a 35-degree angle from that which is normal. A gasp went up from the audience, for if the piano had actually fallen several of Mr. Kropp's toes, if not both his feet, would surely have been broken.

It was with a sigh of relief therefore, that the audience saw Mr. Kropp slowly rise from his stool and leave the stage. A few men in the back of the room began clapping and when Mr. Kropp reappeared a moment later it seemed he was responding to the ovation. Apparently, however, he had left to get a red-handled fire ax, which was hung back stage in case of fire, for that was what was in his hand.

My first reaction at seeing Mr. Kropp begin to chop at the left leg of the grand piano was that he was attempting to make it tilt at the same angle as the right leg and thereby correct the list. However, when the weakened legs finally collapsed altogether with a great crash and Mr. Kropp continued to chop, it became obvious to all that he had no intention of going on with the concert.

The ushers, who had heard the snapping of piano wires and splintering of sounding board from the dining room, came rushing in and, with the help of the hotel manager, two Indian watchmen, and a passing police corporal, finally succeeded in disarming Mr. Kropp and dragging him off the stage.

Perhaps pianists like to repeat tales like these because they deflect attention from the less tangible factors affecting their performance. Every soloist lives with the threat of performance anxiety and memory failure, which can disrupt and destroy the aesthetics of a musical moment as surely as a collapsing piano.

Mountain climbers say that altitude sickness is totally unpredictable: The same climb, under the same weather conditions, can be easy or impossible depending on the body's response. For pianists, the magnitude and effects of anxiety are unpredictable. Many pianists believe that a moderate level of tension before a performance makes it better. Gabriela has said that the worst recital she ever played, years earlier, was preceded by an unusual level of calm. Moreover, they do not believe that high anxiety necessarily leads to poor performance. Just last year, Gabriela says, she was "sick for a week" with anxiety before an important concert with the Hong Kong Philharmonic—a concert where her performance of the *Rhapsody on a Theme of Paganini* drew stellar reviews.

Performance anxiety feels terrible. Noah Adams, host of National Public Radio's *All Things Considered*, has described his first recital as an adult piano student. Adams played a short, easy piece for an audience of other beginners, a long way from the kinds of situations that professional pianists confront, but he well knows how fear feels and how it can affect one's playing:

> There's a coppery taste in my mouth, and my hands are cold. . . . I can play the prelude pretty well, I don't know how to factor in the fear. . . . I walk around the backyard, telling myself that it's only a bit of piano playing in front of people I know and like and that I'm on the radio every evening talking to more than a million strangers. I make a cup of peppermint tea, mostly just to hold and keep my hands warmed. The recital starts. . . . And suddenly I'm at the piano. . . . The name of my piece has been announced, so there's really nothing for me to say. I adjust the knobs on the sides of the piano bench. I take off my glasses. . . . I push the wooden frame holding the music back two inches, place my foot on the right pedal, and push it down to feel the tension. My hands wait above the first notes. I hear the phrase in my mind . . . and begin.
>
> It's like skating very, very fast on dangerous ice, being pushed by the wind with no way to slow down. I don't feel over-the-top nervous, but as I begin the graceful eleven-note run up three octaves with my right hand, it starts to shake. Drastically. I'm still playing the correct keys, I think, but it's scary to see your hand shake like that. I miss a few notes, just leaving them behind. . . . The middle part's coming up; I could collapse right here. I slow down for it, but I can still hear the bad notes clanging like a pinball machine. . . . Then I'm thankfully into the last eight measures. . . . The soft ending chord comes up—I look at the keyboard, so I won't make a horrendous final mistake. . .
>
> A half-hour later I'm standing in the kitchen, drinking a beer, accepting compliments. It's an athletic glow—an after race satisfaction. (Adams, 1996, pp. 197–201)

It is now 3:14 p.m. Audience members are approaching the cathedral, and Gabriela is still out front in her street clothes. We head to the green room. I realize that allowing herself only a few minutes to dress is a deliberate strategy. Keeping busy, she says, helps alleviate anxiety. Right now, my own empathic anxiety is reaching an extremely unpleasant peak. I wish this were all over and we could go home.

Many performing artists develop superstitious routines for the time leading up to performance. Gabriela has her own coping strategies for the entire day of a performance. When I arrived at her house at midmorning, she was busy practicing. Her practice piano, a Kawai grand, had several broken strings, the result of being used for 6 or more hours a day; it sounded tinny and sharp. Because Gabriela has perfect pitch, an out-of-tune piano is not only aesthetically painful, but can interfere with memory retrieval. However, she feels comfortable with her familiar Kawai, her dog Daisy at her station underneath.

She had practiced slowly, playing short sections from the day's program—from a few bars to perhaps 3 minutes in length. When I asked about her strategy, she said that it is aimed at avoiding becoming tired before the performance, "not giving yourself away too soon." Yesterday she had done a "huge workout" on the D minor fugue; today she had "imagined it" instead of actually playing it. This strategy, she said, "works only if you really know it."

Usually she does not eat before a performance, but today she insisted on fixing lunch for me. Quickly, she sliced cucumber, carrot, and a slippery-ripe avocado. Is she nervous, I wondered? Morbid thoughts of the danger to her hands came to mind. Gabriela does not allow herself to do any sports that might lead to hand or wrist injury—no skating, tennis, or racquetball for her. But she is a fearless, creative cook, with an armory of chopping and grinding gadgets and knives and an impatient energy to do complicated tasks *presto*.

After lunch, Gabriela volunteered that she had not been nervous about this recital until about 48 hours before. Her goal, she said, is to be "keyed up," reaching a peak state of being "pleasantly nervous" about an hour before a performance. She confessed that she was more nervous than she should be. She thinks it is because this recital is on home territory; many friends have called to say they will be in the audience. (Afterward, when I asked her to review the course of anxiety and tension throughout the performance day, she remembered this time after lunch, about an hour and a half before the recital, as one of two unpleasant peaks. The other had been earlier, before my arrival, when she had walked Daisy and locked herself out of the house.)

We talk lightly, skipping from one thought to another. Gabriela, prompted by the flower arranging paraphernalia in the green room, instructs me on the best ways to dry flowers from the garden. The dress she wears today is a gift from her friend, the pianist Anna Bronskin, one that Anna has worn for her own concerts and recitals. Gabriela loves its elegance: simple lines, classic white silk. She says she finds comfort in its "stage history." It is good to know that Anna has played beautifully in this same dress. As she slips into her high-heeled sandals, she remembers a concert in Guilford, England, when her sandal strap broke moments before her performance. She walked on stage with it held together by several thumbtacks and played Rachmaninoff with aplomb, but every time she lifted her foot from the pedal, the shoe stayed behind.

Gabriela's husband, the conductor Daniel Spalding, is with us in the green room. In general, Dan's preperformance strategy for both himself and Gabriela is to play down the dangers and difficulties of performing. Of her story of Rachmaninoff and the broken sandal, he says phlegmatically, "Well, all she has to do is sit there."

The director of the cathedral recital series enters, greets Gabriela, and gives her a check with thanks. Then we are alone, and it is nearly time to begin. Regardless of how this performance goes, Gabriela will be awake at 3 o'clock tomorrow morning, remembering every tiny imperfection. "I try," she has said, "to keep a sense of perspective, not to beat on myself for mistakes. But I want to be perfect."

Gabriela smiles a little. "Just waiting," she says softly, "is the worst."

ENDNOTE

1. The review, available at http://charon.sfsu.edu/DISASTER/humic . ml, is said to have been written by Kenneth Langbell for the Bangkok Post.

TWO

Improvisations

Mary Crawford

I t all started with a fax to Katmandu.

Roger and I, on sabbatical in the autumn of 1992, had trekked high into the Himalayas in Nepal. We left Katmandu in early October, flying to Lukla (9,000 feet) and then walking to the Chomolungma (Mt. Everest) base camp (18,000 feet).

The trek is a routine matter for our Nepalese guides. For us—sedentary, middle-aged academics—it is a physical challenge. For 3 weeks, we walk up and down over steep ridges and into cold, narrow valleys. We camp in near-freezing temperatures and bathe in glacial streams. We eat rice, lentils, and our entire supply of thoroughly unappetizing freeze-dried food.

In return for our efforts, we are privileged to enter the world of the Solo Khumbu, where the Sherpa people live in sturdy stone houses with open hearth fires; where the backs of men, women, and yaks are the only means of carrying goods and people; where the Buddhist prayer *Om mani padne om* flutters on strings of prayer flags and whirls on inscribed water wheels. Above us are the great peaks of Ama Dablan, Nuptse, Lhotse, and Chomolungma, Goddess Mother of the Earth. The only way to experience these places and people is to walk there. The only way to return is to walk back out. At times, we are a week's hike from the nearest jeep track. The experience of isolation from Western culture and immersion in an almost medieval world is profound.

Katmandu—motor scooters, noise, markets crowded with baskets of fresh oranges and piles of Tibetan rugs, the smells of food cooking on sidewalk stands, cows and laden porters pushing through the crush of people—is overwhelming after the peace and solitude of the mountains. We are much thinner, slightly spacey from altitude change and the shock of re-entry, and very, very dirty. We enter the Katmandu guest house, dragging our filthy duffels, and learn that we have received a fax from the United States.

The very notion of a fax seems slightly surreal. Dated 2 weeks earlier, the message is from Gabriela, who writes that she has been invited to do a workshop on musical memory for the 1993 meeting of the European Piano Teachers' Association in London. Would Roger like to do it with her? Perhaps they could connect some of the psychological research on memory to musical memory and performance. If he is *not* interested, he should call or fax right away. Otherwise, she will accept the invitation for both of them and they can worry about the details later.

We look at each other. *London, memory research,* and *conference* are concepts from another world. For 3 weeks, we have been hearing the chanting of monks doing *puja* in their richly painted monasteries, sharing food, songs, and fire warmth with our Nepalese friends, thinking mostly about putting one foot in front of the other and dreaming of flying over the snow-streaming peaks. Right now, Katmandu is almost more than we can handle, let alone this intrusion from our Western lives. Roger protests that he doesn't know anything at all about musical memory. But it's far too late to do anything about it. Gabriela must have long since sent Roger's name to London with her own. If it is Roger's *karma* to become an expert on musical memory by next summer, so be it. We shrug and head out for a Nepalese pizza.

AN UNLIKELY TRIO: THE AUTHORS AND THE PROJECT

Gabriela knew about Roger's expertise in memory research almost by chance. Our son Benjamin was a student of hers. When she organized a summer music camp for her students, she asked parents to help with activities, and Roger volunteered to give a minilecture on memory. He introduced the students to concepts such as chunking, retrieval cues, and automaticity—basic psychological constructs that he guessed might aid them in learning to play music without recourse to the written score. Gabriela immediately saw connections with her own ideas about musical memory, and the two began a series of conversations about the demands of memorizing for public performance. In these talks, they explored the similarities and differences between a performer's and a researcher's perspective on memory. Gabriela was learning from Roger about the long tradition of psychological research on memory, and Roger was learning from Gabriela about the traditions of musical performance and the demands that are placed on contemporary performers.

It is only quite recently in history that the performance of serious or classical music in public, and with it the possibility of a career as a performer, has become a feature of social life. Before that, music in Western societies was performed as a secondary part of events in settings where people gathered for other purposes, such as religious or court ceremonies. In these settings, musicians were not treated as important individuals, and virtuosity for its own sake was absent. Those few who were acclaimed as performers were usually composers, and they achieved renown for improvising or performing their own works. Notable examples include Bach and Mozart (Salmon & Meyer, 1992).

The practice of performing from memory is an even more recent innovation begun by Clara Schumann and Franz Liszt. In the mid-19th century, these two pianists created a sensation in the salons and concert halls of Europe by playing without a score. The sensation was warranted; the ability to perform music from memory is a remarkable accomplishment. Some pieces in the piano literature last for over 50 minutes and require the production of over 1,000 notes a minute for extended periods. Performances of such pieces from memory represent a pinnacle of human achievement.

The world of today's performer is very different from the 19th-century artistic milieu into which Schumann and Liszt introduced the new practice of performing from memory. There are many more performers who are skilled and highly trained. Competition is intense, beginning with auditions and public performances for young children. Those who survive the grueling selection process find a limited (and dwindling) market for their skills. Indeed, most are unable to make a living as performers. The stresses associated with becoming a professional performer are immense (Salmon & Meyer, 1992).

Clara Schumann and Franz Liszt's sensational innovation has become a norm, adding yet another source of stress to the performer's life. Today the ability to play without a score is a central feature of a concert artist's professional competence. Even student recitals and regional competitions for young pianists commonly require the music to be memorized. Performing from memory is part of professional life for pianists, as well as other instrumental soloists, singers, and conductors. At the same time, the memory demands represent an important obstacle for many aspiring musicians and a source of anxiety for even the most experienced performers (Salmon & Meyer, 1992). Memory lapses do occur, and they can cripple a performance—a painful experience for artist and audience alike.

Gabriela and Roger's 1993 London workshop, initiated by the fax to Katmandu, was a continuation of their conversations about memory and musical performance and their first attempt to meld Roger's memory expertise with Gabriela's insights as an artist. It drew a standing-room-only audience of pianists and teachers who were eager for new ways to conceptualize and resolve chronic problems of playing from memory, and it led to more invitations to speak about the psychology of musical memory.

Encouraged by the interest from the musical community, Roger and Gabriela wanted to present the same kind of analysis to a psychological audience. A conference on everyday memory scheduled for the following summer presented an opportunity. Roger pointed out, however, that psychologists would want to see some data. At this point, Roger and I were away from home again for the year, so a plan was devised over the phone. Gabriela suggested videotaping herself as she learned a new piece of music. It was decided that she would record her practice of two new pieces. It was left for Gabriela to choose them from among those she would be preparing for performance during the coming year. The pieces should be roughly equal in length; they should be new, and one should be harder than the other to memorize. Otherwise discussion focused on details of where the camera would be placed and the safest way to ship videotapes.

That was the extent of the planning. There was no discussion of how many hours of practice would be involved. (In retrospect, we probably should have chosen something a little less challenging.) Certainly no word was spoken about *hypotheses* or *dependent measures*. These were foreign concepts to Gabriela. To the extent that she thought about it, she imagined the videotapes providing illustrations of the various practice strategies that had been the focus of the workshop. Roger, who might have been expected to have a clearer idea of what was ahead, was busy with the move and with a promising new line of research on learning word meanings. It was only as the tapes began to arrive in the mail that he started to think about what to do with them and, as they continued to pile up, to confront the problem of handling the vast quantity of data they contained. The one virtue of this haphazard beginning was that it ensured that there was no opportunity for Gabriela's learning to be contaminated by preconceived ideas about specific hypotheses that might be tested. By the time Roger had figured out what to do with the data, the learning process was over.

Gabriela had first met Roger and me in 1990, shortly after she had emigrated to the United States. She is Romanian by birth and both Hungarian and Romanian by parentage. She began piano lessons at the age of 5, when her mother took her for private lessons, and soon after she was enrolled in the local performing arts school. Two years later, after her first juried exam, the principal called her parents and urged that if at all possible Gabriela should attend one of the five main performing arts schools of the country. At that time, Cluj was a "closed" city, but the family managed the move there. In the years that followed, the young pianist made her way up the ladder of a conservatory education designed to lead to a career as a performing artist. She made her debut at the age of 16 with the Romanian State Philharmonic and has since soloed with orchestras around the world. A specialist in the Romantic repertoire, including the complete concerti of Rachmaninoff, she recently showed her versatility by recording an all-Bach compact disc for the Connoisseur Society label.[1] It is one of the works on this recording, the Italian Concerto (third movement), that is the focus of our study. During most of the time this book was in preparation, she was represented in the United States by a division of Columbia Artists, playing some 50 recitals annually for audiences around the country.

The first time we heard her play (the Rachmaninoff Second Piano concerto in a 1990 performance conducted by Daniel Spalding), Roger and I realized we were hearing artistry of the highest order. The performance was technically brilliant, musically nuanced, and sensitive. Professional reviewers, too, have noted her "keen musical intelligence," "breathtaking agility," and superb artistry.

As we came to know her, Roger and I were not only impressed with Gabriela's musical skill and sensitivity, but awed by her intelligence and drive. In the first year we knew her, she established a small teaching studio, developed her English from hesitant to utterly fluent, learned to drive, became an American citizen, and developed a new performance career in this country.

One of the most striking aspects of Gabriela's personality is a high degree of aesthetic sensitivity in all realms. We expected her to be a perfectionist at the piano—it is the hallmark of a professional. Yet Gabriela approaches every aesthetic realm with the same high standards, and she seems to have a generalized ability in creative and artistic realms. Whether she is painting, cooking, arranging flowers, or designing jewelry, the process is always intensely absorbing and the product aesthetically pleasing. She is also unusually articulate about her work and the skills involved in playing the piano—a quality perhaps related to her general linguistic abilities (she speaks several languages fluently) and further developed by teaching.

Roger and I are both amateur musicians with very modest performing skills. Roger has played the flute off and on for years, originally self-taught and later with the help of teachers. I studied music as an undergraduate, receiving a degree in music education. However, after leaving that field in my 20s, I did not play or study music until resuming an interest in the piano some 25 years later.

Although we are both psychologists and have been married to each other for more than 27 years, Roger and I have rarely worked together on a research project because our specialty areas are quite different. Roger is a cognitive psychologist who investigates how knowledge is represented in memory. He has worked primarily in basic research on the organization of word meanings in the mental lexicon and on the question of how people learn the meanings of new words. He has also explored more applied areas such as factors affecting the difficulty of GRE analogy items and people's knowledge of their own memory abilities. Born in England, he received his undergraduate degree at Oxford before coming to the United States, where he earned his Ph.D. at the University of Illinois. He teaches courses in cognitive psychology.

Trained as an experimental psychologist, I did research in animal learning before my interests turned to the psychology of women and gender—an area that had been much neglected by psychology. For me, this entailed much more than just a change in research topics; I began to question the epistemological assumptions underlying psychological paradigms such as behaviorism and cognitivism, and to feel a need for innovative research methods and interdisciplinary collaboration. I now direct a program in Women's Studies as well as teach and do research in social psychology.

In summary, the three people who join together to write this book come from different intellectual traditions and personal backgrounds. Far from a meeting of like minds, our work together is characterized by an attempt to bridge our *unlikeness*. We are two social scientists, one artist; two women, one man; two whose intellectual inquiry and job security are protected by academic tenure, and one who earns her living in the marketplace of classical music performance; three different nationalities brought up in three different cultures. Our inquiry is interdisciplinary; because of our differences, our methods are unconventional by both necessity and choice.

Just as each of us had a different starting point, each had a different set of goals for this research project. Gabriela sought to understand the process of memorizing for performance to make her own performance practices more efficient and to reduce the possibility of memory failure for herself, her students, and other pianists. Roger sought to understand memory expertise in a new domain and to contribute to scientific knowledge on this topic.

I sought to document the research process, especially the pleasures and difficulties of interdisciplinary collaboration. In working together to achieve these varied goals, we have attempted to bridge many polarities that characterize the production of knowledge in our culture, and we have encountered complexities that we did not anticipate at the start.

BRIDGING DIFFERENCES

Empiricism and constructivism

Roger approached this project as an empiricist, a scientist. He expected to be able to systematically observe and record relevant aspects of Gabriela's practicing behavior and subject it to quantitative analyses that would reveal its regularities regardless of whether Gabriela herself was aware of them. He expected to correlate specific aspects of practice (such as duration or number of repetitions) with other measures (such as rated difficulty of the passage) and to develop predictions about future behavior based on those relationships.

Roger's metaphors of the process were those of exploration and discovery through the gathering of quantitative data. These metaphors reflect a realist position about the world. From this perspective, reality lies waiting to be discovered; data exist independently of the observer's constructs and can be collected or gathered like fruit for the picking. His underlying epistemological assumptions had been consistent throughout his career in psychology.

Like Roger, I was educated in the empiricist tradition of North American psychology. However, I had moved from an empiricist to a more social constructionist position. Social constructionists make assumptions about the natural and social world that differ from those held by empiricists. They assume that the methods we use to understand the world are social artifacts arising at a particular time in history and within a particular community. Likewise, the acceptance of a particular theory or set of data (or indeed any account of the world) is a social and political process rather than simply a matter of weighing evidence objectively (Gergen, 1985; Potter, 1996).

Debates between empiricists and social constructionists are hardly novel; they are familiar issues in the philosophy and sociology of science. However, the debates have had little effect on the practice of cognitive psychology, which remains the dominant paradigm for North American academic psychology and which continues to rely on empiricist notions of objectivity and method.

Gabriela, educated as an artist in the European conservatory tradition, did not have our investments in epistemological debates. However, the practices that stemmed from Roger's empiricism evoked strong responses from her. Early in the project, for example, Roger presented an informal talk about the research to colleagues and sent a copy to Gabriela in which he listed himself as the author and referred to her as the *subject*. Gabriela found this representation wholly unacceptable. She seemed to feel angry and demeaned and discussed her feelings with me. She then discussed the situation with Roger in a collegial manner. Gently and politely, she explained that she could participate only as an active, thinking partner, not as a passive subject. Roger, who had the highest regard for her abilities, was surprised at her reaction. At that time, he simply had no other way than *experimenter* and *subject* to conceptualize their working relationship. Shaped by the conventions of psychology and their codification in the standardized language of psychological research, and by his own history of research using college students and arbitrary memory tasks, he did not recognize that from her perspective he had imposed an unacceptable hierarchy. Together the two began to work out language to express their collaboration as a pair of equally qualified experts whose expertise happened to be in different realms.

How, then, might an empiricist, a constructionist, and an artist work together? Each of us acknowledged some strengths of the others' positions, and the boundaries among us on this basic epistemological stance were relatively fluid. Roger conceded the value of research methods that allow for individual subjectivity, and he recognized that his own practices as a researcher often did not fit the received view of how scientific inquiry is conducted. (He still felt, however, that other researchers' practices probably did.) He also argued that critiques of mainstream psychology often reflect a stereotype of empiricist inquiry, underestimating the methodological and conceptual sophistication of contemporary approaches to mind and thinking. He felt that Gabriela could learn something useful from his quantitative analyses and she agreed. Gabriela was excited about the prospect of testing her ideas about memorization and performance. At the same time, she saw herself as an artist, not as a researcher, and would not agree to experimental procedures that violated her ideas of what was musically appropriate.

It is tempting to assert that these epistemological differences were resolved in advance of our working together on this project—an empiricist answer to the dilemma. In other words, we might claim that the three of us discussed our personal values and philosophy and agreed that these values undoubtedly influenced our choice of research topic, but once we began doing research they became irrelevant. In actual practice, we have found that our different standpoints affect the way we think about every aspect of the research process. As this project has proceeded, we have muddled through our differences, leaning first one way and then another as we tried to reconcile the goals of all three participants.

Differences and contested interpretations cropped up many times. We continued to be surprised by the extent to which we were each operating from a specific epistemological stance without being aware of it and how these largely unarticulated assumptions influenced our everyday practices as researchers. As a constructionist, I was sympathetic to Gabriela's objections to Roger's empiricist stance, and yet I was also familiar with empiricist research practices, their strengths, and their purpose. I some-times found myself explaining and justifying Gabriela's views to Roger and Roger's to Gabriela. Although this was not an easy task, it did help me understand their differences and empathize with both of them.

In retrospect, the members of this unlikely trio have come to share three important positions. The first is the value of self-reflexivity. In other words, we choose to reflect throughout this work on our own assumptions, motives, and epistemological starting points and how they affect the research process at every stage. The second, related position is a goal of strong objectivity. Sandra Harding (1991) argued that, because values cannot be fully eliminated from scientific practice, all aspects of science should be examined in an ongoing effort to understand their effects (both positive and negative). This includes not only immediate personal goals and values, but those that are so much a part of the discipline or historical period that they may be ordinarily unremarked and socially invisible. Strong objectivity stands in contrast to traditional definitions of objectivity, which Harding called "weak objectivity," and which stress eliminating the values of the researcher from the research process to the point of "annihi-lating the subject position of the knower" (Ewick, 1994). Our third shared vision is one of methodological openness. We decided not to reject either quantitative or qualitative methods, nor would we assume that any one method has the inside track to truth.

Science and Artistry

When we began this project, Gabriela was entirely innocent of any notion of how scientific inquiry is conducted, and Roger had only an outsider's knowledge of the performing arts. I stood somewhere between the two, but closer to Roger, in having a modicum of training in music education (but no performing experience) and a professional identity as a psychologist.

Not surprisingly, Gabriela sometimes had doubts about whether her practice and performance strategies could be captured in what Roger calls data. More than once during the research process, she said to me privately that she could not understand why he wanted to focus so much on the cumulative records and graphical summaries of her practice—summaries that do not interest her as much as the artistic process and her subjective experience of it. At the same time, Roger privately reported to me that he experienced frustration at her reluctance to "sit down and go over the results."

This difference is related partly to basic beliefs in the power of scientific modes of inquiry and partly to more mundane concerns that are rarely acknowledged in scientific discourse. For Roger and me, conducting and publishing research accords professional status and whatever perks may come with it, such as grant money, reduced teaching loads, and increased prestige within our universities and disciplines. We are personally invested in completing the project not just for altruistic reasons of contributing to knowledge, but out of self-interest. At the same time, we know how conservative psychology can be about unconventional methods, its low regard for case studies, and its reluctance to respond to social constructionist critiques (Fine & Gordon, 1989; Kimmel & Crawford, 1999). It would be easier and less anxiety-provoking for us both to stick to more conventional research.

For Gabriela, the cost–benefit ratio is different. Every hour that she devotes to the project is an hour away from the sort of work that will increase her professional standing. Although she shares our altruistic motives, she knows that in her profession publishing a book matters much less than perfecting one's performance, enlarging one's repertoire, or recording a new compact disc. Moreover, her schedule is crowded with performing, recording, and teaching, and she has none of the institutional supports we take for granted.

Despite these differences in background and professional payoffs, Gabriela showed an intense interest and an astonishingly quick grasp of the logic of scientific inquiry. (At least it was astonishing to Roger, who has long labored to teach undergraduates the fundamentals of research design.) In fact, her enthusiasm near the start of the project had to be restrained. She wanted to study more concert pianists right away, add a sample of conductors, and design complicated studies of her students' practice. New to the research process, she did not think about how long it all actually takes. We recognized in her response the intellectual delight of a bright student who comes to understand the power of systematic research and begins to see the world as her laboratory, and we experienced the same kind of pleasure we do when our college teaching evokes such a response.

Yet fundamental differences remain. Although the rhetoric of science concerns itself with revealing nature's truths, the rhetoric of the arts concerns itself with the mysteries of the creative process. The former is a rhetoric of lawful regularities in the natural and social world; the latter is a rhetoric of individual uniqueness and spontaneity.

At times, mundane differences of opinion arose that I believe were due to the lawfulness/uniqueness dichotomy. For example, late in the project, Roger and Gabriela discussed how to organize this book. They agreed that they should provide "the background to the project." Roger assumed that this meant a review of psychologists' research leading to a rationale for the present project in terms of what it would add. Gabriela thought this would be wholly inappropriate. Why, she asked, should we write a book about other people's research? Discussing the issue with her, Roger and I realized that she felt placing our research as part of a long line of similar or related efforts—the adding-a-piece-to-the-puzzle rhetorical strategy of science—demeaned its originality. She argued that the background chapters should start with the words of well-known pianists talking about the problems of memorization and the strategies they use, culled from interviews of the performers. Our project should then be presented as a unique contribution to solving long-standing problems about which little is known. Rather than being a piece of anyone else's scientific puzzle, Gabriela hoped to show that her contribution to research, like her interpretation of a work of music, should be judged on its own merits as a unique creative endeavor. To me, it was fascinating to watch this debate about representation and recognize that there is no right way to represent the research process, only different strategies based on different social goals. (We solved the problem by doing both, see chaps. 3, 4, and 5.)

A related issue of representation involves sustaining the mystique of artistry. There are virtually no systematic observational studies of concert performers, and the interviews in which they discuss their learning strategies are often unrevealing. One reason for this silence is that, within the artistic community, it is widely believed that art demands a certain mystique. Far better to let the audience believe that the artist has a divine gift that is expressed as naturally as the song of a lark than to reveal that he or she sometimes struggles to memorize a work, occasionally has memory lapses, or indulges in superstitious rituals to ward off performance anxiety. Gabriela, whose stage presence has been described by reviewers as radiant, elegant, and glamorous, expressed some of this need for mystique by confiding that she felt self-conscious about being videotaped while practicing in her bathrobe or jeans. She also described acute feelings of vulnerability in revealing to the competitive world of professional musicians just how long and hard she had to work to prepare a difficult piece for public performance: "My self-protective instincts rebelled against the video camera preserving my most personal, private time—practicing. Sometimes I felt terribly inadequate; my mistakes seemed embarrassing" (Imreh & Chaffin, 1996/1997). Thus, our collaboration across the science–humanities divide opened different vulnerabilities and the possibilities of different rewards for each participant, and these differences were played out in dilemmas of representing the research project to its intended audience.

"Experimenter" and "Subject"

Most psychological research is conducted on North American college students (Sears, 1986). Research participants are kept uninformed about the purpose of the study; they may even be deceived. Often they are asked to do tasks that are outside their ordinary experience or even bizarre, and they are tested in unfamiliar environments for brief periods of time. The methods are decontextualized and the situations highly artificial. The data they provide are summarized, analyzed, and interpreted by the expert psychologist. This is the tradition in which Roger was trained and one that he had little cause to question; the approach had provided him with coherent and lawful data over the years, and his work was published in reputable psychological journals.

From a constructionist perspective, there is a clear hierarchy of power in this sort of psychological research, and research is conducted in one direction—downward—in that hierarchy, with "the powerful, all-knowing researcher instructing, observing, recording, and sometimes deceiving the subjects" (Peplau & Conrad, 1989). The inequality of the experimental situation may be especially acute when the researcher is male and the subject is female (McHugh, Koeske, & Frieze, 1986).

Cognitive psychology has adapted its methods and research practices in response to criticism about its artificiality, but has been slower to acknowledge criticism of its power hierarchies. As early as 1976, critics of standard memory research had begun calling for more naturalistic studies of memory (Neisser, 1976). The everyday memory movement that followed forms one context for our project (Searleman & Herrmann, 1994). By now, research on expertise has already looked at individuals with such real-world skills as chess playing, dancing, acting, and figure skating (Ericsson, 1985; Ericsson & Oliver, 1989; Ericsson & Smith, 1991). Working with highly accomplished adults, instead of the college students usually studied in psychology experiments, provides an opportunity to overcome the problems of the traditional experimenter–subject hierarchy. Making the most of this opportunity, however, requires that the problems be acknowledged, and this has not happened. Published reports of expertise studies have either been silent on these issues or have described circumscribed relationships between the researchers and the researched.

I will briefly describe a few examples to show how researchers adopt different strategies for dealing with the potential breakdown of the usual experimenter–subject boundaries in expertise research. The first strategy is to maintain the convention of psychological distance that is traditionally observed in scientific report writing. Helga Noice (1991, 1992) conducted a sophisticated and unique series of studies on the memory strategies and processes of professional actors. Throughout her published reports, she uses the standard experimenter–subject terminology. The expert actors are not named. She reports that some of them were paid a small amount for participating in the research (e.g., Noice, 1991). Interestingly, some of her research is coauthored with her spouse who is a professional actor (Noice & Noice, 1993), and in other studies he is thanked for his help in recruiting actors for study.

A similar strategy is adopted by Kacper Miklaszewski (1989, 1995), who videotaped pianists as they learned new compositions. The pianists are referred to by first name only, and they are described as "volunteers" who "received small fees for their work" (1995, p. 139). After their practice was videotaped, the pianists watched the tapes and added their comments to the sound track, but they did not interact directly with another human being while commenting on their work, nor were they later interviewed about the meaning of their comments. In somewhat different ways, and although they are grounded in different interpersonal situations, both Noice and Miklaszewski employed the strategy of attempting to minimize the effect of personal and professional relationships on the research process.

In contrast, Charles Thompson, Thaddeus Cowan, and Jerone Frieman (1993) reflexively took up the question of their relationship with their "subject," Rajan Srinivasan Mahadevan. Before he became a graduate student in cognitive psychology in the authors' department, Rajan had earned a place in the Guinness Book of World Records by reciting the first 31,811 digits of *pi* from memory. In writing about their 4-year project to study Rajan's memory abilities, Thompson and his colleagues discuss ethical problems (would his intensive participation as a subject interfere with his progress as a graduate student?) and describe the sometimes difficult personal relationships between Rajan and the faculty members of the group. They discuss Rajan's lively sense of humor as well as his "annoying" and "exasperating" ways of not behaving like a docile subject (pp. 16–17). For example, he refused to be tested by paid assistants, insisting on interacting with the project directors. Nevertheless, they describe Rajan as "more than a research subject; we . . . came to know him as a colleague and a friend (p. xi) and a "true collaborator as well as a subject." However, Rajan is not listed as a coauthor of the book that describes the project.

How do psychologists deal with the blurring of boundaries when the subject is also an experimenter and an author of the research narrative? An interesting example is provided by Fernand Gobet and Herbert Simon (1996a, Experiment 3) in a study of expert memory for chess positions. Gobet describes himself in the third person: "A single S (the first author of the paper) has been participating in this experiment for more than 1 year. A former chess professional turned psychologist, he holds the title of International Master." (pp. 21–22).

In addition, he justifies studying himself on grounds of historical precedent and the logic of experimental design:

> In incorporating in the experimental design the collaboration of subject with experimenter to find ways of enhancing performance, we follow the examples of Ebbinghaus, and of the earlier subjects on expert memory for digit strings. . . . In a test of cognitive abilities, with no deception in the experiment's design, and no possibility for subject deception in an upward direction, an expert member of the research team is an appropriate subject. (pp. 21–22)

The rhetorical strategies in this narrative—distancing "subject" from self by use of the third person and providing a double-barrelled justification for studying one's own expertise—demonstrate just how problematic this situation is perceived to be. When college students are studied, a justification of the choice is rarely offered. While it serves to reinforce traditional psychological practices by presenting this case as an exception, the research report subverts these practices and asserts the identity of the "subject." Here Gobet comments on his own motivation, albeit in the third person:

> S was not strongly motivated at the beginning of the experiment, which he took as a whim of the second author, but he was gradually seduced by the task and became curious about how far he could go. His daily performance became an important part of his weekly routine. A bad performance would, in some cases, vex him for the rest of the day, a good one would exhilarate him for a few hours. (pp. 26–27)

The novelty of the subject taking a speaking position to describe his own motivation is underscored by Gobet's reference to the "whim" of the second author. In this case, the second author is Nobel-winning scientist Herbert Simon, one of the world's most eminent memory researchers. Gobet's description of his own motivation, and especially his assertion of choice and control over whether and how to participate in the research, serve to further undermine the experimenter-subject hierarchy.

In summary, the recent research literature in cognitive psychology offers only tantalizing hints on how an experimenter and a "subject" might collaborate as social and intellectual equals. Within the literature on memory expertise, researchers currently adopt different strategies for dealing with the implicit experimenter–subject hierarchy, and they justify their choices in different ways. It is not easy to tell from published reports how successful their efforts are at the interpersonal and social levels. We could find no reports where the participants claimed to have created entirely nonhierarchical relationships among the various parties involved in the research.

The modes of collaboration described in this literature were satisfactory neither to Roger nor Gabriela. As mentioned earlier, Gabriela was not prepared to be a "subject." Obviously, unlike college students, she could not be induced to participate in research by a course requirement, the authority of a professor, or the payment of a small fee for her time. Nor is she indebted to psychology or in awe of its cultural legitimacy. Unlike research participants who were also graduate students in psychology (Gobet & Simon, 1996a; Thompson et al., 1993), she had little to gain in her chosen profession by participating in research. Perhaps most important, she felt that she understood her own memory and practice strategies: what she does, why she does it, and why it works so well. She could articulate her strategies and reasons for adopting them, and she did so regularly in her teaching. Although she saw her research with Roger as a way of systematizing her knowledge and translating it into the vocabulary and concepts of another discipline, she did not expect to discover something entirely new about how to memorize music for performance.

Roger regarded Gabriela's skills with a great deal of respect. He believed that her interpretation of the video record was vital to the project. Indeed, he recognized that he could not have made sense of it without her collaboration. At the same time, he placed more value on what he called *objective data* (quantitative records of behaviors) than what he called *subjective data* (self-reports of intentions and behaviors). In other words, like most cognitive psychologists, he accorded more respect to an "outsider's" perspective on cognitive phenomena. This created a potential for inequality as Gabriela's interpretation might become secondary to his own.

One way that the two reconciled this area of potential tension was by agreeing that the value of insider's and outsider's perspectives on a cognitive event or process depends on the particular phenomenon being studied. Some cognitive processes take place at the conscious level and are quite open to introspective description. Others are not. Moreover, the contents of consciousness in a domain change greatly with learning (Baars, 1988). In general, as learning proceeds, behaviors become more automatic, less subject to conscious control, and more difficult to describe. A familiar and mundane example is learning how to drive a car. At the start, the learner is conscious of turning the steering wheel, going through the sequence of steps required to change gears, and so on. Later, he or she carries out these actions automatically and is conscious of other things such as traffic and road conditions. At this point, the steps needed to actually keep the car on the road—turning the steering wheel, adjusting the accelerator and brake, changing gears—are so automatic that the driver might find it difficult to describe the correct sequence to someone who is just learning.

Researchers in memory expertise have reported instances where highly skilled performance was largely unavailable to conscious introspection. For example, when Rajan Mahadevan was asked to describe how he learned a large matrix of numbers, he said that he just fixated on each number briefly. When asked for more details, he said that being asked to describe how he learned number sequences was like being asked to describe how he rode a bicycle. He was sure that he knew how to do both tasks, but found it difficult to describe how he actually accomplished them (Thompson et al., 1993).

From this perspective, there might be some automatized aspects of Gabriela's practicing that would be more apparent to the systematic outside observer than to her and other, higher order aspects, under conscious control, that would be more meaningfully described and interpreted by Gabriela. In particular, the two collaborators suspected that motor skills and memory would be amenable to outsider analysis, whereas aesthetic goals would be amenable to the performer's own analysis.

The Paradox of Expertise and Aesthetics

Expert performance requires automatic skills. Art requires creativity and freedom of choice. How does a concert artist reconcile these two to produce a technically flawless and aesthetically satisfying performance?

Memorization is central to this process. As motor patterns become automatic, the musician is freed to focus on the performance. At the same time, we will see that how the performer memorizes a piece is intimately related to the interpretation. By studying the memorization of a piece for performance, Gabriela and Roger hoped to make visible the process by which an interpretation is created.

Questions of aesthetics have not often been addressed in research on expert memory because domains involving aesthetic demands have rarely been studied. When the aesthetics of musical performance have been studied, as in the work of Bruno Repp (1998) and Henry Shaffer (1981, 1996), the focus has been on the finished performance rather than on its preparation or memorization. We describe the few studies that have looked at the process of preparing a piece of music for performance in chapter 4, but these provide little information about the aesthetic issues involved in memorization. Either the pianists have been students, the projects have ended at the point where aesthetic considerations were just beginning to be highlighted, or aesthetic properties of the performance were not assessed (Lehmann & Ericsson, 1998; Miklaszweski, 1989, 1995; Nielsen, 1997, 2000; Williamon, 1999; Williamon & Valentine, 2000, 2002). Moreover, given the importance of memory in a pianist's life, there is a striking absence of information within the musical community about the memorization practices of concert artists. Memorization is generally seen as "a rather mysterious process" (Sandor, 1981, p. 194) that differs so much from one person to the next that each pianist must develop his or her own method (Aiello, 1999, 2000a, 2000b).

The absence of information on memory for music and its interplay with interpretation is notable because the most important goal of musical performance is to create an aesthetically engaging experience for per- former and audience, and memorization is an almost universal means to this end. Moreover, it is paradoxical that musical performance requires a precision of execution that, at first glance, appears at odds with the demands of creativity and emotional sensitivity. How does a concert pianist, for example, maintain the emotional coherence of a passage while remembering to hit the beginning of an arpeggio with the correct finger?

Eric Clarke (1995) discussed how researchers in the psychology of music and critical analysts of performance have had little to say to each other because psychologists are interested in general mechanisms and critics in individual manifestations of expressive creativity:

> There is of course much fertile overlap between the two, but cognitive studies of musical performance could legitimately be criticized for having revealed little or nothing about the specificities of interesting and exceptional per- formance. All of the performance models that have been proposed are (necessarily) extremely blunt tools when it comes to investigating individual performances, as they are built upon the premise of general mechanisms and specify the unremarkable background of commonality underlying a vast range of adequate or competent performances—an account of possible significance for those studying general cognitive processes, but surely less interesting to musicians. This does not mean that we should throw up our hands at the complexity and unrelenting specificity of performance, but it

does strike a blow at naively empirical research on expression—leaving trenchant questions about how to do it better. (p. 52)

Gabriela and Roger were determined to develop the sort of multidimensional perspective called for by Clarke. They proceeded from the assumption that the performer's interpretation of a piece develops from the earliest moments of playing through the score, when decisions about fingering and phrasing are made, and continues until the final moment of each performance. The creativity of a musical performance is the result of the entire process of preparation for performance (Nersessian, 1992). In studying this process from both an artist's and a psychologist's perspective, they hoped to make progress in integrating the two.

ENDNOTE

1. A discography is provided in Appendix 1.

THREE

In the Words of the Masters: Artists' Accounts of Their Expertise

Gabriela Imreh with Mary Crawford

Some years ago, I fled all that was familiar, safe, and secure—my family and my native Romania—and started a brand-new life as a free, international artist and the young wife of an American conductor. It was a time of fear, anxiety, and heartbreak as well as tremendous excitement—I was going to America! After many tears, I watched the beautiful landscape of my old country go by. Hours later, I set foot on "free" land for the first time in my life as the train stopped in Vienna. That moment is forever engraved in my memory.

The next stop, Stuttgart, was also a very important one for me. I was able to visit my former piano teacher, Harald Wagner. We hadn't seen each other in over 2 years since he had defected, fed up with being a minority (German) artist in communist Romania. In the past, we had spent many hours together working and listening to music—some of the most helpful, formative hours of my life. We had the sort of strong bond that often develops between master and student after years of hard work. I had spent the past 2 years on my own, finishing my studies with various official teachers, but mostly missing Mr. Wagner and trying to put pieces together from all different times of my musical past like a huge puzzle.

Neither of us wanted to waste that one night sleeping. Eventually, my new husband, Dan, got tired of trying to follow our Romanian or waiting for my broken English translations; he retired. Mr. Wagner and I continued talking. I was worried sick. Was I ready? Everything I had worked for was behind me and I was facing the unknown. Where would I start building a performing career in the United States? If I got a start, how was I going to cope?

With our conversation treading on such anxiety-provoking territory, one of the looming questions was how to prepare a flawless performance for my American debut. Since my application for marriage and emigration a year earlier, all my public performances had been stopped. By now, I felt as if I had never been on a stage.

My studies at the Academy of Music in Romania included years of learning piano pedagogy and the psychology of music, which familiarized me with both general notions of memory and current theories of working with it. Also, I was relying on almost 20 years of stage experience, about 8 of those at a professional level. During our conversation that night, Mr. Wagner brought up a new idea, vague at first, almost too subtle to grasp, but provocative and intriguing. He said he had been thinking about how, in the last weeks before a performance, you must check everything, revise, and rework every detail, but ultimately that there was a special trancelike feeling that allowed a performer to put worries and problems in the background (far enough that they did not interfere, but close enough that they could be reached). This was not something one could just switch on and off; it had to be practiced seriously and painstakingly until it was as automatic and natural as the rest of playing. To enter this state, he said, you had to somehow remap your thinking to emphasize the artistic, inspirational elements without ever losing control. In a way, the ideas he expressed were not new; I felt that on a practical level they were somehow familiar to me. Yet hearing them articulated in a calm, logical way made a lasting impression.

If I had to pinpoint the moment when I became interested in finding more nuanced and reliable answers to the questions that every musician has about memory, it would be the conversation that night in Stuttgart. Like any performer, I had always been interested in understanding and improving my memory; memory is an essential element of a performer's survival and success. Over the next few years, I continued to think about memory as I listened to and read about the great performers of the past. As my English improved, I took advantage of having access to an extraordinary variety and volume of professional literature in America. I read a lot about musicians, especially pianists. Seeking out old, out-of-print books about great performers became a hobby—one that has continued now for more than a decade.

In particular, collections of interviews with great pianists became dear to me. Reading them was a valuable but restricted area of discovery. Sometimes it was frustrating because the performer offered limited information. In some cases, it was obvious that an artist was guarding personal "secrets of the trade"; in others, the artists were extremely inarticulate or naive. In a few of the interviews, the artist had the courage to face tough questions and gave well-thought-out and intelligent answers. Although the interviews were extremely variable, they were all that was available. I kept trying to understand Mr. Wagner's theory, and sometimes by studying the artists' words for a long time I could get a glimpse of understanding. I kept returning to the same questions: How do the great masters prepare for a timeless performance? How do they cope with the enormous stress and complexity of their craft? Are there any rules for how to do it? How general are they? Do they work for everybody?

Studying these interviews also made me realize how different the performer's life is today. I tried to imagine Horowitz, Arrau, Michelangeli, Lipatti, or Bachauer videotaping themselves when they practiced and talking freely about their fears and failures. Even had they had the technology, it seems like an absolutely ludicrous idea. They are the superstars of the past, immortalized in formal black-and-white photographs wearing three-piece suits, sometimes with hats, sitting composedly at the piano or being surrounded by equally fashionable and formal friends. Even the dogs seem more formal in these photographs; they stand quietly on a leash or they heel at the foot of the master. More often, dogs (and children) are missing perhaps because they are too messy for the superstar image.

The great pianists were heroes—strong, invincible, fearless, and charming. Eccentricities were accepted; sometimes they were emphasized or even invented as a publicity device. Problems were a totally different issue. No superstar could admit to hand pains, injuries, performance anxiety, or breakdowns; these were usually swept under the carpet. Sometimes these imposing figures would officially announce an early retirement and go to a sanitarium or move out to the country. Horowitz did both and did not perform in public for 10 years after he snapped from the enormous pressure.

Today, society expects a closer, more intimate look at the performer's life. What has changed today? What makes movies like "Shine" and "Hilary and Jackie" possible? What makes it possible for illustrious pianists like Gary Graffman and Leon Fleisher to talk about their painful, career-wrecking hand injuries and more or less successful treatments? What allows Andre Watts to talk about sometimes paralyzing performance anxiety and how he conquers it? What made me sit in front of a camera, although sometimes (most times) I felt that I was making a total fool of myself in plain view of the world? I think many things have changed. We talk about anxiety, injuries, and fears because we have a much better understanding of psychological processes generally. Performers have learned how much help they can get in return for opening up. Psychology and medicine are more advanced and sophisticated. They really work; they really help. Our image of our heroes has changed. It is acceptable to be human—to be slightly (just slightly) imperfect in the process of achieving the extraordinary.

The superstars are presented to the public more as normal people these days. Managers and agents encourage a much more accessible, simple, contemporary image. Casual clothes like jeans and sweatshirts (sometimes even near nudity for women) have replaced three-piece suits and ties. What are the effects of this new representation of the artist? Are we really free to relax and be ourselves? Can we artists really talk about our problems without losing our audiences and their confidence in us? The answer is ambiguous. We are much more comfortable with self-disclosure than artists of 50 years ago, but there are still taboo areas that can hurt one's image and negatively influence the public's judgment of one's work.

I feel strongly that I come at a time when it is possible to do research of this kind without fearing that the more intimate, self-critical, and self-analytical portrait it reveals of me will wreck my performing career. (I may be wrong, but I hope I am not!) I think of this research as a path toward finding answers to age-old questions that have burdened the piano community. For me, it is also a path toward self-discovery. I still have reservations about what has been revealed willingly (and also unwillingly), but I have full confidence that this is the right time for musical artists to gain new understanding about the difficulties and challenges of their profession. In this chapter, I want to pay tribute to the great masters of the piano by rereading their words in the context of our present work and learning anew from them.

Although the voices of many of the pianists in my out-of-print books date from a different, more reticent era, they have much to tell us about great artists' understanding of the processes involved in learning, understanding, and memorizing music; preparing for public performance; and dealing with pressure and anxiety. For these artists, who had no inquisitive psychologists videotaping them before breakfast, the interview was the only venue for self-disclosure. When one engages in a sort of conversation through reading an interview with someone like Rudolf Firkusny, the soul of the artist emerges. I recommend that anyone who is interested in the art of the piano get to know the artists through reading and rereading their own words as expressed in interviews.

For present purposes, I have used the interviews in a different way. I first identified issues of interest to our research project. We chose to look at the artists' views on five themes: kinds of memory, the process of learning a new piece of music, the memorization process, dealing with performance anxiety, and the experience of public performance. I then read all of the material in my possession—interviews, biographies, books on piano technique, magazines, and journals—looking for mention of the relevant issues. The sources that were most useful were those in which interviewers had asked the pianists to talk about the nuts and bolts of putting together a performance. In the end, it turned out that interviews from a rather small number of books and two articles yielded the most useful material (Brower, 1926; Cooke, 1948; Cooke, 1999/1917; Elder, 1986, Dubal, 1997; Mach, 1991/1980,1988; Noyle, 1987; Portugheis, 1993, 1996). Although the collection is certainly not exhaustive (e.g., Boris Berman's [2000] recent book was not included), it does span the 20th century, and it does provide a good picture of the kind of information that is currently available to the discriminating reader about how concert pianists view their own preparations for performance.

For every source that yielded something useful, I read five that did not.[1] Part of the reason for the scarcity of good material is the cult of the performer, which often allows pianists to get away with drawing a veil over the details of how their magic is produced. There is another reason—one that is central to our hypothesis about how a piece is prepared for performance. A piece has to be analyzed and worked on at many levels. At the final and highest level, the artist manifests his or her own individuality, musicality, personality, taste, sensitivity, and knowledge, all of which are reflected in the details that set one performance apart from others. This is the most rewarding level for the performer and the one that pianists tend to talk about when describing their own performances. Although these descriptions of expressive goals are interesting (e.g., Mark Zilberquit's [1983] fascinating book on Russian pianists), they do not tell us how the performances were put together. For this we need a different and more detailed level of description.

When the interview passages were arrayed by theme, there was a great deal of variability among the artists. This is not surprising—the pianists represent different nationalities and schools of playing, the interviews span different eras, and the age and career stage of the pianists at the time of the interview varied. I had expected to find both general rules and exceptions to the rules. This is such a complex profession, I think it is simplistic and unrealistic to assume that one thing would work for everybody.

There are differences grounded in their unique personalities. Compare Rubinstein's endless joy in life (cigars, wines, luxury, friends) to the rigorous regimes, absolutely stark and methodical, of André-Michel Schub, Misha Dichter, and Janina Fialkowska. Idiosyncrasies include Richter's interest in painting, de Larrocha's in medicine and surgery, Graffman's sense of humor, the unbelievable eccentricities of Glenn Gould, and Michelangeli's total unreliability and rigidity. To me as a pianist, even the most outlandish eccentricities can have reasonable explanations. For example, Michelangeli insisted on traveling with his own Steinway piano. Imagine the financial cost of that—but all of us struggle with the immense problem of adjusting to a new instrument for each performance.

For all the diversity that marks artists' approach to practice and performance, there are a few common denominators. These artists take their practice and profession seriously. They know that their chosen calling requires extraordinary self-discipline and sacrifice. The majority express endless joy, curiosity, and satisfaction in what they do. Quite simply, they love music. Anything less than these qualities would make one unable to cope with the performer's life.

I loved looking at the charts that summarized my content analysis and compared the different accounts. I found it interesting to see that the interviewers had an active role in the outcome of their questions. Sometimes a pianist would answer quite directly, "I don't know how . . ." and it was up to the skill of the interviewer to ask the question in a different way and get exactly what he or she needed: an elaborate, eloquent answer. Sometimes a pianist would answer a question such as, "How do you memorize?" briefly and vaguely, but when asked "How do you practice?" or "How do you learn?" would say exactly what we needed to know about memory. Some books had a set of specific questions that were asked of all the pianists, such as, "Do you practice hands separately or in sections?" In other books, the interviewer did little to direct the conversation, so I had to read between the lines. Perhaps the artists were struggling to articulate ideas that are difficult to express. Whatever the reason, I hated to see my personal heroes give seemingly shallow answers and secretly I was rooting for them.

What follows are the results of my analysis. The pianists' comments on their art have been arranged into five sections. The first consists of their views on memory. The second is their accounts of how they practice and their advice to others on practice strategies. The third section deals with their accounts of how they memorize a work. In the fourth section, they describe the experience of performance anxiety and how they cope with it. The final section contains their accounts of preparing for public performance and the experience of playing for an audience.

The reader should feel free to pick and choose among the entries in each section. There is no need to read each and every one. Every pianist who spoke informatively on a topic is included because we wanted to show the places of agreement as well as disagreement, but this means that the pianists often say the same thing. For the benefit of those who would like to follow the thoughts of a single artist across themes, we have arranged the comments in alphabetical order by artist's name within theme. (Of course, not every artist spoke on every theme.) To help the reader place the artists' words in their historical and cultural contexts, their dates of birth (and death) are listed in Table 3.1, along with the name of the interviewer and the year the interview took place. Since the date is not reported for many of the interviews, the date of first publication of the collection of interviews is also given.

KINDS OF MEMORY

Many of the artists spontaneously made distinctions among different types of memory for music. Muscle (motor) memory, aural (auditory) memory, and visual memory (for both the music and hand position on the keyboard) were frequently mentioned. Building conceptual (declarative) memory was described in terms of using formal analysis, harmonic analysis, and fingering patterns to understand the music. Many pianists observed that memory seemed to develop unconsciously or automatically without deliberate effort. This can be characteristic of any of the different types of memory (motor, auditory, visual, or conceptual). We refer to it as *incidental* memory.

The comments of the pianists about each type of memory, in this and the following sections, are summarized in Table 3.2. The table indicates whether a pianist describes a type of memory as being particularly important (+) or unimportant (-) personally. Several pianists described one or more kinds of memory as being dangerous or unreliable, and this is also represented in the table (—). The table also indicates when a topic was mentioned in a neutral fashion (*) and when it was not mentioned at all (.). (Lack of mention of a form of memory does not, of course, mean that the pianist did not make use of it, only that it was not mentioned in the excerpted passages.) Sometimes it was hard to know if a particular kind of memory was being referred to or not and this is also indicated (?).

Pianists who refer to conceptual or declarative memory are listed in column 4 of Table 3.2. Most of these references are indirect. Only Claudio Arrau and Isidor Philip refer directly to memory in speaking of analytical memory. Other references are more indirect and appear in many guises. Some speak of the role of musical form (Leon Fleisher, Percy Grainger, Edwin Hughes, Victor Seroff), others of the importance of analyzing the

TABLE 3.1
Pianists Included in Chapter 3 With Dates, Date of Interview (When Known), Interviewer, and First Publication Date

(for Collections of Interviews Date Refers to Publication of the Collection)

	Born-(died)	Interview date	Interviewer	First Published in Collection
Martha Argerich	1941		Portugheis	1993
Claudio Arrau	1903-1991	1971	Elder	1982
"	"		Dubal	1984
Vladimir Ashkenazy	1937	1983-86	Noyle	1987
David Bar-Illan	1930		Dubal	1984
Harold Bauer	1873-1951		Cooke	1948
Lazar Berman	1930		Portugheis	1996
Stephen Bishop-Kovacevich	1940		Dubal	1984
Jorge Bolet	1914-1990	1983-86	Noyle	1987
Alexandre Borowski	1889-1968		Brower	1926
Alfred Brendel	1931		Dubal	1984
John Browning	1933	1983-86	Noyle	1987
Alfred Cortot	1878-1962		Brewer	1926
Bella Davidovich	1928	1983-86	Noyle	1987
Jörg Demus	1928	1965	Elder	1982
Misha Dichter	1945	1983-86	Noyle	1987
Alicia de Larrocha	1923	1969	Elder	1982
"			Dubal	1984
Maurice Dumesnil	1886-1974		Cooke	1948
Yuri Egorov	1954-1988		Mach	1988
Janina Fialkowska	1951	1983-86	Noyle	1987
Rudolf Firkusny	1912-1994	1983-86	Noyle	1987
Leon Fleisher	1928	1983-86	Noyle	1987
Ignaz Friedman	1886-1948		Brower	1926
Rudolph Ganz	1872-1972		Cooke	1948
Heinrich Gebhard	1878-1963		Cooke	1948
Walter Gieseking	1895-1956		Brower	1926
Emil Gillels	1916-1985		Mach	1988
Percy Grainger	1882-1961		Cooke	1948
Myra Hess	1890-1965		Brower	1926
Josef Hofmann	1876-1957		Cooke	1948
Stephen Hough	1961		Mach	1988
Edwin Hughes	1884-1965		Cooke	1948
Ernest Hutcheson	1871-1951		Cooke	1948

TABLE 3.1 *(continued)*

	Born-(died)	Interview date	Interviewer	First Published in Collection
Lili Kraus	1905-1986	1969	Elder	1982
"			Mach	1980
Benno Moiseiwitsch	1890-1963		Brower	1926
Elly Ney			Brower	1926
Mitja Nikisch	1855-1922		Brower	1926
Guimar Novaes	1896-1979	1970	Elder	1982
Garrick Ohlsson	1948		Mach	1988
Isidor Philipp	1863-1958		Cooke	1948
Murray Perahia	1947		Mach	1988
Ivo Pogorelich	1958		Mach	1988
Moriz Rosenthal	1862-1946		Cooke	1948
Artur Rubinstein	1887-1982	1970	Elder	1982
Olga Samoroff	1882-1948		Brower	1926
Emil Sauer	1862-1942		Cooke	1913
André-Michel Schub	1952		Noyle	1987
Rudolf Serkin	1903-1991	1970	Elder	1982
Victor Seroff	1902		Cooke	1948
Ernest Schelling	1875		Cooke	1913
Abbey Simon	1922	1983-86	Noyle	1987
Ralph Votapek	1939	1983-86	Noyle	1987
Tamás Vásáry	1933	1976	Elder	1982
Andre Watts	1946	1983-86	Noyle	1987
Mark Westcott	1946 c.	1971	Elder	1982

harmonic structure (Janina Fialkowska, Rudolf Firkusny, Leon Fleisher, Myra Hess, Lili Kraus). Many of the pianists report that they engage in mental practice (indicated by a # in Table 3.2), which certainly exercises conceptual memory. Jörg Demus is speaking of conceptual memory when he says that "if your heart fails you, your brain will come to the rescue," and Isidor Philipp seems to be referring to the same thing when he says that he memorized "by sections" after his memory was weakened by illness. In most cases, no connection is made between thinking about a piece in a particular way and memorization. We will have more to say about conceptual memory later. Here we note only that there is clearly a

TABLE 3.2
**Pianists Who Mentioned Different Types of Memory in
Their Interviews**

	TYPES OF MEMORY			
	Motor	*Auditory*	*Visual*	*Conceptual*	*Automatic*
Claudio Arrau	*	*	*	*	.
Vladimir Ashkenazy	—	*	*	*	*
David Bar-Illan	—	*	.	+	.
Harold Bauer	.	.	.	.	+
Jorge Bolet	.	+	.	#	*
Alexandre Borowski	.	-	+	.	.
Alfred Brendel	+	+	-	.	.
John Browning	*	*	+	#	.
Alfred Cortot	+	.	.	+	+
Bella Davidovich	*	+	+	*	*
Jörg Demus	*	.	.	*	*
Misha Dichter	—	*	-	+	—
Maurice Dumesnil	.	.	.	*	*
Alicia de Larrocha	—	.	—	+	*
Yuri Egorov	.	.	.	.	*
Janina Fialkowska	*	*	*	*	.
Rudolf Firkusny	.	+	.	#	*
Leon Fleisher	—	*	+	#	.
Ignaz Friedman	*	*	*	*	.
Rudolph Ganz	*	*	*	*	.
Heinrich Gebhard	—	—	—	+	—
Walter Gieseking	.	+	+	#	.
Percy Grainger	*	.	.	*	*
Myra Hess	*	*	+	*	*
Josef Hofmann	*	*	*	+	.
Stephen Hough	*	*	*	+	*
Edwin Hughes	.	*	.	+	.
Ernest Hutcheson	+	+	-	+	*
Lili Kraus	*	*	—	#	*
Benno Moiseiwitsch	.	.	.	?	.
Elly Ney	.	.	.	#	.
Mitja Nikisch	.	*	+	#	*
Guimar Novaes	.	*	*	?	*
Isidor Philipp	.	.	—	+	.
Moriz Rosenthal	.	.	.	+	.

TABLE 3.2 *(continued)*

	Motor	Auditory	Visual	Conceptual	Automatic
			TYPES OF MEMORY		
Artur Rubinstein	.	.	+	*	.
Olga Samoroff	*	+	-	#	.
André-Michel Schub	.	.	.	.	*
Rudolf Serkin	—	.	.	*	*
Victor Seroff	+	*	—	#	.
Ernest Schelling	*	*	*	.	.
Abbey Simon	.	.	.	.	*
Tamás Vásáry	+	.	.	+	.
Ralph Votapek	—	.	.	+	.
Andre Watts	*	*	.	+	.
Mark Westcott	*	.	.	*	.

+   particularly strong or important personally
-   particularly weak or unimportant personally
—   dangerous, insecure, not to be relied on
reports using mental practice, indirectly mentioning conceptual memory
*   topic mentioned
?   ambiguous as to whether topic mentioned or not
.   topic not mentioned (N.B., this does not mean that the pianist did not make use of this
    form of memory, only that it was not mentioned.)

need for such a concept. Most of the pianists refer to it, but there is no generally agreed upon term.

An interesting sort of response came from pianists who said that their memory worked unconsciously or naturally, (Table 3.2, column 5) but then proceeded to give explicit and articulate descriptions of their memory-enhancing strategies and routines. For example, Rudolf Serkin says that memory is an unconscious process of going over the work until it "sticks," but then talks about relying on the architecture of the music. Even more strikingly, he mentions that his fingerings vary unpredictably. In other words, he does not rely on motor memory. I think the only possible conclusion is that he is relying heavily on conceptual and aural memory, yet he describes his memory initially as "unconscious." Heinrich Gebhard and Percy Grainger both describe a "nonmental" or "automatic" memory, but then specify elaborate conceptual strategies such as sectional memorizing and careful analysis of form, rhythm, and harmony. Bella Davidovich denies "sorting out the analytical stages", instead relying on her instinctive knowledge of music, but goes on to acknowledge that her instinctive response comes from many years of study of musical form and structure. What seems to be going on here is that these artists think of motor and aural memory as memory and do not realize that analyzing the formal and harmonic structure is also a form of memorization.

In contrast to the varied terms and concepts used to discuss conceptual memory, the pianists were much more consistent in talking about the other forms of memory. Muscle or motor memory (Table 3.2, column 1) is an unambiguous concept mentioned by many of the pianists. Ernest Schelling describes it as "training the fingers to do their duty no matter what happens." Several caution that, although motor memory is universal, it is the least reliable form of memory for performance. Rudolf Serkin calls it "irritating" and "dangerous". Alicia de Larrocha also warns that relying on the "memory of the fingers" is "dangerous". As Leon Fleisher says, "It's the finger that deserts one first." Victor Seroff expresses a minority opinion when he says that motor memory is particularly useful when the performer is nervous.

There is also clear agreement about auditory memory (Table 3.2, column 2), although it is by no means mentioned by every pianist. I would guess that auditory memory is so vital and automatic that it is often simply taken for granted. I would expect it to be noticed only when the performer is learning polyphonic or atonal music, where the profusion or lack of expected aural patterns can cause serious difficulty.

Visual memory, in contrast, is not taken for granted (Table 3.2, column 3). Many of the pianists mention that they either have it or they do not. Claudio Arrau, Guiomar Novaes, Artur Rubinstein, and John Browning mention having "photographic" memory; Myra Hess describes how she can "see" and "read" the printed page when playing from memory; Leon Fleisher is aware of "interference" when he switches to a differently printed score. In contrast, Alfred Brendel, Lili Kraus, Ernest Hutcheson, Misha Dichter, Heinrich Gebhard, and Janina Fialkowska say that they rely little on visual memory either because their visual memory is poor or because they do not find it useful. The consistency in these accounts is that, whether they use it or eschew it, these master pianists all are familiar with the concept of visual memory and use quite similar terms to talk about it. The term photographic memory is often used, although psychologists now believe that no one's memory is truly photographic. Among the pianists, however, only Leon Fleisher expressed any skepticism about the concept, noting wryly, "I'm always inclined to ask what kind of film they use: I got an answer once from Seiji Ozawa, 'Fuji film'" (Noyle, 1987, p. 97).

> *Claudio Arrau:* I have four kinds of memory: muscle, photographic, sound, and analytic. I use analytic memory last, after the work has gone into my body—my muscles, my ears, my vision. (Elder, 1986, p. 45)

Alexandre Borowski: It is visual memory with me. I see the notes and signs on the printed page before me as I play. No, I do not seem to hear them so much as I see them. (Brower, 1926, pp. 219–220)

Alfred Brendel: I have a good aural and kinesthetic memory, but my memory is not visual at all. I don't see the score as I play. (Dubal, 1997, p. 73)

John Browning: I have a partial photographic memory. I think the old rule of thumb was, the memory has to be aural, through the ear, visual, tactile. (Noyle, 1987, p.32)

Bella Davidovich: In looking at the score, I have a sense in my mind of what the piece will involve, what the important elements are, and what I want to be telling the audience through this music. I don't make a habit of separately sorting out the analytical stages. For me, it is a process that all takes place at once. If it is a Beethoven or a Mozart sonata, I already know it instinctively, having studied music for so many years. I know what it involves, so there's no actual conscious thought that has to go into it. (Noyle, 1987, p. 39)

Jörg Demus: The expression "playing by heart" is the key to . . . your subconscious musical feelings and instincts. When you are young, you play almost unconscious of what you are doing, other than expressing what you feel about the music. But at a later age . . . this unconscious approach doesn't work any more so we have to support the heart by the "brains" and use much of Gieseking's mental method: analyzing, realizing this entry comes here, this voice does this, here is the first big climax, here is an augmentation, a diminution, a stretto and so on. You have to have a detailed knowledge of what you are playing. Then if your heart fails you, your brain will come to the rescue. (Elder, 1986, p. 129)

Alicia de Larrocha: First, there is natural memory. There are passages . . . that memorize themselves. Without your realizing it one day you know them by heart. But this kind of memory is dangerous.

Second, there is the kind of memory which for me is almost the most important—musical form memorization. I analyze the work—the phrases, the intervals, the cadences, the form, and so on.

Third, there is the memory of the fingers, which is also dangerous but which can help.

Fourth, there is a kind of memory which helps me a lot . . . the memory of the accents (so frequent and important in Spanish music)—a phrase where there is an accent, or a phrase where there isn't. . . .

And fifth, there is a kind of memory which can help and which is also dangerous: the visual memory of the keyboard—what the hands and arms have to do, the distance to be here, to get there. Memory is complex. You must have all these kinds. . . . (Elder, 1986, p. 109)

Misha Dichter: I don't have a photographic memory, and that's why I need a system. . . . I can only rely on aural memory in a pinch, because I have good relative pitch. It's probably close to perfect pitch . . . if I'm looking down and my memory tells me this is an F half diminished chord in the left hand if my memory has gone blank at that moment, I can hear the chord and then play it, which is very helpful. (Noyle, 1987, pp. 52–53)

Janina Fialkowska: I'm lucky enough to have visual memory. I also do [have] a harmonic memory. But I can just sit here and see the music in front of me. That doesn't work when you're performing, though, because you see it too late. . . . I'm big on knowing all the harmonies so that you can't get lost. . . . Then of course, there is the muscular memory. That's the longest in that you just have to practice and practice until your fingers know it by heart. And finally, I do something that is from my French training, because early French training is very big on solfège[2]. In many works, such as Mozart or Bach, I can actually solfège the notes. (Noyle, 1987, p. 64)

Rudolf Firkusny: After reading it through, I would start getting acquainted with the general ideas of the piece and start to work. By work, I mean analyzing the harmonic structure, the formal structure, the dynamic structure of the piece. Then I would try to put it in shape in my mind and then try to do the same thing at the piano. After completing this process you have the feeling that you basically know the piece and its most important elements. (Noyle, 1987, pp. 81, 83)

Leon Fleisher: Memorizing depends on the circumstances. Ideally speaking it should be some combination of aural, visual, and tactile. . . . I think probably the least reliable, in terms of public performance, is finger memory, because it's the finger that deserts one first. So I would think in terms of structural memory, a structure memory in terms of bar periods, how long the phrase is. I have a certain amount of photographic memory, it's a part of the equation but it's not all of it. I think I have that because when I see the piece I'm playing in another edition that has it placed on the page differently, I get confused. So I think to a certain extent I use visual memory. I close my eyes and I see it on the screen of my eyelids, plus I have an understanding of the structural and harmonic form. (Noyle, 1987, p. 97)

Ignaz Friedman: One must know the piece, its construction and harmony, through careful study. There are four sources of memory: the eye, to see the notes on the page or keys—that would be visual memory; the fingers, to find the keys easily on the keyboard—digital memory; the ear to hear the tones—auricular memory, and lastly though we may say it should be first, the mind to think these tones and keys—or mental memory. (Brower, 1926, p. 52)

Heinrich Gebhard: In my own memorizing and teaching my pupils how to memorize . . . there are three kinds of memorizing which I condemn:

First—the "automatic" memory; that is, when the student just practices automatically for weeks on a piece until finally, by "multiple digital repetitions" the fingers get used to the motions required to strike the right keys.

Second—relying on your ear and emotions to reproduce the sounds. . . .

Third—painfully visualizing each printed note on the page.

I consider these three methods unreliable.

The method that I use might be called the "keyboard geography method." Before we begin to memorize a piano piece, we study the notes carefully, all through, analyzing the form of the piece, the character and outline of the melodies, the rhythms and harmonies. When that has been fairly well digested . . . we memorize how the piece *lies physically on the keyboard*, as we study a map in geography, and finally we hear how the music *feels physically on the keyboard*. (Cooke, 1948, pp. 82–83)

Percy Aldridge Grainger: To have a secure concert memory I find it needful to approach memorizing from several different angles, so that if one form of memory fails, there are other forms to fall back on.

1. Physical (non-Mental) Memory. This is the subconscious memory of hand and finger acquired from playing a passage through countless times. I do not consider this form of memory established unless I can read a book at the same time, or be read aloud to by somebody else. . . . This memory "tides one over" when one's mind "becomes a blank".

2. Form-Conscious Memory. Awareness of the structure, form-shapes, and key changes. . . .

3. The ability to spell out each note [away from the keyboard]. . . .

4. Sectional memorizing. Special memorizing of the beginning of each section, so that one is always able to begin *securely* with the beginning of the next section, if anything goes wrong with the memory in the section one is in.

5. Awareness of Bar Groupings. . . . In practicing this kind of memorizing one says to oneself: "Four group, bar 1, bar 2, bar 3, bar 4, etc. . . . If one's memory fails, inside a bar group one knows how many bars to wait (silently, or orienting oneself by soft playing) until the next bar group, or section, begins.

6. Transposing Memory. To be able to play all one's passages and pieces in any key. This gives one a special grasp of the tides of modulation within a piece. (Cooke, 1948, pp. 84–86)

Myra Hess: When I take up new work, I try to see it from all sides. By this I mean that I study out the harmony, the chord and key progressions, the technical requirements, then the meaning and necessary interpretation. (Brower, 1926, p. 194)

As is well known there are three kinds of memory training: that of the eye, the ear, and the fingers. Although I use all three, I depend, I think, more on the first than on either of the others. I can really see the printed page before me, mentally, and can actually read it as I play, just as though it were on the music-desk before my eyes. (Brower, 1926, p. 197)

Edwin Hughes: Knowledge of musical form, of the patterns of musical composition, is always a valuable asset. (Cooke, 1948, p. 96)

Ernest Hutcheson: Unfortunately I have no visual memory whatever. That is to say, I cannot form mental photographs of the printed page. I realize this is a deprivation. . . . My own memory is largely aural and kinesthetic, partly just pure memory, unassociated with the senses. (Cooke, 1948, p. 98)

Lili Kraus: I have an excellent visual memory, but when I am playing I try to eliminate it because I want to remember with my ear, not my eye. I don't want to see the music but to hear it, to live it. I have to remember the sound and identify with the harmonic, thematic, rhythmic, and mechanical aspects so completely that I don't want to see the picture. . . . (One) must know the piece from every aspect—harmonically, melodically, and rhythmically. . . . But first and last a reliable memory is possible only if an absolute identification with the piece in living experience has taken place. (Elder, 1986, p. 67)

Guimar Novaes: (Interviewer: Is your memory strongly aural or photographic?) Both. I like to look at the music very intentionally. . . . I have photographic memory. (Elder, 1986, p. 25)

Isidor Philipp: If I don't think that visual memory is useful, I am sure that analytical memory is a basis of secure memory. (Cooke, 1948, p. 112)

Artur Rubinstein: My memory is mostly photographic, inherited from my father. When I play I turn the pages in my mind; I even see the coffee stains. My knowledge of the architecture of a work, how it is built, helps too. (Elder, 1986, p. 4)

Rudolf Serkin: I memorize by remembering—unconsciously. After a while the work sticks. . . . You can't perform any work without knowing its architecture. . . . Finger memory is irritating really, a dangerous, unreliable thing. With me it would be disastrous because I change fingerings constantly, at the spur of the moment sometimes, according to the piano, the hall, my disposition, how I slept, and so on. (Elder, 1986, p. 57)

Victor Seroff: Musical memory consists of at least four elements: (1) Sight Memory; (2) Physical or Touch memory; (3) Intellectual Memory or Memory of Form and Content, and (4) Ear Memory.

Memory varies with the individual, and some musicians with a great capacity for it possess only one of the many elements. However, there is much greater security in having all four highly developed. Touch memory is indispensable to the performer, and is particularly useful if he is nervous or distracted by something. The fingers alone will usually bring him out of the woods. . . . Sight memory is the least secure. . . . (Cooke, 1948, pp. 122–123)

Ernest Schelling: There are three ways [of memorizing]. 1, By sight; that is, seeing the notes in your mind's eye; 2, memorizing by "ear", the way which comes to one most naturally; 3, memorizing by the fingers, that is training the fingers to do their duty no matter what happens. Before performing in public the student should have memorized the composition in all of these ways. Only thus can he be absolutely sure of himself. If one way fails him the other method comes to his rescue. . . . (Cooke, 1913/1999, pp. 276–277)

Tamás Vásáry: When one is playing, the mechanical movements of the hands and the mental work of the memory go hand in hand. Sometimes you don't know which is operating, sometimes both, sometimes only one. It is dangerous when only either the hands or the brain is operating. So I prefer that both fingers and brain be solidly there. Then if one gets tired, you can reach to the other. (Elder, 1986, p. 138)

HOW TO PRACTICE

How to practice—how often, how much, how methodically—is an emotionally loaded topic for pianists, one that induces guilt, denial, and other strong feelings. I believe that this is so for a variety of reasons. First, many concert performers began their study as very young children. Although they were surely motivated to play, some recall being forced into long hours of excruciating practice long before they could understand or internalize the reasons for such discipline. Martha Argerich reports the "cheating" she did as a small child to divert herself from practice, and Lazar Berman says poignantly, "I had no childhood, no youth." Like Martha Argerich, I too sometimes used to read as I practiced scales or exercises. While I do not recommend this, it did provide good practice in dividing my attention.

A second reason for the emotional intensity surrounding practice is that most pianists, as students, were trained to believe that more practice is always better. As André-Michel Schub says, "There's no way of getting around those hours at the piano." As adults, they still believe that they should be practicing long hours each day, but most do not. Moreover, describing one's practice routines to an interviewer could reveal weaknesses, such as technical limitations, lack of discipline, compulsions, superstitious routines, and anxiety-induced blocking of memory or concentration. For all these reasons, I believe we can expect a certain amount of dissimulation—I like to think of it as "fibbing"—when pianists are interviewed about this issue. At the least, many are more evasive and guarded than when they are discussing less sensitive topics.

The range of expressive language and emotion words used by the pianists was greater than when they talked about memory. The diversity of their feelings was striking. Claudio Arrau and Janina Fialkowska claim that practicing is "fun," while John Browning compares it to dishwashing. Others—Lazar Berman and Jorge Bolet—say they dislike it. At the extreme of negative emotional reactions, Browning reports rage, frustration, even swearing and hitting the piano. The range of habits is striking too. Reported amounts of practice range from Bella Davidovich's 8 one-hour segments each day to Claudio Arrau, who, in his old age, was still practicing "two or three hours a day."

Despite the range of feelings about practice, there is considerable agreement that it is serious business. Leon Fleisher and Misha Dichter talk about the importance of mindful practice—focused, concentrated, and highly attentive. Jorges Bolet agrees that mindless practice is a waste of time, like "chewing one's cud." The strategies mentioned most frequently (hands separate, slow practice, and mental practice) are certainly activities that require concentration. In the same vein, Bella Davidovich stresses the importance of being fresh and well rested, while John Browning points out the importance of working on weaknesses.

When I read these pianists' accounts, I recognized some of my own practice strategies. For example, I rely on relearning a piece before public performance—a strategy we describe more fully in later chapters. The accounts also gave rise to feelings about whether I practice too much or too little. My own (perhaps self-serving) belief is that pianists who practice long hours tend to be those who become known as more methodical, precise performers; those who practice less gain reputations as more spontaneous, creative, and exciting performers. For me, no less than for other pianists, practice creates dilemmas of guilt, responsibility, and self-definition.

Martha Argerich: (Remembering her childhood) Officially, I was supposed to practice three hours but, in reality, it was less because I cheated. What I really liked was reading, so I used to read while pretending to be practicing. If I heard the door I would put whatever I was reading under my skirt. . . . (Portugheis, 1993, p. 5)

Claudio Arrau: I think it's beautiful to practice; I *love* to practice. On the average I do now two to three hours a day. (Dubal, 1997, p. 15)

Vladimir Ashkenazy: I think you have to live with a piece to assimilate it, and sometimes you have to live with a score all your life to assimilate everything. But superficially speaking, just to get the form, you have to know, basically, what happens in the piece of music. You know, the relationship of the individual parts and so on. That comes very quick. I don't even need to play it. (Noyle, 1987, p. 5)

You can take one measure, you can take two notes and practice musically. Everything I practice, in that case, becomes musical. Sometimes I play a passage which is difficult and try to get it right, but within it I try to play it musically. . . . (Noyle, 1987, p. 7)

David Bar-Illan: (Describing his method of silent practice in which he presses the keys so slowly that they make no sound) I found this to be a marvelous way of checking on how securely I had memorized the pieces. . . . This kind of practice gives you a margin of strength and security on stage, where we may be performing somewhat below our optimum level. . . . Do understand that during my soundless practicing I do hear the music in my mind. One can all too easily play music without actually listening to it. Through this kind of work I ensure that my music making is not merely automatic. (Dubal, 1997, pp. 40–41)

Lazar Berman: I was forced to practice and very often it was not a pleasure. I had to practice a lot as I was younger than the other students but was expected to play like them. I had no childhood, no youth. (Portugheis, 1996, p. 11)

Jorge Bolet: I practice at the piano only when I feel it is required—no more than an hour and a half at any one time. (Noyle, 1987, p. 14)

The general principle of practicing hands separately, I think you can apply to everyone. . . . Practicing slowly is another general principle that is very important. . . . I don't really get the results of what I practice today, the next day, or the next day, but probably from ten days to two weeks later. . . .

Whatever I do at the keyboard gives me enough practice material so that I can practice mentally, for twelve, fifteen, twenty hours, whenever I'm awake. I always have something running through my mind. (Noyle, 1987, p. 17)

John Browning: First of all, every artist gets angry in practicing. He gets angry at the music, or he gets angry with himself for his own stupidity. So there are times that you hit the keyboard, and there are times you swear four-letter language. It's hard work. It's like dish washing. It isn't fun. (Noyle, 1987, p. 30)

If one is looking through a brand-new piece, I think it's an intuitive thing. I read through it and I get an idea of where the problems for me are going to lie. . . .

Also, the successful performer is the one who has a kind of intuition as to what may not seem to be giving him trouble but what will give him trouble in the performance. It's like insurance. . . . You insure, you over-prepare, so that if you are distracted during a concert, if you're not feeling up to snuff, you have so much backlog of preparation that it will carry you through automatically. (Noyle, 1987, pp. 28–29)

Alfred Cortot: In the early days the student has to do considerable technique practice, but the material for this should be so carefully chosen as to eliminate all unnecessary effort. Avoid useless repetition; rather get at the principal – the heart of the thing you want to conquer, and cut away whatever is superfluous.

Take the difficult portions and passages of the piece you are study-ing. . . . Make new material for technique practice out of them. . . . The passage may, in various ways, be developed in such a style as to fix it deeply in the mind, besides making it valuable for finger, wrist and arm technique. (Brower, 1926, p. 26)

I consider it absolutely essential for the piano student to commit everything he attempts to learn, to memory. If he wishes to enlarge his acquaintance with music by getting the works of various composers and playing them through, there is certainly no harm in that. But this is very different from attempting to learn the pieces. With this end in view, one must study seriously, analyze the music, see how it is made up, consider its form and tone texture, and what the composer evidently intended to convey through it. (Brower, 1926, p. 30)

Bella Davidovich: The best hours for practice are the morning hours when a person's mind is fresh and the ears are fresh. . . . I find that a one-hour period is where I achieve the utmost in terms of concentration. I work very intensively for one hour and then take a ten, fifteen, or twenty-minute break during which I will occupy myself with something completely different, whether it's to eat or something else. This method works out well so that I can continue for eight hours, in one-hour periods. . . . In general, the more you practice, the better. That's really true. But the best is to practice with a fresh head, a rested mind, otherwise, you're not going to be productive. (Noyle, 1987, p. 43)

Misha Dichter: I try to never remove musical meaning from what I'm going over. (Noyle, 1993, p. 50)

After I've learned the piece, I do mental practicing away from the keyboard. I've had some of my greatest revelations while jogging, or on the tennis court. (Noyle, 1987, p. 57)

I hate to think of the time I wasted as a student. Now it's just so easy to see certain shortcuts that would have saved thousands of hours. (Noyle, 1987, p. 57)

In practicing, never daydream. Never use the piano as a vehicle for simply moving the fingers and passing time. If you have only one moment when you're not aware of what you're doing musically or technically (and usually both), you're wasting your time. . . . (Noyle, 1987, p. 59)

Janina Fialkowska: For me, the best time to learn something is in the morning. I, absolutely, at my advanced age cannot learn a new piece, I cannot memorize, in the afternoon after lunch. I don't know why, I cannot. . . . (Noyle, 1987, pp. 67–68)

If I'm learning a new work, say it's Schumann, basically, at this point in my career, I know all these pieces in my head, and even if I haven't played them, I know exactly what I want to do with them. So I don't really have to rush out and buy a lot of recordings to listen to, which I used to when I was learning a piece. I would buy all of the recordings of all my favorite pianists and play them, and hear, What's he doing here? How does this piece go? Now, you'll find me doing that far less. Actually, about halfway through my practicing of a piece, I am always terribly curious to hear how people that I admire play the piece and compare it with what I'm doing and steal their best ideas. (Noyle, 1987, p. 63)

Rudolf Firkusny: Concentration is very tiring. . . . Sometimes one or two hours of concentrated practicing is much more tiring than playing seven or eight hours. That's just the way it is. (Noyle, 1987, p. 81)

I believe in practicing slowly . . . because you can have much more control of what you are doing. At other times you have to play in tempo to really get the feeling of the piece. However, when you play a piece slowly and in tempo you are prepared for most things. I believe slow practicing is very helpful and very useful.

When I say practicing, I do not only speak of the purely technical aspect of the work . . . but also the melodic line, the pedaling, all of which are very important. The touch is important. I've studied it and have found out that it somehow expresses most of your ideas which may be right or wrong, I don't care, but which at any rate, they are your own. To find out what to do with the piano mezzo forte, forte, piano, the touch control; this is what I call global practicing.

Very often I practice away from the piano, sometimes before I actually learn the score. I read the piece away from the piano just to get the ideas that I would like to have, then I go to the piano. (Noyle, 1987, p. 83)

Leon Fleisher: With a new piece one should sit down, probably in a chair away from the piano, and learn it, look at it, take it apart, try to understand it structurally, harmonically, and in all its elements as much as possible. Sing it to yourself. Sing the various components, the various material. Get some kind of idea. It's not an idea that you have to be wedded to for life, but get some kind of idea of what you think it should sound like, of what you want it to sound like. Then, when you have gotten as far as you can in this manner, when you've become as specific as you can about the material in this manner, then take it to the keyboard, because then you have a goal. (Noyle, 1987, p. 92)

Learn a piece as best you can up to a certain point, and then drop it. Drop it for whatever, nine months, a year, or more, then come back to it, and in that period of having been dropped, it will have matured, grown, ripened in your subconscious and when you come back to it, it will have evolved. It will have changed. You will see it with different eyes, you will hear it with different ears. Relearn it again, or go on from where you left off, and I would recommend dropping it the second time. And only when you pick it up for a third time do ... you really have a chance ... of presenting something in public that has become genetically part of you. (Noyle, 1987, p.91)

(Mindless practice is) very dangerous. You spend time at the instrument and the fingers are going up and down and the sound is coming out of the instrument, but it is without intent behind it, it's as though you're in automatic ... suddenly you become consciously aware of "God, what am I doing here? I went through so many hours of this without really thinking about it." It means your fingers do it, without realizing that under the stress of public performance, they're the first thing that goes, if you are nervous. (Noyle, 1987, pp. 94–95).

Stephen Hough: (A) stratagem I find useful is to practice with my eyes closed. The brain is trained to use all of the senses. The piano, though, seems confined to the sense of touch and hearing, obviously, and also the sense of sight – looking where you're playing on the keyboard. If you remove one of those senses, you make the other one develop more strongly, because it has to overcompensate. (Mach, 1991, vol. 2, p. 136)

Emil Sauer: One hour of concentrated practice with the mind fresh and the body rested is better than four hours of dissipated practice with the mind stale and the body tired. With a fatigued intellect the fingers simply dawdle over the keys and nothing is accomplished. I find in my own daily practice that is best for me to practice two hours in the morning and then two hours later in the day. (Cooke, 1913/1999, p. 238)

André-Michel Schub: People forget the hard work they put in. When you read that this one didn't practice hard, don't believe it. I know that I did, and I know that other people did too. ... There's no way of getting around those hours at the piano if you practice to play correctly. It is what it does for your equipment and for the control of sound. What's even more important than how many notes you play is what you do with those notes.

The more time you spend at the piano, the more control you have. Practice has a lot to do with quality but there has to be a certain number of hours of playing just to maintain a level. (Noyle, 1987, p. 108)

(On learning new music): I tend to play through things as much as possible. I read quite well, although there are people who read better. Barring a Rachmaninoff concerto, I can get through a piece and make some musical sense out of it. I quickly become aware of the mechanical spots that need to be worked on in greater detail. But I'm more interested in how this all fits into a musical concept. . . . In starting out, I try to grasp the whole piece as opposed to just seeing where hard spots are. (Noyle, 1987, pp. 103–104)

Abbey Simon: I try to put out of my head, or out of my ears, everything I ever heard about the music. I approach every piece of music as if I have never heard it before in my life, whether it is a piece that I have played since childhood that I am reviving, or whether it is a new song. (Noyle, 1987, p. 119)

. . . I practice not more than two hours at a time because I get tired. After that there is no concentration so it is not worthwhile. (Noyle, 1987, p. 122)

Ralph Votapek: I would rather, after the initial reading, start by practicing very slow at a tempo where I know I won't go wrong. I don't like to divide the music up into segments: notes, tone, dynamics, phrasing. . . . I think studying a piece for three weeks is sufficient time to learn the work. After that, I get very impatient. (Noyle, 1987, p. 129)

I think it all boils down to your concentration in practicing. If you concentrate when you are practicing, chances are nothing will go wrong with memory. If once you've memorized a piece. . . . then the danger is to play without thinking too much. And if I find I do that too much and then I go to play a piece. . . . I sometimes have a few memory slips at the performance. Usually they are minor ones, in the left hand, that are quickly covered up, but the fear is there lurking. (Noyle, 1987, p. 134)

Andre Watts: Practicing is really up in your head, and this comes first. . . . You have to have the ability to think and make decisions and to have a belief that when you've made a decision you will be able to implement it. The next is to have the ability to hear as you play, to hear and judge at the same time so that you can listen to what you are producing. You try to control it, but also judge at the same time and decide, no, that's not what it should be. (Noyle, 1987, pp. 145–146)

Mark Westcott: I don't feel good inside if I miss much practice. Even going on a vacation is hard for me. I'm not a masochist about it or anything, but I love to practice. Practicing excites me. I do about seven hours a day on the average. (Elder, 1986, p. 176)

HOW TO MEMORIZE MUSIC

The requirement of playing from memory is a source of tremendous anxiety for pianists. More than one concert artist has argued that playing from memory should be abolished (Williamon, in press). For example, Percy Grainger once wrote, "Music has been greatly worsened by public performances without notes" (Cooke, 1948, p. 86). Yet no pianist today could have a successful career without extremely well-developed memorization skills.

Given the difficulty of playing long, complicated programs flawlessly from memory and the public humiliation that attends memory lapses, it is surprising that there are so few agreed-on principles of memorization. Among the multitude of books about piano technique and piano pedagogy, few have much to say about memorization. The topic is either not mentioned or dealt with in cursory and formulaic fashion. Rita Aiello (1999) and Aaron Williamon (in press) listed as exceptions only Bernstein (1981), Gieseking and Leimer (1972), Hughes (1915), Matthay (1926), and Rubinstein (1950). In the interviews in my collection, many of the pianists claim that they pay little attention to memorizing—that it is easy, automatic, and nonproblematic for them. Over and over, they say that they do not need to worry about it. Lili Kraus says she does not know the meaning of the word. Memorization "just happens," according to André-Michel Schub. Yuri Egorov claims that, "all at once it comes to me." It comes "naturally," says Guiomar Novaes, so naturally that "it's like breathing" (Jorge Bolet). "I suddenly realize that I know it," echoes Mitja Nikisch. It's "very simple" (Walter Gieseking), "very easy" (Benno Moiseiwitsch, Rudolf Firkusny), "subconscious" (Harold Bauer).

One way to explain this chorus of denial is to say that memory failures are problems only for amateurs; world-class artists have such highly developed memorization skills that they are beyond thinking or worrying about how they do it. I would say that the opposite is true: The more eminent, accomplished, and sought after one is, the more dangerous and humiliating the possibility of a public memory failure. It may be true that early in their careers many pianists rely on automatic memory processes, but it is just a matter of time before some scrape with disaster brings home the need to work more deliberately. To perform time and time again, one needs to prepare safety nets. I believe that many of the artists are engaging in major denial when they discount the possibility of memory lapses in their interviews. Ralph Votapek is, I think, unusually insightful when he says that memorization is a "bane" that performers relegate to their "subconscious" rather than confront their anxieties. Abbey Simon seems to illustrate the validity of Votapek's (and my) viewpoint when he says emphatically that he has no idea how he memorizes and does not want to know. John Browning, too, is candid. He states flatly that memorizing is an issue for every pianist. "And I don't care what anybody says, every performer, no matter how secure, always thinks about the possibility of memory slips."

There are clues to unacknowledged anxiety in the artists' words. For example, some—no less talented and accomplished than others who deny it—speak indirectly of anxiety about memorization. Vladimir Ashkenazy warns that it is "dangerous" to rely on muscle memory. Most revealing are those who mention that they are "blessed naturally" in the memory department (Myra Hess) or boast of their memory feats. Alexandre Borowski claims to have memorized "the most difficult piece ever written" with no noticeable effort. Jorge Bolet recounts a tale of memorizing Liszt's virtuoso *Mephisto Waltz* in an hour and a quarter (Noyle, 1987, pp. 19–20). If playing from memory were really as natural and automatic as breathing, such stories would have no point.

Pointing up pianists' concerns about memory is an anecdote told by Guy Maier about a pianist who ate lime because he read that memory problems are caused by a "lack of lime in the system." Maier advised:

> Before ossification or alarming complications set in, I hasten to urge you to desist from your lime diet! The only possible utilization of your theory would be to offer packages of lime drops to your students as rewards for good lessons. You are by no means alone with memorization difficulty. (Cooke, 1948, p. 100)

The view that every pianist memorizes differently seems to be widely held. Although only Benno Moiseiwitsch, Elly Ney, and Moriz Rosenthal are explicit on this point, many of the pianists describe characteristics of their own memories in ways that make an implicit contrast with the memories of others. When Rudolf Firkusny says, "My memorizing is only aural, I never see the printed page," he implies that the memorizing of others is different. This is borne out by the summary in Table 3.2. Most of the pianists make some mention of other forms of memory.

So too with strategies for memorizing. Everyone seems to be different, and this variety seems to lend credence to the view that everyone's memory is different. Jörg Demus builds muscle memory by using consistent fingerings. Olga Samaroff recommends memorizing by sections. Moriz Rosenthal recommends memorizing the structure first away from the piano. John Browning, Walter Gieseking, and Victor Seroff also make use of "mental practice". Rudolph Ganz advises memorizing hands separately, but Ernest Hutcheson "practically never bothers" with this. Jorge

Bolet, Alicia de Larrocha, and Isidor Philipp suggest that strategies change with age or the state of one's health.

I believe that there must be a lot more similarity in the way that pianists' memories work than their comments suggest. We all make use of the same memory systems, and we all have to perform under similar conditions. Surely everyone is using auditory memory when they hear a wrong note in their playing, and everyone must rely on the automaticity of motor memory. There may be a real difference in use of visual memory, but I am sure that every concert artist has a clear memory for the melodic and harmonic structure of the pieces he or she plays.

This last type of memory—conceptual memory—is important for me personally. Many of the pianists also acknowledge its importance when they talk, like Elly Ney, of studying a piece and thinking about its meaning. For Edwin Hughes and Moriz Rosenthal, it is the first thing to be memorized. But there are many others who do not mention it, like Walter Gieseking, who talks only of hearing the music. Does this mean that he does not use conceptual memory? I doubt it very much. Although it is certainly possible for students to memorize using just motor and auditory memory—we see them do it all the time—I do not believe that professionals would ever put themselves in that position even if they were able to. The risk of a memory lapse would be too great. The test would be to ask a pianist like Walter Gieseking to describe the harmonic and structural form of a piece he has memorized. Of course he could do this. He is one of the pianists who report engaging in mental practice which exercises conceptual memory more strongly than anything else.

> *Vladimir Ashkenazy*: I think it's a combination of things. It's memorizing the musical progression of music. There is something mechanical about it, too. The fingers memorize things, but it should be a combination. If you rely on your fingers, it's very dangerous. It is everything, mind, visual, aural, everything. (Noyle, 1987, p. 8)

> *Harold Bauer*: It is only very rarely that I have consciously employed any system in memorizing music. In the vast majority of instances, the process seems to be quite a subconscious one, and only when it has been necessary for some special reason for me to prepare a new composition in a very short time for public performance have I undertaken the mechanical labor of "committing to memory." When I have done this, the process has usually been that of mere reiteration. It is not a speedy process, but it works. I dare say other methods may be better.
>
> The important thing, however, is that I have never felt that I knew a piece of music unless the memorizing of it has been absolutely subconscious. (Cooke, 1948, p. 77)

Jorge Bolet: My memorization is almost one hundred percent aural. It's a question of ear. To me, it's like breathing. You never have to think about breathing. It's something that you do automatically twenty four hours a day, period. Memorizing to me is just that natural. (Noyle, 1987, p. 19)

Alexandre Borowski: I am told I have an unusual memory. Perhaps this may be true, for I feel my ability to memorize is somewhat out of the ordinary. Of course you know Balakireff's Islamey. It has been called, the most difficult piece ever written. I both learned and committed it to memory in five days. (Brower, 1926, p. 219)

John Browning: Memorizing is an issue with everybody because we have to play from memory. And I don't care what anybody says, every performer, no matter how secure, always thinks about the possibility of memory slips. . . . Everybody has to work at memorizing. . . .

I think mental practice is crucial for performers. You're not likely to have problems with memory if you can sit in a chair or lie on a bed and go through the entire work, no matter how complicated, and call it out in your mind. I really don't feel I'm ready to play a work in public until I can do this. (Noyle, 1987, p. 32)

Bella Davidovich: If it's a piece that I have heard and am familiar with, then the approach is to get it immediately memorized and into the hands at the same time. . . . I hear the main melody, the secondary lines, the base line, the reprises, etc., in my mind. It's thoroughly, clearly imaginable. (Noyle, 1993, p. 39)

The piece is retained first in the mind and then the fingers, but you cannot separate how you learn. Everything happens all together, the mind, the ears, the fingers, the feet. My photographic memory is actually quite good. Very often, during a concert, I'm able to visualize the page and the notes which I'm playing at that moment. I have it in my head. If I am in the middle stage of studying a new work, very often I will find myself walking down the street and hearing certain passages separately, echoing in my mind. So the memory is working away when I hear fragments of this music. But not in the beginning stage. At the beginning stage it's in the ears. A photographic memory does help, but it is the hearing and the ears that do the major part of this retaining process. (Noyle, 1987, p. 43)

Alicia de Larrocha: I study the music carefully first to form an idea of what it is all about. Then I seek passages or sections which offer the most difficulty, especially in regard to fingering. . . . Sometimes, too, I have to play a piece very slowly to solidify the memorization of the part. Slowness also helps to check note accuracy and phrasing . . . you see every detail and at the same time reinforce the memory. You are able to see chords more clearly, the form, the design, the harmonic groupings, and so on. It helps enormously to know the phrases, the ritardandos, an accent here, an accent there, an ending phrase, a starting phrase, that is, all the details.

This memorization of the rhythmical accents in every phrase is a very important memory aid, but not quite as reliable as the memorizing of the phrases, cadences, and form. I don't believe much in vision memory. It seems unsure and leaves me feeling rather insecure. Also, I don't practice above the keys, omitting the aural aspect, that is. (Mach, 1991, vol. 1, pp. 58–59).

(Interviewer: How do you memorize?) This is another thing that was once very easy and little by little has gotten more difficult. First, I sight read and then I look at the structure of the work and work on the fingering and write it in. I used to play without writing it in but now I have to do that. Then I memorize the piece from a visual point of view; and then the harmonies. (Dubal, 1997, p. 148)

Jörg Demus: (In response to a question about learning Bach's Well-Tempered Clavier) I found fingering very important. Because I can't have time to go over them every time before I play them, it is important that the hand positions and finger movements be built into my hand, even in the easy pieces. My hand somehow knows where to go automatically. It is hand, head, and heart which have to function. (Elder, 1986, p. 129)

Misha Dichter: I happen to be a rather fast learner, and I have memory systems that work for me. And yet, as I get older, I don't trust this rather superficial gobbling up. Experience has shown that these are the pieces I forget first, when I don't allow things to sink in. I (prefer to allow) . . . a period of at least three months from the first reading of a piece. I leave it and go back to other things, or learn new things. Then I come back to that, and there's a new layer of understanding because all that filigree work has fallen into place, into the larger blocks, in fact, that I think were the composer's intention. (Noyle, 1987, p. 49)

I'm eventually going to write my own book about memorizing because I realize that it has become such a system. . . . It all emanates from the circle of fifths . . . these little circular motions of fifths, one leading to the next, left hand to right, right to middle voice, and that sort of thing, which has been the skeletal understanding of the piece. (Noyle, 1987, pp. 52–53)

Maurice Dumesnil: If one practices a piece thoroughly and patiently, without undue hurry or time limit; if one studies the difficult passages with rhythms and transpositions (here the hands separately are in order); if one devotes much time to the study of proper phrasing, tone coloring, and expression in "cantabile" passages, there is bound to come a time when the whole piece is memorized without having become conscious of it. In short, "repetition" seems to me to be a safe and sound way to commit music to memory, and by adding a few "flag-posts" along the way, one is sure to feel pretty secure; by the latter I mean, for instance, the full knowledge of the variance between repeats one and two in the classical sonata, and of the harmonies which lead to the middle section or to the coda. (Cooke, 1948, p. 79)

Yuri Egorov: There are two concessions, however, I make to myself when practicing the music I'm going to play. The first is that I like to practice slowly, much more slowly than I would like to play at the concert. I keep the same movement though, that I use in the regular tempo. . . . I also like to practice pianissimo. This forces more concentration. . . .

   If you are speaking of memorizing the piece, that I don't do. I play the piece over and over for practice, and all at once it comes to me that I know the music by heart. But I don't sit at the piano and memorize one page of the music. Not at all! (Mach, 1991, vol. 2, p. 48)

Janina Fialkowska: The very first thing I do is memorize it. Before anything, I memorize it. I memorize it at the keyboard. . . . I never consider that I can begin to know a piece if I don't know it by heart. I think it's cheating to look at the music . . . I'm a tremendously fast learner. Here I'm showing off, but it's true. I never take more than two or three days to memorize a real full-scale work or a concerto. (Noyle, 1987, p. 64)

Rudolf Firkusny: For me, it is very easy. When I play the piece a couple of times, I know it. My memorizing is only aural, I never see the printed page. (Noyle, 1987, p. 84)

Rudolph Ganz: I believe in the most minute, the most detailed memorizing, but never the notes alone—dynamics and musical phrasing must go along. . . . There is memorizing melodically, harmonically, and polyphonically. A mental photograph of the page must be achieved to a certain extent. Aural memory or kinesthetic memory is helpful. The final result of memorizing must be the ability to put the entire composition down on music paper, with the indications of tempo, dynamics, signs, and phrasing. (Cooke, 1948, pp. 80–81)

Walter Gieseking: To commit to memory is a very simple matter with me, unless the composition happens to be very difficult. A great deal can be accomplished by reading the music through away from the piano. As I read it the eye takes in the characters on the printed page while the ear hears them mentally. After a few times reading through, I often know the piece, can go to the piano and play it from memory. (Brower, 1926, pp. 66–67)

Myra Hess: Fortunately I am blessed naturally with an excellent memory, and after I have made a careful study of the piece, noting the points we have dwelt upon, I nearly know it already, without giving special attention to that side of work. (Brower, 1926, p. 197)

Josef Hofmann: Complicated parts of a musical piece require more attention; therefore, they should be repeated oftener than the easy parts.

Pianists who master the keyboard sufficiently will fare better to try memorizing a piece in its entirety: viz.. depicting it with both hands from the outset, thus obtaining a 100% instead of a 50% musical impression.

I dare say that memorizing, in general, consists of three factors: namely the acoustic picture, the optical picture, and the acquired habit of musical sequences. (Cooke, 1948, pp. 91–92)

Edwin Hughes: In memorizing a new composition, the first step should be to play the work through slowly, in order to find out how it sounds and to become acquainted with its general form and construction. Start to memorize it immediately, even though at first you may be able to retain only a few salient points. . . . Play understandingly—and listen. . . .

Play the hands separately at first, noting and analyzing everything, letting the keyboard images, the feeling for the fingering-groups, and above all, the sound, impress themselves on your mind.

Remember that the best memorizers are ear-memorizers. (Cooke, 1948, pp. 93–95)

Ernest Hutcheson: In memorizing I usually take the piece as a whole, but often sectional practice is useful too. In practicing by sections, it is advisable to let them overlap a little, so that the "joints" will be secure.

I practically never bother to memorize the hands separately. . . .

The most important thing is to memorize as naturally and effortlessly as possible, without hurrying the process unduly, and then to trust entirely on the subconscious memory, except for correction of mistakes or improvements of interpretation. (Cooke, 1948, pp. 97–98)

Lili Kraus: Memorize- there again I don't know that word. By the time I can produce what I want to hear, by the time I am satisfied with the interpretation and it is technically correct, I have known it a long time by heart. (Elder, 1986, p. 67)

Benno Moiseiwitsch: Each pianist seems to have his own method of committing music to memory. It has always been very easy for me, so perhaps that is why I have no cut-and-dry manner doing it. I generally do memory work at the piano, by playing the piece in sections and studying them out in detail. (Brower, 1926, p. 173)

Elly Ney: There are so many ways of memorizing. Some pianists play the piece over and over a great many times, until they know it. Others begin to learn the notes first of all, before thinking much of their meaning. I go at it differently. For me it must be the music first and the meaning of it. So I begin by thinking, thinking, thinking, studying the tones, the phrases which embody the music I wish to reproduce. I can do this away from the piano. For I don't care to hear too much the sound of the piano- not too much repetition. Better to use my mind and accomplish what I seek by mental means instead of mechanical ways. (Brower, 1926, p. 210)

Mitja Nikisch: Perhaps I have not thought definitely enough as to just how I really do memorize my music. It seems to come to me almost unconsciously after studying the piece, and I suddenly realize that I know it, without the need of the printed page. I can say this, however, that I visualize the notes and signs on the printed page, and can really see them before me as I play. I believe that is the most reliable way to learn and retain the notes of a composition. Of course I hear the tones also, so, in fact, I both see and hear them at the same time. Yes, I can memorize away from the keyboard when necessity requires. (Brower, 1926, pp. 188–189)

Guiomar Novaes: (Interviewer: How have you memorized?) Very naturally; I have never forced my memory. (Elder, 1986, p. 25)

Isidor Philipp: I amazed my school fellows because I had memorized 48 Preludes and Fugues of the "Well-Tempered Clavichord". Later, very ill for months, my memory weakened, and I was obliged to memorize by sections. . . . (Cooke, 1948, p. 112)

Moriz Rosenthal: To memorize a work of music depends entirely on the individual's talent and his musical knowledge gained by the study of theory, harmony, and composition, and even then everybody develops their own method of memorizing.

In my opinion, the best method is the musical approach; that is, to understand the structure of the work and to find the meaning the composer endeavored to give to his composition. This should be done first, thus memorizing the work away from the piano. . . .

The best time to develop the memory is as a child. (Cooke, 1948, p. 114)

Olga Samaroff: I always memorize a composition in sections. To give an example: Suppose we take a passage of eight measures. I practice this until it is committed to memory. Proceeding to practice the following passage, I always begin, not at the beginning of the second eight measures, but two or three measures back. In this way the joining-on measure between passage one and passage two gets double practice, and one has, so to speak, a cue before every passage, which greatly aids in sureness. . . . Then there is thinking through a piece mentally, away from the piano. I can do this sometimes as I walk along the street. Of course, I think it in the same movement and tempo as though I were actually playing it at the piano. This is also ear memory. . . .

Of course I have my own little devices for contrasting themes or passages—the likes and unlikenesses, and other things to help fix the composition in mind. I do not visualize the page, as I saw it before me, as some players do. The ear plays the biggest part; I remember through the ear. I hear it all mentally, not thinking ahead, or expecting what is coming—because that divides the attention, but just hearing the music as it unfolds under my fingers. I think there is a good deal of virtue in having finger memory too. If you know the piece well enough and have played it long enough, the fingers find the keys themselves. And sometimes you can just leave them to do it, while you let up the tension, as it were, sit back and let the music pour forth without care.

I think one should live with a work for some time before venturing to perform it in public—several months at least. (Brower, 1926, pp. 149–150, 155–157)

André-Michel Schub: It just happens. I can't tell you how. Once you've spent X number of hours with a piece, it's memorized. (Noyle, 1987, p. 106)

Victor Seroff: An excellent device to develop memory is to learn the pieces silently, by heart, before once playing them on the instrument. (Cooke, 1948, p. 123)

Abbey Simon: I have no idea, no clue as to how I memorize. There are all sorts of musicians. . . . I have never been able to tell anyone how I memorize. I don't know nor do I even want to know! (Noyle, 1987, p. 122)

Ralph Votapek: I don't like to think about memorizing because I think it's the bane of many performers and if they don't admit it, it's because they put it in their subconscious. (Noyle, 1987, p. 134)

Andre Watts: The first thing is to go from beginning to end, slowly, and maybe even sloppily or badly, in order to get a general sense of the whole body of the piece. . . . Then I just go back and I start learning the notes, start planning to play. I try to learn the notes and do the initial combination of memorizing and getting it into the hands and the body, but not in a rote way or a non-musical way. . . . By the time I'm halfway through learning the piece, I'm quite entrenched for the moment in all my musical ideas and what I want out of the piece. (Noyle, 1987, p. 144)

Mark Westcott: I like to memorize a piece right off cold. I do that first, and then usually I'm a little saturated with it. I memorize at the piano, usually phrase by phrase, the first thing. For me, a piece never starts to mature, to develop subconsciously, until it's memorized. (Elder, 1986, p. 176)

COPING WITH ANXIETY

Not long ago, I asked a large group of students at the New Jersey Governor's School for the Arts to write down anonymously their biggest fears about performing. No need for statistical analyses here—the answers were virtually uniform. With hardly a variation, two themes were voiced: "I will forget" and "I will make a fool of myself."

Great performers are not often asked about their fears and trepidations. Notice that the comments in this section are fewer and briefer than in previous sections. Interviewers typically do not steer the talk in this uncomfortable direction. If they did, they might encounter the performer's reluctance to admit his or her fear and lack of confidence. Each artist is aware that his or her career hangs in the balance when performance anxiety becomes unmanageable and visible to the public.

Nevertheless, a few of the artists do describe their feelings about performance anxiety, and they use very strong terms. Myra Hess speaks of great stress and mental agitation. In the course of a single brief comment, Janina Fialkowska refers to "terror" three times. In a second-hand account, Mitja Nikisch, speaking of Anton Rubinstein, talks of "nervous excitement" and "going to pieces" from fear even when playing relatively easy and familiar music.

The artists describe several coping strategies. Mental rehearsal is mentioned by Vladimir Ashkenazy, Yuri Egorov, and Janina Fialkowska as a good form of psychological preparation. Reflection and meditation are endorsed by Emil Gilels. Less sanguine is Mitja Nikisch's account of Anton Rubinstein's excessive anxiety-related smoking, which led to his death.

Claudio Arrau: I don't say I never feel fear before a performance but I have learned to channel it. This is important, to channel feelings of fear, of anxiety, to use them—it makes you more sensitive. (Dubal, 1997, p. 5)

Vladimir Ashkenazy: I find it a very good idea to imagine that you're performing, so that you get into shape what you need on the stage. (Noyle, 1987, pp. 10–11)

Lazar Berman: I remember, at a hotel, a woman came to me and, kneeling down, begged me to play the piano. I responded by kneeling down and begging her not to make me play. For me, every time I play in front of an audience, it is a very important and difficult affair, both physically and spiritually. I am never sure that it is going to end well. This is why I prefer to play when I feel like it. She (his mother) decided to make a pianist of me so that I could fulfill her dreams. This is why all of my life I have been unsure of myself. I don't like to perform; I am afraid of performing badly. (Portugheis, 1996)

Yuri Egorov: I have to admit that sometimes before a concert I get nervous. I try to avoid the jitters by preparing myself psychologically for the event. I begin my preparation about a week before the concert. I imagine myself already on the stage actually playing the concert. . . . I also concentrate, as I would on the night of the concert, on the music itself, and review one more time just how I will perform it. (Mach, 1991, vol. 2, p. 47)

Janina Fialkowska: Playing a concerto for the first time is the most terrifying experience in my life. That's why I'm glad when I think there are only two major concertos left for me to perform that I ever want to perform: The Brahms D Minor and the Emperor. I will be absolutely terrified the first time I play them. . . . The first sound of playing them with an orchestra will be terrifying. (Noyle, 1987, p. 65)

I simply cannot go on the stage and play without that very day having gone through the pieces that I'm going to play. Otherwise, it's a psychological thing, I feel unsure. Sure, at some times I'd play well, but I would always have that terror of forgetting. (Noyle, 1987, pp. 73–74)

Emil Gilels: I have always been nervous before concerts, and I continue to this day to be so. I've never found a cure for it. But I've found that by being reflective and meditative about it all, I can do it. (Mach, 1991, vol. 2, p. 123)

Myra Hess: There have been times of great stress, when I was mentally agitated and could neither see the notes before me or even hear them, yet my fingers would go on and continue to play of themselves. (Brower, 1926, p. 197)

Stephen Hough: Quite apart from (technique) is the whole other question of nerves and the different ways that nerves can affect the performer. First, there are the nerves, or the nervousness, one feels before a performance which dissipate when the concert begins. Then there is the confidence which suddenly fails the artist as he or she walks on to the stage. Or the failure can come in the middle of the performance whether through tiredness or distraction. . . . The mind and the nerves can play various sorts of tricks on anyone. I know; at different times, I've been the victim of all of them.

Yet I can't say that I suffer from any kind of chronic nerves really, certainly not like some who are really paralyzed and unable to give their best. It's funny that for me the size of the concert or the place of the concert often have relatively little to do with it. Sometimes it can be the smallest date somewhere, where nothing's really hanging on the outcome, that a bad case of nerves sets in. . . . Sometimes you just have to look at yourself as a human being and realize how small you are in the context of the world and in the context of the universe, and see how ridiculous it is to be nervous. . . .

Now, I know that it's hard to rationalize these things in the context of a performance when you know that your career is often riding on how you play when you go out onto the stage. However, the performer must try to be divorced from all of that. . . . Each of us has to go out there with a crazy mixture of self-confidence and humility and whatever talent we have and try to do what he or she feels the music demands, and do as much as he or she can. Of course, all this is wonderful, philosophizing as we are over lunch, but of course when it comes to putting it into practice while actually standing in the wings, well, that's something else again. (Mach, 1991, vol. 2, pp. 137–138)

Mitja Nikisch: It is really sad that there should be such fear about playing from memory; this attacks all kinds of artists. If it could be done away with—wiped out—what a boon for us all! Some suffer from the fear much more than others. One of the greatest pianists of any time – Anton Rubinstein- was a prey of fear in the most severe form. I have heard my father tell about going to his dressing room before a concert, and finding him in a high state of nervous excitement. To try and calm himself and become numbed to this condition, he would be smoking one cigar after another in rapid succession. The air would be so thick that one could hardly distinguish the great artist from the smoke. He died of excessive smoking, you know. The fear that memory would play him false would affect him in unexpected moments: even in a Chopin nocturne—can one fancy it?—He would go to pieces. (Brower, 1926, p. 189)

ON PREPARING FOR
OPTIMAL PERFORMANCE

This topic, more than any other, led to completely idiosyncratic comments from pianists. While they describe their reliance on thorough preparation (Claudio Arrau, Stephen Bishop-Kovacevich, Janina Fialkowska), they also speak of what psychologists call *flow* (Csikszentmihalyi & Csikszentmihalyi, 1988): a feeling of immersion in the moment, spontaneity, creativity, and total absorption. An optimal performance involves a state of flow. It doesn't always happen. Emil Gilels notes ruefully, "Sometimes I even have to force it." Yet when an artist is in a flow state during performance, I believe that the audience can always tell. After all the preparation, analyzing, memorizing, and drilling the fingers, this is what makes a great performance.

Their words falter as pianists try to describe the sensation of flow. Garrick Ohlsson says, "I'm ahead of myself, but I'm also with myself in the present and a little bit behind myself." Emil Gilels says that each performance is different because of an element of playful "fantasy"; Tamás Vásáry speaks of a "half dreaming state" that allows fingers and brain to work together. Ivo Pogorelich best captures the feeling of immersion in the musical moment: "The notes have become you and you have become the notes."

Stephen Bishop-Kovacevich: I wish I could tell you that I had found a formula [for how to prepare for a concert on the day of the event] after all these years. . . . For me there are no rules. . . . I find that it's a good idea not to touch any of the pieces you're due to play, but to practice other things instead; get to know the piano, find your way into the new keyboard. And then rest.

But if you are very well prepared, no matter what state of mind you're in, your preparation will save the day.

My preparation is always savage. Then again, there are sometimes various demons to cope with in one's head. I recently went to the hall the day before I was to give a concert and I found myself practicing the fugue of Beethoven's Sonata Op. 101 for four hours. That's a piece that I can usually play without practicing at all. But that day, it wasn't going very well and I was scared like hell. (Dubal, 1997, p. 56)

Misha Dichter: I've had endless discussions with colleagues about analyzing the harmonic structure. They see my music all marked up, the notes are almost obliterated, and they say, "Well, that's very nice to study, but what do you think of during the concert?" And I say, "Exactly this. . . . " If I break a new piece up into its smallest components, if I understand why a composer wrote a certain note in that measure that fits into a larger picture, then suddenly I'm seeing a piece and its basic harmonic units as the composer intended. These are the things that I'm thinking about constantly, which causes the tension and relaxation in a performance. (Noyle, 1987, pp. 49–50)

I'm constantly practicing a work as if I was performing it. I don't mean, "Oh, my goodness, in one week this is going to be on the program, and I'm nervous." Nothing like that. I consciously recreate in the room, as close as I can, the mental impulses that will be going on, that have been going on since I learned the piece, that are going on that week before or the day before, and that will be going on during the concert. "What am I thinking of right now?" If I stop concentrating on these things and start to be aware of extraneous things, I'll introduce nerves that are totally unnecessary. If I've built in this concentration, I never lose sight of that structure for a moment. (Noyle, 1987, p. 55)

Janina Fialkowska: If it's a solo work, usually I allow myself a year. . . . I learn the piece in June and I'll probably start performing it in September or October of the same year, but in smaller places, using them as guinea pigs. That doesn't mean that I'll give them the worst performance. It means that I will be less nervous. It will mature and develop, and the piece will reach its peak, usually (this is the way it has happened to me) the following March. That is the best it'll be, at that time. I will drop it then in April or May. And if I take it up the next year, it'll probably be really good. It'll be solid. (Noyle, 1987, pp. 64–65)

Emil Gilels: When I am in top form, I imagine the music in almost a quasi-fantasy manner. But then, when I perform a work, each time I also play it differently. The ideas are always different. Sometimes I play with greater changes in the dynamics, sometimes with less. . . I must say that it is different each time I play, and it is a process which I would say includes the mastery of the work, knowing the detail, being comfortable with it, and then adding the fantasy . . . when I am not feeling very well, I have to try harder to get all the elements together. Sometimes I even have to force it. (Mach, 1991, vol. 2, p. 123)

Lili Kraus: (Before going on stage) I am so excited that I have the feeling of being so faint, so helpless, as if the very candle of my life is going to snuff out. I feel as if I couldn't lift an arm, move a finger, and as if I'd never seen a piano; it is as if I'm lost and don't know what to do. But when I walk out and see the friendly grin of those eighty-eight keys reassuring me, inviting me, I love them, and then everything falls into place. Whenever I perform, my happiness hangs on every note. . .

During the performance, this person you see before you, this Lili Kraus, ceases to exist as an individual.I exist only in the music I project to the audience. My mortality is eclipsed. (Mach, 1991, vol. 1, pp. 151–152)

Garrick Ohlsson: As I'm playing, the only way I could describe it is that I'm ahead of myself, but I'm also with myself in the present and also a little bit behind myself because these are the three evaluation points. Maybe the chief one is moving into the future with your mind, and of course with your body, which is how you play the piano. (Mach, 1991, vol. 2, p. 186)

I guess you could call it taking more of a positive mental attitude than sheer courage, bravado, or competitiveness. Even when I'm walking on the stage to play, I try to think courageous thoughts. I think only of smiling at the audience. What kind of feeling is it? I call it defensive optimism. (Mach, 1991, vol. 2, p. 193)

Murray Perahia: I love the playing, and most of all I love playing a piece many times. I feel this is a most important attitude for an artist to have, because I feel that to learn a piece one doesn't simply play it in one's home; one must play it in public. This is very important, because until one has played the work in public, one doesn't know all of the nuances of the piece. Playing the piece in public brings new knowledge of the music. One can learn it, one can sing the words, one can even feel it, but unless one has sung the song to somebody, in the presence of people, one hasn't really experienced the song. (Mach, 1991, vol. 2, p. 215)

Ivo Pogorelich: I believe a composition can only be performed well if it is entirely yours; you know not only every note from memory, but the notes have become you, and you have become the notes. Then the composition is yours. And then comes the belief in yourself. (Mach, 1991, vol. 2, p. 244)

Tamás Vásáry: (Interviewer: What do you think about as you play?) I constantly revise what I think about. Nowadays I cut out my concentration on notes. I find that if I concentrate too much on what is coming next, I will spoil the thing. But on the other hand, I need to know the work so well that my fingers can play it without my thinking or my brain can reproduce it without my playing.

When one is playing, the mechanical movements of the hands and the mental work of the memory go hand in hand. Sometimes you don't know which is operating, sometimes both, sometimes only one.

It is dangerous when only either the hands or the brain is operating. So I prefer that both fingers and brain be solidly there. Then if one gets tired, you can reach to the other. Of course, when both fingers and brain get tired, you may have a memory lapse. . . . If I remain in a half dreaming state, I know what is coming very clearly. But if I concentrate too hard on what is coming next, I have a sort of mental cramp. (Elder, 1986, p. 138)

CODA

We noted at the start of this chapter that reading the words of the great pianists may help us understand the soul of the artist. Problem-solving strategies, techniques, and tricks of the trade are interesting, to be sure, but sometimes a deeper kind of truth emerges from artists' disclosures to interviewers. The most moving story in my collection was told by Lili Kraus. On a concert tour in Indonesia in 1940, Kraus was arrested by the military secret police and imprisoned on a phony charge after the Japanese occupation of Djakarta. Deprived of her freedom, her family, and her music, Kraus kept hope alive through constant mental rehearsal. She recalled her imprisonment and its effects in an interview with Elyse Mach (1991):

At the beginning, I guess I was just too dazed to think or feel anything. I never became used to the yelling and cries of pain that echoed through those subterranean cells. I would sit with my hands over my ears to help shut out the screams. I imagined that Dante's Inferno was a tea party compared to this place. . . . I had little time to think of myself. Occasionally, though, I did take a long, wistful look at my hands and wondered what might become of them. But the hands did not suffer. On the contrary, my hands became so superb *because* I did the forced labor after being moved to a POW camp, although the other women in the prison offered, with sincere generosity, to take over my duties. Obviously, I couldn't possibly accept any such sacrifices on their part. As long as I was there with them I felt compelled to do my share. . . . In this particular prison, there were no faucets and so there wasn't any running water. About forty buckets had to be pulled up in the morning, forty at noon and forty in the evening. At the end of my first day of doing this, my finger joints were so swollen and so painful that I couldn't open the fingers. I was as frightened as I was shocked. But only for a moment, because the thought came again that, if I am going to play the piano again, I will; and if it isn't meant to be, I won't! So I worked on. And as a consequence, my hands became wonderfully strong.

However, it wasn't the manual work or possible damage to my hands that bothered me so much. What really ate me up was the longing for my music and my family. I could never decide which anguish was more tormenting; however, I was consumed by the desire to sit down at the piano and play and play. This longing almost drove me mad. So I resorted to a kind of "recall" from the subconscious realizing that I had to materialize all the music within me—the composition and the projection—silently. I worked so hard at doing this that scores and technique, which seemed to have been buried many fathoms deep, now appeared so real, so present, that I knew that if I were seated before a piano I could play pieces I hadn't practiced since childhood, and in doing so discover new wonders that never seemed so apparent before.

Later, at another prison, when the Japanese brought in a piano at Christmas time, I was commanded, not asked, to play for the other prisoners. It was as if a crystal source had sprung up from the sand of the Sahara before a man who had spent days and days wandering in the desert; I just poured over that piano and, without any music, I played on and on with my whole heart, in pain and joy. I don't even remember how long, but I don't recall repeating any piece, nor do I remember making any mistakes while playing them. It was as if I could play anything and everything ever known to man—what merciful madness. (vol. 1, pp. 149–150)

CREDITS

Excerpts from *Modern Masters of the Keyboard*, by Harriet Brower are reprinted with permission by Ayer Company Publishers.

Excerpts from *Pianists on Playing: Interviews with Twelve Concert Pianists*, edited by Linda Noyle are reprinted with permission by Scarecrow Press.

Excerpts from *How to Memorize Music*, by James Francis Cooke are reprinted with permission by Theodore Presser Company.

Excerpts from *Great Pianists Speak for Themselves*, edited by Elyse Mach are reprinted with permission by Dover Publications, Inc.

Excerpts from *Pianists at Play*, by Dean Elder © The Instrumentalist Co., reprinted with permission. Subscribe to *Clavier* for 10 issues yearly at $19 ($27 for delivery outside the U.S.A.) by writing to 200 Northfield Road, Northfield, Illinois; telephone 847–446-8550 (fax 847.446.6262).

ENDNOTES

1. The additional sources that I consulted in this search were:

Badura-Skoda, P. (1993). *Interpreting Bach at the keyboard*. Oxford: Oxford University Press. (First published in German, 1990, Laaber Verlag.)

Brendel, A. (1981). *Tünödés a zenéről*. [Musical Thoughts and Afterthoughts]. (Translated to Hungarian by David Gabor). Budapest: Zenemukiado. First published in Great Britain, Robson Books Ltd.

Brendel, A. (1990). *Music sounded out, essays, lectures, interviews, afterthoughts*. New York: Farrar Straus Giroux.

Chasins, A. (1961). *Speaking of pianists*. New York: Alfred A. Knopf.

Cooke, C. (1941), *Playing the piano for pleasure*. New York: Simon & Schuster.

Cooke, J.F. (1925). *Great men and famous musicians, educational conferences on the art of music*. Philadelphia: Theo. Presser Company.

Cutting, L.K. (1997). *Memory slips*. New York: HarperCollins.

Ewen, D. (1949). *Men and women who make music*. New York: Merlin Press.

Friedrich, O. (1989). *Glenn Gould: A life and variations*. Toronto, Canada: Lester & Orpen Dennys Limited.

Gerig, R. R. (1974). *Famous pianists and their technique*. Washington: Robert B. Luce.

Gieseking, W., & Leimer, K. (1972). *Piano technique*. New York: Dover. (First published as *The Shortest Way to Pianistic Perfection*, 1932, Bryn Mawr: Theo. Presser Company.)

Horowitz, J. (1982). *Conversations with Arrau*. New York: Alfred A. Knopf.

Jacobson, R. (1974). *Reverberations: Interviews with the World's Leading Musicians*. New York: William Morrow & Company.

Kaiser, J. (1971). *Great pianists of our time*. New York: Herder & Herder. (Translated to English by G. Allen.) German Edition, Munich: 1965, Rutten & Loening Verlag GmbH.

Lenz, W von. (1983). *The great piano virtuosos of our time, a classic account of studies with Liszt, Chopin, Tausig & Henselt*. London: Kahn & Averill, 1983. (First published in German, 1872.)

Lhevinne, J. (1972). *Basic principles in pianoforte playing*. New York: Dover Publications, Inc. (First published 1924, Philadelphia: Theo. Presser Company.)

Mackinnon, L. (1938). *Music by heart*. London: Oxford University Press.

Neuhaus, H. (1967). *Die Kunst des Klavierspiels* [The Arts of Piano Playing]. Köln: Musikverlage Hans Gerig.

Parrott, J., with Ashkenazy, V. (1985). *Beyond frontiers*. New York: Jasper Parrott.

Pasculescu-Florian, C. (1986). *Vocaţie şi Destin Dinu Lipatti*. [Talent and Destiny, Dinu Lipatti] Bucuresti: Editura Muzicala.

Rubinstein, A. (1973). *My young years*. New York: Alfred A. Knopf.

Sbârcea, G. (1984). *Întîlniri cu Muzicieni ai Secolului XX* [Encounters with Musicians of the Twentieth Century]. Bucureşti: Editura Muzicala.

Schonberg, H. C. (1963). *The great pianists from Mozart to the present*. New York: Simon & Schuster.

Schonberg, H. C. (1988). *The Virtuosi, classical music's legendary performers from Paganini to Pavarotti*. New York: Vintage Books.

Şoarec, M. (1981). *Prietenul Meu Dinu Lipatti* [My Friend Dinu Lipatti]. Bucureşti: Editura Muzicala.

Speranţia, E. (1966). *Medalioane Muzicale* [Musical Portraits]. Bucureşti: Editura Muzicala a Uniunii Compozitorilor.

Whiteside, A. (1955). *Indispensables of piano playing*. New York: Coleman-Ross Company.

Zilberquit, M. (1983). *Russia's great modern pianists*. Neptune: NJ: T. F. H. Publications, Inc. Ltd.

2. Solfège is a system used by singers to identify the notes of the scale.

FOUR

Expert Memory

Roger Chaffin

W hy is it that some people can memorize and others cannot? I am one who cannot. Or is it, "Will not"? I have tried. If the music is simple enough, I can do it. But the effort is so great, for such paltry results, that it does not seem worth it. This makes it tempting to think of memory ability as a special gift or talent. The history of music is filled with examples of extraordinary feats of memory that seem to lend credence to this view. The story of the young Mozart writing out Allegri's *Miserere* from memory after two hearings was seen, at the time and ever since, as a conclusive and final proof of his genius (Cooke, 1917/1999). Jorge Bolet tells of memorizing Liszt's *Mephisto Waltz* in an hour and a quarter (Noyle, 1987). Cases like these, and many others, seem to support the widely held idea that musical ability is a gift, given to the few, who stand out from the rest of us by virtue of their extraordinary natural endowment.

This explanation flatters those who have the gift and lets the rest of us off the hook, relieving us of the obligation to try. Unfortunately, at least in the area of memory, talent is too easy an answer. Like any other ability, the ability to memorize is the product of a complex interaction between biological endowment and experience (Bronfenbrenner & Ceci, 1994; Crawford & Chaffin, 1997; Simonton, 1999) . Like any other ability, the ability to memorize requires practice—a lot of practice. Those of us who do not memorize have simply not learned the skill or we have not practiced it effectively. This is the conclusion of more than three decades of research on the nature of extraordinary memory (Ericsson & Smith, 1991).

Mozart's and Bolet's feats of memory are astounding, but they are not superhuman. They are the entirely predictable result of years of intensive training and experience. We can all perform similar feats in areas in which we are similarly experienced. Consider first the span of working memory—the mental scratchpad that holds our current thoughts for the few seconds that make up the subjective present. For all of us, geniuses and just plain folk alike, the capacity of working memory is 7±2 (Miller, 1956). This means that when we are asked to immediately repeat a list of items, such as digits or letters, most of us are able to recall between five and nine items. If you have not tested yourself before, try it with the following list. Read the letters over once and then close the book and repeat them to yourself in order.

HEQ FPM RD TBVAZGI KD LFWROXS

You probably managed something less than seven. This is normal. Now try again with the following list.

YOU ARE AN EXPERT AT READING

You do not even have to try it to know that you will remember all the letters. Why? The answer is obvious. You can read. You are an expert at reading. You have stored in your long-term (as opposed to working) memory somewhere between 50,000 and 100,000 words that you can immediately and automatically recognize, pronounce, and understand (Landauer & Dumais, 1997).[1] This makes it possible for you to perform feats of memory with strings of letters that would seem astounding to someone unfamiliar with reading.

When we see a familiar word, we recognize it as a unit, not as individual letters. This is called *chunking*. The existence of a familiar pattern in long-term memory allows us to recognize that pattern and treat it as a single *chunk* of information. Each word can be a single chunk in working memory. Because the capacity of working memory is 7±2 chunks, you can remember almost as many words as letters. [2] The ability to chunk information allows us to recall much more information in a memory span task for familiar materials than in the same task with unfamiliar materials. It is not that our working memory capacity has changed; it is still 7±2 chunks. It is just that we are able to handle information in bigger chunks when we have more experience with it.

Chess masters shown a chess board in the middle of a game for 5 seconds with 20 to 30 pieces still in play can immediately reproduce the position of the pieces from memory. Novices, of course, are able to place only a few. Now take the same pieces and place them on the board randomly and the difference is much reduced (Chase & Ericsson, 1982). The expert's advantage is only for familiar patterns—those previously stored in memory. Confronted with unfamiliar patterns, even when it involves the same familiar domain, the expert's advantage disappears.

The beneficial effects of familiar structure on memory have been observed for many types of expertise, including music. People with musical training can reproduce short sequences of musical notation more accurately than those with no musical training when notes follow conventional tonal sequences, but the advantage is much reduced when the notes are ordered randomly (Halpern & Bower, 1982; Sloboda, 1985). Expertise also improves memory for sequences of movements. Experienced ballet dancers are able to repeat longer sequences of steps than less experienced dancers, and they can repeat a sequence of steps making up a choreographed sequence better than steps ordered randomly (Allard & Starkes, 1991). In each case, memory span is increased by the ability to recognize familiar sequences and patterns.

Committing information to long-term memory is a different kind of challenge for expert and novice. Because novices must work with smaller chunks than experts, they have more to store. The task for experts is simpler. Because they work in larger chunks, there is less to be remembered. I do not mean to minimize the expert's accomplishment—we are, after all, talking about things like young Mozart's ability to recall the *Miserere*—but this is why memorization for experts is so often effortless. This is one reason that many of the pianists in chapter 3 report that memorization happens automatically or unconsciously. When memorization occurs without effort, it is because the expert can recognize that the music is largely made up of familiar patterns and familiar ways of varying novel patterns.

Many people find this explanation of memory ability a little hard to believe. One way to convince the skeptic might be to take someone with normal memory abilities and follow their progress as a training program turns them into an expert memorist. This was the approach of William Chase and Anders Ericsson (1981, 1982), who employed a college student, identified only as "SF," to come into the lab regularly over a period of 18 months and do digit-span tasks. Each day, SF heard strings of numbers that he had to repeat back from memory. With practice, the number of digits he could recall increased steadily. He began with a normal working memory span of 8 digits and ended up, after 18 months, with a span of 80—far outside the ordinary range.

This is the kind of ability that, if you did not know where it came from, would make you think that you were dealing with some kind of genius. Yet SF was not a genius. He just worked hard for a long time and developed a specific memory skill. SF's memory abilities were specific to his domain of expertise. When he was tested with letters, his abilities were at the same normal level that his memory for digits had been at the beginning of the experiment. Like the chess experts, SF had developed the specific ability he had practiced.

How did he do it? SF started by building on knowledge he already had. The two kinds of number strings that he was most familiar with were dates and running times. He was a runner and knew a lot about records for running different distances, so he organized strings of digits into running times and dates that he could recognize. Here is his account of how he recalled a digit string starting 08033806321431 (Ericsson & Oliver, 1989):

> I made the 803 in the beginning a 2-mile. I put a zero onto it, so I just remembered the 803 as a 2-mile time then the 380 was difficult, very difficult, to remember because it was not a time. I had to concentrate especially hard, then I made six-thirty-two a mile time, then I made fourteen-thirty-one a 3-mile time. . . .

By chunking the digits into meaningful sequences in this way, SF reduced the number of different things he had to remember. He provided himself with a set of retrieval cues that told him what to look for in memory at each step. For example, the retrieval cue "A 2-mile time" reminded him of the opening sequence "0803."

SF further reduced the number of things he had to memorize by always using the same organization of digits into times and dates. For example, at the point when he was able to recall about 30 digits, he would always organize the digits into four 4-digit numbers, followed by three 3-digit numbers (see Fig. 4.1). This retrieval scheme reduces the amount of new information that has to be stored still further. The memory task is now to recall four 4-digit running times followed by three 3-digit times in the correct order. The task is reduced to storing seven chunks in long-term memory. During testing, a few additional digits could usually be recalled from working memory bringing the total memory span to around 30.

Every expert memorizer uses some type of retrieval scheme. The scheme does not have to be hierarchically organized like SF's. One waiter who was able to take long, complex orders without writing them down

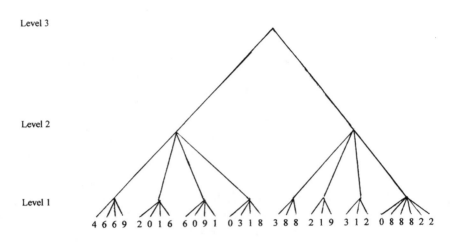

Level 3

Level 2

Level 1

4 6 6 9 2 0 1 6 6 0 9 1 0 3 1 8 3 8 8 2 1 9 3 1 2 0 8 8 8 2 2

FIG. 4.1   The Retrieval Scheme used by SF for Recalling Strings of up to 30 Random Digits (4 Groups of 4, 3 Groups of 3, Plus the Contents of Working Memory). Adapted from "A methodology for assessing the detailed structure of memory skills" by K.A. Ericsson and W.L. Oliver, 1989, in A. M. Colley & J. R. Beech (Eds.), *Acquisition and performance of cognitive skills*, p. 201. Copyright 1989 by John Wiley & Sons Limited. Adapted with permission.

organized each order as a matrix of guests (in order of seating) and food groups (starch, protein, vegetable; Ericsson & Polson, 1988). Rajan, the memorist described in chapter 2 who could recall more than 30,000 digits of the mathematical constant pi, also used a matrix organization. This enabled him to start at any point in the string—for example, at the 20,000th digit—and list the digits in either forward or backward order (Thompson et al., 1993).

Concert soloists are skilled memorizers. Any musician will recognize that chunking occurs—that notes can be organized into familiar patterns such as scales, arpeggios, and harmonic progressions. Do pianists also use elaborate retrieval schemes of the sort used by SF and Rajan? The pianists in the previous chapter who insisted that memorizing "just happens" seem to suggest otherwise.

Clearly, memorizing for piano performance is different than memorizing digits and dinner orders. For one thing, piano performance involves motor (procedural) memory in a way that memorizing digits or chess boards does not. Motor memory develops automatically and, with practice, its functioning becomes largely unconscious (Kihlstrom, 1987). It seems perfectly plausible that concert pianists could rely on the automaticity of motor memory to sidestep the need for a highly practiced retrieval scheme. The deliberate creation and practice of a retrieval scheme is something that is necessary for conceptual (or declarative) memory, but may not be necessary for motor (or procedural) memory (Anderson, 1983). This seems to be what the pianists in chapter 3 are saying when they report, like André-Michel Schub, that memory "just happens". Many of the pianists seem to be saying that they do not make deliberate use of a retrieval scheme in the way that SF and Rajan did.

However, three considerations suggest that these disclaimers are not the complete story. First, the formal structure of classical (and most other forms of) music, with its divisions and subdivisions into movements, sections, themes, and motives, provides a ready-made hierarchical organization of the sort that SF had to create for himself (Snyder, 2000). Even if a person did not set out to create and use a hierarchical retrieval scheme, it would be remarkable if a highly trained musician did *not* use this structure to organize his or her understanding of a piece. Second, some understanding of the formal structure seems essential if a performer is to avoid confusing the different repetitions of highly similar thematic material that form the basis for the formal structure of any piece. It seems that the pianist must somehow keep track of the current location in the formal structure while playing to distinguish one repetition of a theme from another. Third, almost all of the pianists in chapter 3 admit to knowing the formal structure, if not to memorizing it. They acknowledge the importance of analytical memory or of knowing the architecture, musical form, or harmonic structure.

In the chapters that follow, we see many indications that the formal structure was important in Gabriela's practice. In chapter 9, we argue that it provided the framework for a retrieval scheme much like that used by SF. Despite the huge differences between memorizing strings of random digits and strings of notes at the keyboard, the mnemonic strategies used by Gabriela and SF had important similarities. Both used a highly practiced hierarchical organization to retrieve chunks stored in long-term memory in a particular order.

The retrieval cues that a pianist uses we have called *performance cues* because the pianist thinks about them during performance (Chaffin & Imreh, 1997, 2001 in press). The idea that what the performer thinks about during a performance are retrieval cues helps us to better understand Gabriela's conversation with Harald Wagner in Stuttgart described in chapter 3. The suggestion was that a performer must practice thinking about the "artistic and inspirational elements" of a piece until the thought of these expressive goals for the piece become as automatic as the motor activity of the hands. The performer has to learn to use the inspirational elements as retrieval cues, but this cannot be just switched on and off; it has to be practiced until it becomes automatic. This is the lesson that Chase and Ericsson drew from the study of SF. A particular retrieval organization has to be practiced over and over until its use is entirely automatic. This allows the limited resources of working memory to be devoted to the needs of the moment, forming digits into chunks in SF's case, attending to the ongoing performance in the case of a pianist. With sufficient practice, retrieving information from long-term memory becomes so automatic that it requires minimal attention from the performer.

This translation of the idea of automatically functioning memory cues into the realm of creative performance adds a new wrinkle to Chase and Ericsson's account. How is a pianist to retain the creative freshness and sparkle that is the hallmark of a great performance when the piece has been played over and over again to achieve the necessary automaticity? The solution is to select as retrieval cues the interpretive and expressive features of the music that the performer wants to bring to the attention of the audience. The goal of practice in the final weeks before a performance is to make sure that it is these features that come to mind automatically during the performance, not the difficulties and trouble spots. It must be the pianist's expressive and interpretive goals that serve as retrieval cues, not the problems.

This calls for a reorganization of the upper levels of the retrieval hierarchy during the final polishing for performance so that it is the higher level musical goals that the pianist thinks of. Any remaining difficulties have to be rechunked and given an interpretive gloss. Interpretive decisions are recast in terms of their larger, expressive effects, e.g., a sudden "*forte*" becomes "surprise". The pianist practices while thinking of these expressive goals so that they come to mind during the performance to act as retrieval cues, eliciting the finely tuned motor responses. Only when the expressive cues have become automatic can the pianist hope to achieve that trancelike state in which the worries and problems of the piece recede into the background and attention is focused entirely on the music and the emotions it conveys. At this point, the pianist is (ideally) able to perform while thinking about the piece entirely in terms of the higher level expressive goals. This kind of reorganization of thinking about a task to focus on high-level goals is a normal feature of the development of any highly skilled activity (Wegner & Vallacher, 1986).

Unpacking this account of the role of retrieval cues in performance is one of the main themes of the chapters that follow. We return to the idea of performance cues in more detail in chapters 7 and 8, where we look at their development over the course of learning a new piece, and in chapter 9 where we focus on their role in memorization.

ENDNOTES

1. The everyday term *memory* refers to long-term memories. These memories last anywhere from minutes to decades and their number is vast. Long-term memory is distinguished from working memory, the mental scratchpad, which lasts for only a few seconds and has a limited capacity (7 ± 2). One way to think of the relationship between the two kinds of memory is that the contents of long-term memory that are currently activated are in working memory.

2. Because there is a small cost for chunks that take longer to pronounce, the capacity of working memory is slightly smaller for words than letters (Baddeley, Thompson & Buchanan 1975).

FIVE

The Way to Carnegie Hall

Roger Chaffin

As every musician knows, the way to get to Carnegie Hall is to practice. What surprises most people is just how much practice is needed. The training of a professional musician requires more than 10,000 hours of music practice and a minimum of 10 years before the young musician is ready to begin a career (Ericsson, Krampe, & Tesch-Römer, 1993). In Lauren Sosniak's study of a group of American pianists who had reached the finals of one or more major international piano competitions, the average number of years of musical training was 17 and ranged from 12 to 25 (Sosniak, 1985). For composers, the preparation is generally even longer—20 years from first exposure to music until their first notable composition (Hayes, 1981; Simonton, 1991). In music, as in other fields, a minimum of 10 years of dedicated and intensive practice and preparation is needed to achieve eminence.[1]

It has been one of the goals of psychology, since its earliest days, to understand the nature of extraordinary talent. The question is important because of the significance of talent to society and because the question of where it comes from has provided a proving ground for arguments about the contribution of nature and nurture to human development (Simonton, 1999). Francis Galton, who first framed this debate, believed that talent has an important biological component, as the title of his book *Hereditary*

Genius (Galton, 1979/1869) suggests, and this belief is still widely shared today. A great deal of scientific effort has been expended in the effort to identify the genetically based traits and abilities of which talent is composed and many likely candidates have been identified (e.g., Coon & Carey, 1989). Success in predicting outstanding achievement from such components has, however, been relatively meager (Simonton, 1999, 2001; Winner, 1996a). The jury is still out on the issue. It may well be that the lack of success has been due to an overly simplistic view of how traits combine to produce extraordinary talent (Simonton, 1999), but it remains to be seen whether more sophisticated approaches will ultimately prove successful in demonstrating the biological basis for talent that most people take for granted.

One response to psychologists' lack of success in predicting achievement from the measurement of traits and abilities has been to look more closely at the contribution of the environment. This work has confirmed Galton's initial analysis that, whatever the role of inherited ability, a capacity for hard work and the motivation to work toward a particular goal are also prerequisites of outstanding achievement (Ericsson, 1996; Ericsson & Lehmann, 1996; Howe, Davidson, & Sloboda, 1998). Particularly crucial is the role of what Anders Ericsson and his colleagues have called *deliberate practice* (Ericsson & Charness, 1994; Ericsson et al, 1993). Although the willingness of some individuals to devote their early years to sustained practice remains to be fully explained, there can be little doubt that extended, deliberate practice is essential to outstanding achievement.

In every area of human achievement that has been examined, the biographies of those who have attained eminence indicate that a minimum of 10 years of intensive practice preceded the achievements that made them famous (Ericsson et al., 1993; Ericsson & Charness, 1994; Howe, 1990; Sloboda, 1996). This is true for fields like running that call mainly for physical skills, for fields like chess and mental calculation that depend on intellectual skills (Staszewski, 1988), and for fields like musical performance (Ericsson et al., 1993; Sosniak, 1985), ballet, and figure skating (Allard & Starkes, 1991) that require a combination of both. Ten years is a minimum, exceeded only in a very small number of cases, and then by only a year or two. For the majority of the small number of people who achieve eminence, the path is longer and often much longer.

This 10-year rule applies even to child prodigies, although the myths that surround their early years often suggest otherwise—that their abilities appeared suddenly in fully developed form (Ericsson & Charness, 1994). Even Mozart, the paragon of childhood genius, needed more than 10 years to develop the musical skills that earned him his enduring reputation. His early compositions would never have earned him this acclaim. They are remarkable for a young child, but his first work to clearly stand on its own as a masterwork was not composed until he was 17, by which time he had already been composing for 13 years (Schonberg, 1970; cited in Hayes, 1981).[2]

Even musical savants—people whose musical abilities contrast strikingly with their generally low level of functioning—require extensive practice. Their abilities often appear to emerge suddenly and without the opportunity for practice. When studied more closely, however, savants turn out to have put in years of dedicated practice just like other people. It is just that in the case of savants recognition of their skills is often delayed and happens suddenly (Ericsson & Faivre, 1988; Howe, 1990, 1996; Sloboda, Hermelin, & O'Connor, 1985). Prodigies and savants may progress with extraordinary speed, but even these special cases put in years of practice. There are no well-documented exceptions to the principle that "practice makes perfect."

NO PAIN, NO GAIN

Not only does the development of musical skill require practice, but the level of skill attained is directly related to the amount of practice. The more the practice, the greater the achievement. This was the conclusion of a series of studies by Ericsson and colleagues (1993). They obtained retrospective reports of the amount of practice during each year from childhood to the present from pianists and violinists representing different levels of achievement: successful professional musicians, conservatory students nominated as having the potential for careers as international soloists, other student musicians, future music teachers, and accomplished amateurs. The level of accomplishment was clearly related to the amount of practice. By age 18, the professionals and conservatory students had accumulated approximately 7,000 hours of practice, the student musicians 5,000 hours, future music teachers 3,000 hours, and amateurs 1,000 hours. This is not to say that achievement is uniquely determined by the amount of practice. It is almost certainly not the case that anyone who puts in the required number of hours would achieve the same high level of skill. More accomplished musicians may practice more because their abilities make practice more rewarding or because they are more motivated. The relationship between practice and achievement simply suggests that practice is an important, probably essential, part of the road to high achievement.

The same conclusion is supported by a study of student practice at the high school level by John Sloboda and colleagues (Sloboda, Davidson, Howe, & Moore, 1996). They compared a group of *elite* students enrolled in a selective, specialist high school for music with four other groups matched in age and sex. (The group names that follow are ours.) The *applicant* group was comprised of unsuccessful applicants for a place at the school. The *interested* group included young musicians whose parents had inquired about applying to the school, but who had not completed an application. The *nonspecialist* group were students taking music lessons at a comparable nonspecialist school. The *unsuccessful* group were children at the same nonspecialist school who had stopped taking music lessons. The students and at least one parent were interviewed about how much time the students devoted to four kinds of activity (formal practice, improvisation, playing through previously learned pieces, and "messing about") during each year. In addition, a subset of children in the elite, interested, and nonspecialist groups kept diaries of their practice for 9 months.

The more accomplished musicians practiced more. The elite students started out practicing 30 minutes a day on their primary instrument, whereas the others started out at 20 minutes. By their fourth year of study, the elite students were doing an hour and a half a day, the applicant and interested groups were doing 30 minutes, and the nonspecialist and unsuccessful students had never increased their practice time. By age 13, the elite group had accumulated an average of 2,500 hours of practice. By comparison, the applicant, interested, nonspecialist, and unsuccessful groups had averaged 56%, 56%, 31%, and 17% of this number, respectively. When progress was measured by success on the Associated Board exams (a national system of standardized music exams), the five groups showed similar differences. They started out together and rapidly diverged, with the elite students progressing through the grade levels faster than the other groups and the unsuccessful students not progressing at all.

As in the Ericsson et al. (1993) study, amount of practice was clearly linked to level of achievement. Moreover, it seemed that it was hard work and the motivation to do it that made the difference. First, the amount of practice required to pass each grade level of the Associated Board was the same for the elite students as for the other groups. If anything, the elite students put in more time. So it was not a matter of talented students breezing through the exams on the basis of natural ability alone. What were the elite students doing differently? It was deliberate practice that made the difference, not the other kinds of more informal (and less arduous) practice. The elite students did no more informal practice than the three other groups of successful musicians. Moreover, deliberate practice was hard work for the elite students as much as for the other groups. It was not a matter of practice coming more easily to them. Students in all groups practiced more when they were taking lessons and less during vacations. Tellingly, the largest decrease during holidays occurred in the elite group for technical practice (scales and exercises), the

most arduous kind of practice. This strongly suggests that the achievements of the elite students were a product of hard work.

Once a person has put in the 10,000 or more hours of practice needed to
acquire the skills of a concert pianist, still more practice is needed to
maintain those skills. The relationship between amount of practice and
level of skill continues to hold, even for professional pianists, and even
after a lifetime of playing (Krampe & Ericsson, 1996). One place where we
can see the effects of continued practice is in the many striking examples of
prominent musicians who continue their professional careers well past
normal retirement age—Artur Rubinstein, Vladimir Horowitz, and
Sviatoslav Richter to name just three. Are these musicians immune to the
normal effects of aging? No! They suffer the same general decline in mental
and motor functioning in old age as everybody else (Krampe & Ericsson,
1996; Krampe, 1997). It is just that skills that are continually exercised are
largely preserved from the effects of aging. Age-related declines in job
performance appear to be negligible in every kind of occupation, even
those like simultaneous translation and musical performance that require
rapid response and complex cognitive skills, so long as the skill continues
to be exercised (Krampe, 1997).

Ralf Krampe and Anders Ericsson (1996) looked at age-related changes
in musical and nonmusical skills in professional pianists. They obtained
retrospective reports of the amount of practice during each year and diary
reports of current practice from two groups of expert pianists, professionals in their 60s and students in their 20s, and from two groups of amateur
pianists matched in age with the experts. As we would expect, the experts
practiced far more than the amateurs. The novel result was that the
difference continued into old age. The experts' practice peaked at age 25 at
just over 30 hours a week and then decreased gradually over the years to
just over 10 hours a week by age 60. For the amateurs, practice remained
constant across the lifespan at less than 3 hours a week. The differences in
accumulated practice time for the groups were striking: close to 60,000
hours for the older experts, 20,000 hours for the younger experts, 10,000 for
the older amateurs, and 2,000 hours for the younger amateurs.

It seems that the older expert pianists were doing just the amount of
practice needed to maintain their high level of skill. Although they
practiced less than the younger experts, they worked more and had less
leisure time. Their practice time was carved out from the other demands of
a busy schedule as a professional musician. When the groups were tested
on laboratory tasks (some music related, others not), both experts and
amateurs showed the usual age-related declines in abilities unrelated to
music. In contrast, music-related abilities only declined in the amateurs.
For the experts, music-related abilities showed no decline with age. Even

more striking, among the older experts, those who practiced more performed better on the musical ability tasks. Even after a lifetime of playing, ability was still influenced by the amount of practice.

In summary, the development and maintenance of musical skills requires practice, a lot of practice. To reach the finals of international piano competitions, young pianists must practice regularly from childhood, increasingly dedicating their lives to music. Estimates of the amount of practice required for high achievement are remarkably uniform—about 2,500 hours by age 13, 6,500 by age 17, and approaching 10,000 by age 21. Those who practice less achieve less. This is true for students, and it is true for professionals even after a lifetime of performing and dedication to music.

THE NATURE OF EFFECTIVE PRACTICE

Practice Must Be Deliberate

Are some ways of spending practice time more effective than others? Common sense suggests that the answer to this question must be "Yes." The existence of throngs of avid amateur musicians, golfers, joggers, tennis players, swimmers, and so on is testimony to the fact that just messing around is not enough. Even the repeated exercise of a skill for professional purposes does not necessarily lead to improvement. An early study of Morse Code operators showed that operators generally reached a plateau in speed of transmission and only improved beyond this point when they were motivated to make a deliberate effort to do so by the offer of a promotion or pay raise (Bryan & Harter, 1899). Improvement requires *deliberate practice* (Ericsson et al., 1993).

John Browning says of practice in chapter 3 that, "It is hard work. It is like dishwashing. It is not fun" (Noyle, 1987, p. 30). Whether they love to practice, like Claudio Arrau, or only practice when necessary, like Jorge Bolet, none of the pianists in chapter 3 disputes that practice is hard work. This is why Bella Davidovich, along with several other pianists in chapter 3, prefers to practice in the morning and limits herself to 1-hour periods of practice separated by breaks (see also Ericsson et al., 1993). The rewards of practice are in the future—the addition of a new piece to the repertoire or an increased proficiency. The goal is improvement, which requires experimentation and trial and error. New and better ways of doing the same thing have to be discovered. As soon as a problem is solved, it is time to move onto something else (Ericsson, 1997). This requires a self-critical stance and is probably why Leon Fleisher, in chapter 3, described mindless practice as "dangerous" (Noyle, 1987, p. 95).

The relationship between effort and improvement was evident in John Sloboda's study of student musicians. It was the time spent in deliberate practice that distinguished elite students from the interested and nonspecialist students, not the time spent in messing about, playing favorite tunes, or improvising (Sloboda et al., 1996). Moreover, the elite students devoted a larger proportion of their deliberate practice to scales and technical exercises, the most arduous kind of practice, than the nonspecialist students. The elite group members were also more regular in their practice especially of scales. They also did a higher proportion of their scales in the morning, while the other two groups did more scales in the evening. If Bella Davidovich is right—that practice is more effective in the morning (see chap. 3)—this would mean that the elite students were devoting more prime practice time to the most demanding form of practice.

Practicing Is a Skill

The ability to practice effectively is a skill that develops with training (Gruson, 1988; Hallam, 1994, 1997a, 1997b). Misha Dichter remarked in chapter 3, he could have "saved thousands of hours" of practice if he had known as a student the short cuts that he knows now (Noyle, 1987, p. 57). Sozniak's (1985) pianists reported that their teachers gave them explicit instruction about how to practice. "She would very clearly outline practice methods. . . . She would write it down in a book" (p. 50). When the pianists began studying with a master teacher between the ages of 12 and 19, the teacher continued to exercise a decisive influence on practice by assigning work and setting standards. These master teachers "assigned an enormous amount of material and they expected it to be learned to the high standard they set." Practice was shaped by the need to meet the teacher's expectations. "You played a concert, you didn't play a lesson. You walked in prepared to play a performance. . . . You would get torn apart for an hour" (p. 63).

If practicing effectively is a skill, then it seems likely that some people will be better at it than others. This is suggested by the large differences in the amount of practice reported by the elite pianists in Sloboda and Sosniak's studies. In the Sloboda et al. (1996) study, there were large differences within each group in the amount of practice reported. Among the elite students, there was "a small handful of outliers who do vastly greater amounts of practice than anyone else" (p. 301), and there was a handful of students in each group who managed on very little practice— less than 20% of the group average. At each grade level, there were students in each group who passed the exam with one fifth as much practice as the other students, and there were others who did four times as much practice. Similarly, there were large differences in the amount of practice reported by the pianists in Sozniak's (1985) study. In their early years, some spent every free minute at the piano, whereas others practiced as little as possible (although with practice enforced by parents this was still a substantial amount). As the pianists became more serious about their practice in their middle years, the differences narrowed, but still ranged from 2 to 4 hours a day. These differences in the practice time needed to achieve the same level of skill may have been due to differences in ability, but they could equally well have been due to differences in the effectiveness of practice or both.

Does practice change and become more effective with training? One way to answer this question is to compare students with different levels of experience to see how practice changes. This was done in an ambitious study by Linda Gruson (1988) of 40 pianists who each practiced three different pieces representing different musical styles. The pianists represented the complete range of levels in the Canadian system of graded exams for music students as well as three concert pianists. Each pianist audiotaped a practice session (in which they worked on all three of the pieces for the first time) and were interviewed about their practice. In addition, 12 of the students, representing three different levels of experience, recorded an additional nine sessions of practice. Twenty different behaviors were recorded, including repetitions of practice segments of different lengths (note, bar, section, and piece), comments of various kinds, and total practice time.

There were clear differences in practice as a function of experience. The biggest was that more experienced pianists worked in larger units and seemed to be thinking more in terms of the piece as a whole. When they made an error or encountered a problem, less experienced pianists tended to repeat the note in question. More experienced pianists, on the other hand, were more likely to repeat sections. They also played through the entire piece more. A second difference was that the more experienced pianists worked harder. They paused less frequently and practiced longer. The third major effect of experience was on students' understanding of their own practice and what they were trying to achieve. More experienced students made more self-guiding comments during practice (e.g., "I made a mistake, I'd better try again"). In the interviews, the more experienced students mentioned more different strategies and described them in more abstract ways (e.g., "I get a feel for the piece" rather than "I work on the fingering" or "I play each piece three times"). These differences all point to the conclusion that the ability to practice develops with experience. Effective practice is a skill that has to be learned.

Studying Expert Practice

One way to identify characteristics of effective practice is to observe the practice of professional musicians. There are not many studies of this sort. Despite the current fashion for taking the audience behind the scenes (chap. 3), performers are often reluctant to be too forthcoming about how their art is created. Revealing the hard work that goes into preparing a performance is inconsistent with the illusion of effortlessness and spontaneity that is an important part of the artists' mystique. Besides, professional musicians have busy schedules. Practice time is precious. Concentration is important and distractions can be ill-afforded. For all these reasons, most professional musicians are reluctant to reveal too much about their practice. Nevertheless, some investigators have been able to persuade them to talk about how they practice (e.g., Aiello, 1999; Hallam, 1995a, 1995b).

Interviews With Professionals. In the most wide-ranging study of professional musicians' practice habits, Sue Hallam (1995a, 1995b, 1997a) interviewed 22 musicians selected for their reputation among their fellow musicians in London for their technical and musical excellence. They represented a wide range of experience, musical activities (solo work, chamber music, orchestral playing, conducting, and teaching), and instruments (all the major orchestral instruments as well as the organ and conducting). Not surprisingly, all the musicians demonstrated a high level of skill in their practice and a keen awareness of their own strengths and weaknesses. All described a wide range of practice strategies that they applied flexibly according to the needs of the moment, deliberately and strategically managing their own learning, practice, motivation, and emotional state.

Each musician was shown a score that was new to her or him and asked about the activities she or he would undertake to learn it (Hallam, 1995a). Musicians differed in how analytically they approached the music and whether they took a holistic or piecemeal approach. Three quarters reported consistently using an analytic strategy of first getting an idea of the structure, tempo, and technical problems in an initial overview, either playing it through or examining the score. Only one musician reported consistently using the opposite—intuitive—approach of starting right in without an overview, working through the music bit by bit, and allowing the overall picture to emerge gradually. Most of the musicians who used the intuitive strategy did so as part of a mixed approach, sometimes relying on one strategy, sometimes the other.

Those who always started out with an overview continued to take an analytic, problem-solving approach to working out the thematic and harmonic structure.

> You spend most of your time delving into the reasons of it. . . . I find I spend far more time in dealing with construction and analysis and I learn quite a lot of my works without actually playing them. (p. 120)

Those who always or sometimes skipped the initial overview tended to take a more intuitive approach—not thinking too deeply about form and structure, but letting the piece gradually emerge without too much conscious intervention.

> I like to think that the musical aspects will take care of themselves towards the end of your practice schedule. (p. 120)
> Musical interpretation is not consciously planned and is probably learned subconsciously as practice continues, because when it comes to performance it actually has been pretty carefully worked out. Very little is left to the last minute. (p. 120)

The two different learning styles were also apparent in the musicians' approach to technical difficulties. Approximately half the musicians used an intuitive approach, repeating passages at gradually increasing tempi. Another quarter adopted a more analytic approach, changing rhythms and slurs, inventing exercises, and avoiding simple repetition. The remaining quarter used a mixture of the two approaches (Hallam, 1997a).

The same differences in learning style appeared in the musicians' approaches to interpretation. The more intuitive musicians ($N = 7$) allowed their interpretation to evolve unconsciously and intuitively. They avoided deliberate analysis and planning and avoided listening to recordings of works they were learning. In contrast, the more analytic musicians ($N = 2$) relied on deliberate, conscious analysis of the piece that began before starting physical practice. They made comparisons with other music, including recordings of the piece they were learning and made connections with disparate musical ideas. They saw themselves as trying to discover the underlying meaning of the music. Those who took a mixed approach ($N = 10$) adopted the two approaches interchangeably, although usually with a clear preference for one or the other.

When memorizing a work, most musicians used a combination of the two approaches. Many reported, like many of the pianists in chapter 3, that memorization often occurred automatically, without deliberate effort, during the process of learning to play a new piece—an intuitive approach

(Hallam, 1997a). When additional practice was needed, two thirds continued to use an intuitive strategy, first repeating short sections without the music and then linking them together into larger units until the whole piece could be played from memory. Half of the musicians also reported that when they were ready to memorize they would use an analytic strategy of cognitive analysis to provide a conceptual framework for their memory. At this stage, one musician reported taking the score to bed for several nights to read through before falling asleep.

The conceptual frameworks used by these musicians included harmonic structure, key changes, length of rests, difficult exit points, and the like. The conductor reported relying entirely on cognitive analysis, using repetition only to "screw it down" after it had been memorized. He likened his analysis to seeing a building go up:

> You see the squares with nothing else. But then they're going to be divided into three parts, or another square perhaps left as it is because it's a big room . . . a score is like that . . . there's a certain square there, you are in a certain section . . . and then a certain way through this the trumpets and timpani actually have something to play . . . and it never lets you down. You always know. (Hallam, 1997a, p. 91)

In addition to conceptual memory, the musicians reported using a combination of aural, motor (kinesthetic), and visual memories, with individuals differing in the importance of each type. A good aural memory allowed one musician to play from memory by busking (improvising). Others reported strong visual memories, sometimes seeing actual notes and at other times seeing with less detail:

> You need to know whereabouts it is on the page in your mind's eye . . . according to which entry it is. . . It helps me tremendously. (Hallam, 1997a, p. 92)

Other musicians reported relying more on motor memory particularly once a passage was begun:

> Once you are into a moving passage . . . then the ear tends to take over, the fingers, the movement, you get into the swing of playing the passage so that there is no time, no need for visualizing positions, or counting mathematical number, the music simply flows. (Hallam, 1997a, p. 93)

Hallam's interviews indicate that expert musicians have a wide range of practice strategies available that they use flexibly to address every aspect of the task in front of them: learning new repertoire, maintaining skills, preparing for performance, and managing the physical and emotional demands of their challenging careers. It would be important, if possible, to verify these conclusions by directly observing the practice of at least a small number of expert musicians.

Flexible Use of Practice Strategies. To find out more directly how expert musicians deploy their repertoire of practice strategies in practice, Siw Nielsen (1997, 2000) observed the practice of two organists—students in their third year at the Norwegian State Academy of Music. They were each videotaped during a practice session as they worked on pieces they were preparing for recital. As they practiced, they reported what they were thinking about. At the end of the session, they watched the tape and further described their problem-solving activities.

Both organists used a variety of practice strategies with great flexibility. For example, they focused on new patterns as they were introduced in the piece, separating them out for practice and then merging them with preceding patterns. For each new pattern, they decided whether to begin by playing the two hands and the pedal parts separately and whether to play up to or below tempo. As they practiced, they evaluated their playing, selecting weak spots for additional work, building toward larger units and toward performance tempo. This may be pretty standard stuff for experienced musicians, but it is different from what beginners do (Hallam, 1994). It provides some confirmation that skilled musicians really do engage in the flexible use of practice strategies that Hallam's professional musicians reported.

Allocation of Practice Time. Another kind of flexibility was evident in a diary study of a student pianist preparing a graduation recital. More or less by chance, Andreas Lehmann and Anders Ericsson (1998) encountered a student pianist who had been keeping a practice diary while preparing a recital. This allowed them to examine how the pianist allocated her practice time among the different pieces of the program on the basis of difficulty. The pianist, GM, was preparing her graduation recital for a master's degree in piano pedagogy and had been keeping a practice diary for 6 months. The 45- to 50-minute program consisted of a Haydn sonata in two movements, three transcriptions for piano by Prokofiev of music from the ballet "Romeo and Juliet," and Debussy's "Estampes," also a set of three pieces. In her diary, GM recorded the starting and ending time of her practice on each piece and sometimes metronome markings; she also provided reports on the history of her musical development, practice habits, and a ranking of the difficulty of the eight pieces. GM's report of her practice habits since her earliest years indicated that her accumulated practice time, up to this point in her life, was comparable to the expert pianists studied by Ericsson et al. (1993)—approximately 10,000 hours.

GM's preparation for the recital certainly documents the long hours of practice reported by the expert musicians in the studies described earlier. She started in the fall and worked throughout the academic year, with only a 3-week break for Christmas, finishing in the spring. Over the course of 9 months, she practiced her recital program for 531 hours, averaging 17 hours a week (slightly less than 3 hours a day with no practice on Sundays). Because the music took 37 minutes to play in recital, this amounts to 14.5 hours of practice for each minute of performance.

GM also demonstrated the kind of flexible adjustment of practice to the demands of the particular piece of the sort noted by Sue Hallam in her interviews with professional musicians. GM altered her allocation of practice time to allow more practice of the two most difficult pieces during the spring semester. This strategic flexibility in the use of practice time reflects an ongoing appraisal of her progress and the task remaining. It also may indicate a failure to make sufficient allowance for differences in difficulty in her initial allocation of practice time.

Another kind of flexibility in the use of practice strategies was evident in the way that GM went about memorizing her program. She memorized the program twice, relearning it after the Christmas break. The second time her goals were somewhat different than the first. After the break, she worked on preparing ways to recover from slips in performance by memorizing the two hands separately so that she could continue playing with one hand if she made a mistake or had a memory failure for the other hand. She also strengthened her memory by engaging in slow practice from memory, and she prepared for a possible memory failure during performance by practicing starting at different points in the piece so that, in case of a problem during performance, she could skip forward and start afresh. We will see all of these strategies being used in Gabriela's practice.

Learning New Piano Repertoire. The most detailed accounts of the practice of experienced pianists comes from two studies of Kacper Miklaszewski's (1989, 1995). The first of these describes a pianist learning Claude Debussy's *Feux d'Artifice*. The pianist was a gifted student in his second year at the Chopin Academy in Warsaw who went on to a career as a concert pianist. Although he had performed other preludes by Debussy and was familiar with this one from live performances and recordings, he had not undertaken any special preparation before the start of the study. He videotaped his entire work up to the point at which he was ready to play through the piece for his teacher. In addition, he watched the tape of his first practice session and commented on his work (Miklaszewski, 1989).

The practice consisted of four sessions, the first lasting 90 minutes and the others lasting 48 minutes each. The pianist worked in short segments and did not play through the complete work until the end of the fourth session. In Sessions 1 and 2, he systematically worked through the piece from the beginning in short sections of one to four bars in length, frequently repeating sections several times, and then linking the repeated section with the sections immediately before it. Two sessions were required to complete this process for the entire piece. Thirty-five minutes into Session 1, he visually inspected the remainder of the score. Session 3 recapitulated the process, starting at the beginning again and playing through the piece a section at a time, but with fewer short segments. In Session 4, the same process was repeated in reverse order, starting with the last section and working back to the beginning one section at a time. Again, the length of the practice segments increased over the previous sessions, many being 5 to 20 bars in length. In the last 15 minutes of the session, he played through the whole piece several times with minimal interruption.

The pianist was using Hallam's (1995a) analytic approach. Because he was already familiar with the piece, there was no need for him to begin by getting an overview, but he did make a visual survey of the rest of the piece a third of the way into the session. He also took an analytic approach to the learning of each small section. From the pianist's comments, Miklaszewski concluded that he "first of all intended to build up a clear idea of the music (its pitch and rhythm combinations, its texture and expressive value) and as quickly as possible to support it by an image of how his hands would perform it" (Miklaszewski, 1989, p. 103).

What features stand out as potential hallmarks of expert practice? First, the use of formal structure to divide the piece into segments for practice. Miklaszewski (1989) reported that "the divisions of the musical material introduced by the subject agree with the basic formal units of the composition" (p. 106) and suggested that they "exist in some independent way in the musician's mind" (p. 106). This was demonstrated most dramatically in Session 4, when the pianist worked through the piece backward section by section. Unfortunately, Miklaszewksi provided no further detail, either about the formal structure or its use in organizing practice. We will see the same thing in Gabriela's practice (chap. 8) and will argue that it played a crucial role in memorization by establishing section boundaries as retrieval cues for recalling the next section from long-term memory (chap. 9).

Second, the flexible use of practice strategies reported by Hallam (1995a, 1995b) was readily apparent. For example, Bars 35 to 38 of the prelude presented particular technical difficulties for the pianist and received more attention than other sections in Sessions 1 and 4, but not in Sessions 2 and 3. In practicing this passage, the pianist alternated the use of hands separate and hands together and slow and fast tempi. As he became more proficient, hands together and fast tempo playing became more predominant. This alternating pattern of practice was not repeated in Sessions 2 and 3, but reappeared briefly in Session 4 when the difficult section was played in conjunction with adjacent bars, "presumably to smooth his performance of this difficult passage" (Miklaszewski, 1989, p. 106). Further evidence of the flexibility of practice strategies comes from the steady increase in the length of practice segments across sessions. The pianist commented that he had to practice in small segments because of the complexity of the prelude, suggesting that the length of practice segments was calibrated to the difficulty of the music and the degree to which it had been mastered. Again, we will see evidence of similar effects of musical complexity on Gabriela's practice (chap. 8).

Third, practice was organized around identifying and eliminating problems through cycles of what we call *work* and *runs* (chap. 6). The practice of Bars 35 to 38 is a case in point, with its alternation of fast and slow playing and hands-together and hands-separate practice. Miklaszewski suggests that these cycles can be seen as examples of the TOTE (test-operate-test-exit) sequences that are characteristic of planned, deliberate activity (Miller, Galanter, & Pribram, 1960). The pianist would first attempt to play a section up to tempo in a long run to identify any problems (test). He then worked on the problems, making notes on the score about his decisions and practicing slowly to implement them (operate). The cycle concluded with another run in which he attempted to play the section up to tempo again (test). If the final test was not satisfactory, the cycle would be repeated until the problem was solved.

The TOTE cycle was also reflected in the distribution of comments during the practice of each section. The comments initially concerned the ability to play the section (test). Next they focused on the remedial actions that were needed (operate). Finally, they concluded with an evaluation of success (test). The final test of the difficult Bars 35 to 38 was accompanied by a smile of satisfaction as the pianist concluded his practice of this section.

A fourth potential characteristic of expert practice was the pianist's explicit concern with his long-term goal of performing the work. The pianist was not simply developing an automatic sequence of motor responses, but was actively looking ahead, thinking about the piece, and developing a plan for how he was going to perform the work (Shaffer, 1976, 1981; Sloboda, 1985). For each section, the pianist first formed an overall idea of the texture and expressive value and then decided how to perform it, making many comments about fingering during the process.

Use of this kind of analytic approach, at least some of the time, was reported by all but one of the musicians interviewed by Hallam (1995a), suggesting that it is a fairly general characteristic of expert practice. We will certainly see many kinds of evidence of the same approach in Gabriela's practice.

Differences Between Pianists: Effects of Experience? The same features of expert practice also emerged in a second study that examined individual differences among three pianists as they learned two pieces—a late Romantic miniature, *Vom Erlengrund,* by Fr. Zierau and a set of three variations from a cycle of *30 Variations on Paganini* by 20th-century composer Rafal Augustyn (Miklaszewski, 1995). Two of the pianists (Jaroslaw and Lukasz) were seniors at the Chopin Academy, each giving 10 to 15 recitals per year. The third (Karol) was more experienced, having received his master's degree 8 years earlier, and was giving around 40 recitals per year. All three are described as *very high* in musical achievement. The pianists were asked to act as if they were to perform both pieces in public and to stop work when they were ready for public performance. They videotaped their practice.

To compare the practice styles of the three pianists, two types of runs and two types of work were distinguished. Runs were divided into (a) "concert" playing, which involved performance of an entire piece up to tempo and with a clearly expressed interpretation; and (b) "fluent shorter" concert playing, which consisted of similar playing of segments consisting of at least two phrases. Work was divided into (a) "playing with repetitions," which involved playing longer sections at close to final tempo but with many repetitions of short fragments of up to two bars in length without pause, and (b) "concentrated playing and loops," which involved multiple repetitions of the same section. The number of concert attempts increased over sessions, whereas "playing with repetition" and "concentrated playing and loops" decreased.

The pianists all found the Romantic music easier than the contemporary, and this was reflected in their practice. They devoted more time to concentrated playing and loops for the contemporary piece (27%) than for the Romantic piece (8%), and they spent more practice time on the harder pieces (a mean of 4 hours) than on the easier ones (2½ hours). Also, all three pianists prepared to perform the easier, Romantic piece without the score. Only one prepared to perform the contemporary work without the score, and another "practically did not finish" work on the third variation (Miklaszewski, 1995, p. 141).

Miklaszewski noted consistent differences among the three pianists in the use of concert playing and concentrated playing. These differences appear to reflect consistent individual learning styles because they occurred in the practice of two works involving different types of music. Two of the pianists were described as "mov[ing] from a general approach to details" (Miklaszewski, 1995, p. 144) and thus appear to have adopted an analytic approach (Hallam, 1995a), The other pianist (Jaroslaw) appears to have taken a mixed approach. Initially he was described as "catching the whole composition through gradual mastering of shorter segments" (p. 144), suggesting use of an intuitive approach. However, he later spent an entire practice session in visual examination of one of the pieces, which indicates an analytic approach. It seems that this pianist falls into Hallam's *mixed* category.

This study provides an opportunity to compare the practice of a more experienced pianist (Karol) with two less experienced pianists (Jaroslaw and Lukasz), although Miklaszewski does not do so, perhaps out of consideration for the feelings of those involved. We make the comparisons with apologies to the musicians. The more experienced Karol is clearly distinguished from the other two pianists in three ways. First, he made a sharper distinction than the other two in the amount of time he spent on the two pieces. He spent approximately 2 hours on the Romantic piece and 5 hours on the contemporary work—2½ times longer on the harder one. In contrast, Jaroslaw and Lukasz both spent only 1¼ times longer on the harder piece. Second, Karol made a sharper distinction in his practice between runs (testing) and work (operating), doing more concentrated playing and loops than the other two. Third, the difference between Karol and the other two pianists in the amount of concentrated playing was more marked for the harder, modern piece (two thirds more) than for the easier, Romantic pieces (one third more).

Of course, we cannot be sure that these differences are due to Karol's greater experience. They could just be idiosyncrasies of his practice that have nothing to do with experience. For the moment, however, this is the only published study that permits detailed comparison of the practice of highly accomplished pianists with different amounts of experience.[3] It suggests that more expert pianists are able to make finer distinctions between levels of difficulty—either because the overall level of difficulty of any given piece is lower for them or because their ability to recognize and anticipate difficulties has increased.

In summary, Miklaszewski's two studies provide the most detailed account we have to date of how expert pianists go about learning a new piece. The studies confirm Hallam's (1995a, 1995b) characterization of expert practice as involving the use of an analytic approach and the flexible use of practice strategies. They also provide additional support for the idea that experts strategically allot more practice time to more difficult pieces, as suggested by Lehmann and Ericsson (1998). In addition, Miklaszewski's studies allow us to expand the notion of strategic allocation of effort to suggest that expert practice is organized into cycles of work on short passages containing difficulties interspersed with longer runs to assess the effectiveness of the work. There is also the tantalizing suggestion that the ability to organize practice this way continues to develop with experience. Finally, Miklasewski's (1989) study suggests that the use of the formal structure of a piece to organize practice may also be characteristic of experts. We have already suggested that the formal structure plays an essential role in the memorization of a new piece, and we pursue this observation in chapters 8 and 9.

CONCLUSIONS: CHARACTERISTICS OF EFFECTIVE PRACTICE

By examining the practice of experienced musicians, we can identify the characteristics that make their practice effective. It may be possible to use this information to improve students' practice skills. Even small improvements in the effectiveness of practice are important because of the enormous amount of practice time required to develop high levels of musical ability. More generally, a better understanding of the nature of effective practice should provide the basis for a more detailed understanding of expertise and its development. Not that we expect students to practice just like professionals. The improvement of practice skills is necessarily an iterative process, with each skill depending on other skills that must be learned. However, having a clear idea of the practice strategies used by highly skilled musicians provides a set of goals toward which students can shape their own practice.

Deliberate practice:

- Is a skill that has to be learned,
- Is hard work and takes time,
- Is aimed at improvement,
- Requires constant self-evaluation, and
- Involves a continual search for better ways to do things.

Expert musicians:

- Flexibly apply a wide range practice strategies to the problem at hand,

- Strategically allocate practice time on the basis of difficulty,
- Organize practice into TOTE cycles of work (operate) and runs (testing), and
- Use the formal structure of the music to organize their practice.

We see ample evidence of each of these characteristics in the following chapters as we describe how one experienced concert pianist went about learning a new piece for performance. In chapter 11, we return to this list of characteristics of expert practice to expand and revise it in the light of what we have learned.

ENDNOTES

1. The one exception may be the visual arts (Ericsson et al., 1993; Winner, 1996b).

2. Arnold Schonberg (1970, cited in Hayes 1981) describes Mozart as a "late developer". Other composers really have pushed the boundaries of the 10-year rule. Two exceptions cited by Hayes (1981) are Satie's *Trois Gymnopédies*, composed after 8 years of experience, and Paganini's *Caprices*, composed after 9 years. These are popular pieces, but they are not master works. Early compositions with stronger claims to the status of master works are Alban Berg's Sonata, op. 1, and Dmitry Shostakovich's *Symphony No. 1*, both created when the composers were 19 years old and had been composing for 9 years. In any case, the small number of these exceptions and the limited extent to which they erode the 10-year limit support the "10-year rule" (see Simonton, 1991).

3. Aaron Williamon and Elizabeth Valentine have looked at the effects of experience on the practice of student pianists (Williamon, 1999; Williamon & Valentine, 2000, 2002).

Lessons From J.S. Bach: Stages of Practice

Roger Chaffin and Gabriela Imreh

W e began with two questions. First, how does a performer memorize a new piece? We have seen that one of the hallmarks of expertise is a remarkable ability to memorize. Yet studies of expert memory have all been done in areas involving conceptual skills, with chess masters, mathematicians, physicists, and the like (Ericsson & Smith, 1991). There has been little work on expert memory in domains involving complex motor skills and none on expert memory in musicians. Do the principles developed for other domains apply to piano performance? Second, what does a performer think about while playing? At what level are the details of the performance consciously controlled (Wegner & Vallacher, 1986)? The performer has to reconcile two apparently contradictory goals. She has to play accurately, hitting all the right notes and keeping track of where she is, and she has to convey to her audience the emotions expressed in the music. How does a pianist meet both the technical and aesthetic demands of her art? How can a person mindfully perform a highly overlearned skill?

To answer these questions, we observed Gabriela learning a new piece all the way from the first time she opened the score at the piano until the final, polished performance. For the study, Gabriela selected the third movement (*Presto*) of a work she had scheduled for performance during the coming year, J.S. Bach's *Italian Concerto*. She knew the piece of course. It is a staple of the piano repertoire; she had taught it to a student 3 years before, but she had never learned it herself. The *Presto* was a good choice for our purposes because it is a fairly difficult piece that Gabriela knew would be hard to memorize. This meant that there would be plenty of opportunity to observe memorization and practice.

For comparison, we also selected a second piece that would be easier to learn, Claude Debussy's *Clair de Lune*. This proved to be so much easier that it was relatively uninformative. So much so that, in the account that follows, we have chosen to focus entirely on the *Presto*. *Clair de Lune* took 4 hours to learn compared to 33 hours for the *Presto* (Chaffin & Imreh, 1996).

The *Presto* was a good vehicle for addressing the questions that concerned us. Its fast tempo and *moto perpetuo* style place heavy demands on memory, requiring the performer to retrieve each passage from long-term memory with little time for reflection or anticipation. This means that the performer needs to devote a lot of practice to memory retrieval. Gabriela needed to practice attending to particular features of the piece so that these would automatically come to mind at the right point during the performance. These performance cues are described in chapters 8 and 9. Performance cues function as retrieval cues for recalling the music from long-term memory. They also answer the question of what the pianist attends to during performance.

In this chapter, after introducing the music, we sketch out the stages of the learning process. We then begin to fill in this outline by describing quantitative changes in practice across the course of learning: changes in number and length of practice segments, number of repetitions per bar, playing time, average tempo, and rate of practice. The following chapters continue to fill in the picture by describing Gabriela's comments as she practiced (chap. 7) and the effects on practice of different types of musical complexity (chap. 8). We then use what we have learned to answer the questions with which we started: How does a pianist memorize? What does a performer think about while performing? (chap. 9). Chapter 10 returns to the stages of the learning process, integrating insights from the intervening chapters. Finally, chapter 11 considers what we have learned about memorization, expert practice, and the process of collaborative, interdisciplinary research.

THE MUSIC

The *Presto* consists of 16 major sections, most of which are divided into subsections, giving 37 sections and subsections (referred to collectively as *sections*), each between 4 and 20 bars in length. It has 210 bars, notated in 2/4 time, and lasts 3 to 4 minutes at performance tempo. Gabriela's recording lasted for 3 minutes and 4 seconds (Imreh, 1996).[1] The score used by Gabriela is reproduced in Appendix 2.

The *Presto* is fairly short and contains no more than a normal share (for Bach) of technical difficulties. Gabriela judged it to be less difficult than two other pieces she was preparing for the same recording—the Chromatic Fantasy and Fugue in D minor and Busoni's transcription of the Chaconne in D minor. Hinson (1987) rated the *Italian Concerto* as being of medium difficulty on a 4-point scale ranging from *easy* to *difficult*, whereas Faurot (1974) described the *Italian Concerto* as *difficult*.

The difficulties of the *Presto* come from four sources. First, the music is polyphonic and the voices shift between the two hands, sometimes with a third or fourth voice to bring out as well. Second, like most of Bach's keyboard music, it does not follow standard conceptual or motor patterns. He continually defies expectations, veering away from the usual continuation of a familiar pattern so that the music does not sit easily in the hand. As a result, each bar, even each half bar, must often be learned of itself. Third, the fast tempo gives the performer no time to think about what is coming up next; there are no sustained notes or pauses for the pianist to collect her thoughts. This is compounded by the fourth source of difficulty—the complexity of the formal structure.

The *Italian Concerto* takes its name from the musical form of the *Presto*, which is in Italian Rondo form. In the prototypical Italian Rondo, an A theme repeats six times, each separated by different themes. In the *Presto* of the *Italian Concerto*, each repetition is slightly different. As if this does not provide enough opportunity for confusion, Bach doubles up on the A theme (repeats it twice in succession) at the beginning, middle, and end, giving nine repetitions altogether (see Fig. 6.1). On top of this, the B theme repeats three times, and one of these repetitions is doubled, making four repetitions. The C theme occurs twice. Only Section D, a fugue, occurs once. This is the kind of elegant complexity for which Bach is justly famous. Keeping track of these multiply embedded repetitions, with no time to think about the next one, adds an element of horizontal complexity to the vertical complexity of the polyphony that makes the *Presto* very difficult to memorize.

Each time a theme is repeated, there comes a point at which it diverges from other repetitions of the same theme. These points of divergence we call "*switches*". A switch is a place where two (or more) repetitions of the same theme begin to diverge. For example, there is a switch between two repetitions of the Ba theme in Bars 29 and 171. The two bars are identical except for an octave jump on the second note of the left hand in Bar 171.

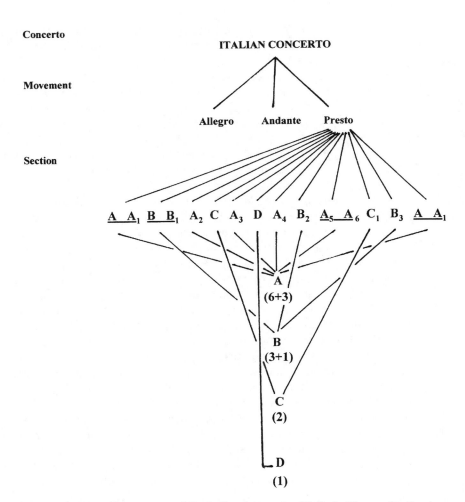

FIG. 6.1 The formal structure of the *Italian Concerto* by J.S. Bach. Themes (sections) are represented by capital letters with different variations represented by subscripts. Themes that are doubled (repeated twice in succession) are underlined. In parentheses are the number of repetitions (first number) and doublings (second number) of each theme.

This note (in both bars) is the switch. Not making the jump puts the pianist in Bar 29; making it puts her in Bar 171. Keeping track of which way to go at switches is one of the main challenges of playing the *Presto* from memory.

RECORDING PRACTICE

Gabriela taped her practice from the first time she sat down at the piano with the score until the piece was ready for the recording session. The *Presto* was learned for an all-Bach CD professionally recorded in September 1994. Preparation of the program for this recording, including the work on the *Presto*, was fitted into a busy professional schedule. During the 10-month period that the *Presto* was learned, Gabriela was also preparing the rest of the program for the CD while maintaining a full schedule involving 30 performances of two different recital programs and preparing five different concerti for piano and orchestra, two of them for the first time. Before the recording session, she tried out the *Presto* once in public, substituting it into a recital program about two thirds of the way through the learning process.

While Gabriela was learning the *Presto*, we had not yet formulated the specific hypotheses to be tested. Indeed, the whole idea of quantifying behavior and testing hypotheses was foreign to Gabriela. The plan was simple: to collect data so that the points we had made in our workshop could be illustrated in a conference on everyday memory (Chaffin & Imreh, 1994). The description of the formal structure on which Figure 6.1 is based was provided at the end of Session 12 in response to a request from Roger about how she had divided up the piece for practice. He had just received the videotapes of the first practice sessions and was having trouble identifying which sections were which. Gabriela responded by marking a copy of the score with the section boundaries and switches, labeling each section and subsection to indicate the theme and its variation.[2]

Work on transcribing the first practice sessions began at this time, and the cumulative records of practice described later were developed. The last important development in the method occurred during preparations for the conference presentation about the research (Chaffin & Imreh, 1994). The *Presto* was getting its final polishing with the recording session about 7 weeks away. For the conference, Gabriela provided a description of her decision making for one section of the piece (see Fig. 8.1). The account was so valuable that Roger asked her to provide the same information for the whole piece, which she did several months later, at a time when she was listening to the tapes of the recording session as part of the production process. This description of features of the piece organized on 10 dimensions provides the basis for the measures of musical complexity whose effects on practice are described in chapter 8.

Preparation for the recording session involved 57 practice sessions, 45 of which were taped. The taped sessions represent almost the entire learning process. Most of the sessions that were not taped took place immediately before the recording (Sessions 45–48 and 51–57). At this point, Gabriela considered that learning had been completed. Practice consisted simply of playing through the piece once or twice to maintain it at a high level of readiness until the recording session. However, these sessions are included in the description of the learning process. Gabriela made a note of how many times she played through the piece, and the duration of each session was estimated from this record. One other session was not recorded. In Session 23, Gabriela played the entire concerto through twice—once with a student as an audience and once before the student arrived. One session that was recorded was not included in the analyses because it was atypical. In Session 25, Gabriela played the *Presto* twice for Roger during a discussion of the research project.

Taping was done mostly on videotape with the camera positioned to the pianist's right and slightly behind her so that her hands and the score were visible. Audio recordings were made for practice Sessions 25 to 35 because of problems with the microphone on the video camera. The same problem with the microphone also resulted in the loss of data for Sessions 18 and 19, for which the entire audio track was inaudible, and in the loss of Gabriela's comments during the whole of Sessions 14 to 16 and for parts of Sessions 13 and 20 to 24.

The 57 practice sessions, totaling 33 hours, were clustered in three distinct periods, separated by two long intermissions during which the piece was not played (see Table 6.1).[3]

The first learning period consisted of 12 practice sessions, totaling more than 11 hours, over a 4-week period. There was then an interval of almost 4 months before the beginning of the second learning period. (*Clair de Lune* was learned during this interval.) Two sessions of practice on the *Presto* (Sessions 13 and 14) occurred midway through this interval, separated from the main body of the second learning period. Including these two sessions, the second learning period consisted of 12 practice sessions, totaling 8 hours. Apart from the first two sessions, the second learning period lasted for 14 days and concluded with the first public performance of the new piece. After the performance, there was another interval, this time of 2 months, before the beginning of the third learning period. The start of the main body of sessions was again preceded by two isolated sessions toward the end of the interval, occasioned this time by a meeting of the authors. The final learning period consisted of 26 sessions lasting 14

TABLE 6.1
Summary of Practice Sessions for the *Italian Concerto (Presto)* by J.S. Bach

| Learning Period | Sessions | Week | N | Duration in hours and minutes | | | |
				Total	Mean	Max.	Min.
1	1-3	1	3	2:57	0:59	1:12	0:41
	4-5	2	2	2:35	1:17	1:25	1:10
	6-9	3	4	3:47	0:57	1:47	0:31
	10-11	4	2	1:24	0:42	1:07	0:17
	12	5	1	0:36	0:36	.	.
Total	1-12	1-5	12	11:19	0:57	1:47	0:17

Intermission 1

Learning Period	Sessions	Week	N	Total	Mean	Max.	Min.
2	13	13	1	0:57	0:57	.	.
	14-17	20	4	2:56	0:44	1:02	0:20
	18-21	21	4	2:31	0:38	1:01	0:28
	22-24	22	3	1:42	0:34	0:51	0:08
Total	13-24	13-22	12	8:06	0:41	1:02	0:08

Intermission 2

Learning Period	Sessions	Week	N	Total	Mean	Max.	Min.
3	25-27	30	3	0:55	0:18	0:24	0:14
	28	32	1	0:26	0:26	.	.
	29-32	33	4	3:11	0:48	1:34	0:14
	33	34	1	0:59	0:59	.	.
	34-35	35	2	0:46	0:23	0:25	0:21
	36	36	1	0:33	0:33	.	.
	37	37	1	0:22	0:22	.	.
	38-39	38	2	1:11	0:35	0:49	0:22
	40-41	39	2	0:55	0:27	0:30	0:25
	42-44	40	3	0:47	0:16	0:23	0:03
	45-52	41	8	2:37	0:20	1:00	0:12
	53-57	42	5	1:18	0:16	0:30	0:12
Total	25-57	30-42	33	14:00	0:25	1:34	0:03
Total	1-57	1-42	57	33:25	0:35	1:47	0:03

hours, spaced over 12 weeks, and ended with two performances of the *Presto* during a recording session.

STAGES OF THE LEARNING PROCESS

Wicinski (1950; reported in Miklaszewski, 1989) identified three stages in the process of learning a new piece for performance: preliminary ideas, work on technical problems, and trial rehearsals (see Table 6.2). These stages were distilled from interviews with 10 eminent Russian pianists, including Sviatoslav Richter, Emil Gilels, and Heinrich Neuhaus, on how they went about learning a new piece. In Wicinski's first stage, the pianist gets to know the music and develops preliminary ideas about how it should be performed. This is followed by a stage of hard work on the technical problems. The third stage is devoted to trial rehearsals, in which the ideas developed in Stage 1 are combined with the technical skills developed in Stage 2 to produce the final interpretation.

Gabriela independently described her process in learning the *Presto*, using a similar but more detailed scheme involving five stages: scouting it out, section by section, the gray stage, putting it together, and polishing. The relationship between the two schemes is shown in Table 6.2. Both start with a preliminary scouting of the piece (1) followed by section-by-section work on technical problems and fingering (2a). Gabriela then describes a gray stage (2b) in which the transition is made from thinking about every detail to playing automatically. For a technically demanding piece like the *Presto*, the transition is slow, whereas for a piece with few technical challenges, like *Clair de Lune*, this stage is almost absent. Wicinski's third stage of trial rehearsals is divided by Gabriela into putting it together (3a) and polishing (3b). Again, polishing may be perfunctory for an easy piece with a simple structure like *Clair de Lune*, but was important for the more demanding and complex *Presto*. A final stage of maintenance practice (4) is included in Table 6.2, although it was not mentioned by either Gabriela or Wicinski. *Maintenance* refers to the period after a piece has been learned and before it is performed. We needed to add this stage to give a full account of the preparation of the *Presto*.

Stage 1. Scouting it Out (Session 1)

For Gabriela, the first step in learning a new piece is to scout it out—sight reading the whole work from beginning to end to get an idea of the large-scale structure.

TABLE 6.2
Stages of Learning a New Piece for Piano Described by
Imreh and Wicinski (1950)

Stage	Imreh	Wicinski
1	Scouting it out	Preliminary ideas
2a	Section by section	Work on technical problems
2b	The gray stage	
3a	Putting it together	Trial rehearsals
3b	Polishing	
4	Maintenance	

This will typically be done in a single run through the entire piece at the beginning of the first practice session. For me, the first read through the piece is typically done at a slow tempo with many hesitations and pauses to find the right notes. The goal is to simply hear the piece to get an idea of its overall shape. Knowledge about the type of piece and the composer already provides a fairly detailed schema for the architecture of the piece. The initial scouting identifies how the music on the page maps onto this schema and identifies any surprises. At this time I also make a preliminary evaluation of the work of the editor and of any fingerings notated in the score.

This was the procedure for the *Italian Concerto*, although Gabriela already had a general idea of the structure of the piece from having taught it 3 years earlier and from a general knowledge of its musical form. In the first session, Gabriela began by playing slowly through the entire concerto, with many hesitations and pauses but without stopping to practice anything. The scouting run allowed her to identify the main outline of the formal structure, locate the technical difficulties and other issues that would have to be dealt with, and see how to divide up the piece for the next stage. Like the pianist studied by Miklaszewski (1989) and most of the musicians interviewed by Hallam (1995a, 1995b), she took an analytic approach.

Stage 2a: Section by Section (Sessions 1–6)

The next stage began, 20 minutes into the first session, immediately after the initial scouting expedition and continued through to the end of Session 6.

The next step is to get the music into the fingers. This is done by playing small sections. The harder the music, the smaller the sections. Then the small sections are joined together linking them, backwards and forwards, into larger units. This provides multiple starting points in case of memory failure or mistakes in performance. . . . Memorizing can start at this stage.

Gabriela began working through the *Presto*, a few sections at a time, making decisions about fingerings and working them into the fingers. At the beginning of Session 6, she was able to announce,

Okay, so the plan for today was to pretty much to wrap up the rough draft, so let's see if it is happening.

Apparently it was because after this there was a break for a few days while Gabriela worked on the first movement.

Stage 2a learning was largely completed. The transition from one stage to another is not, of course, clear cut. Transitions occurred at different times for different passages and problems. The process of testing fingerings, for example, continued until the entire piece could be played through at performance tempo, as in the following episode in Session 8.

I am trying to use [a] fingering that may not work. I may just let it go because it is just too much trouble. It may be just the new fingering that I put in that's not working. Okay, what I am going to do. . . . This is so frustrating. I feel like really cursing. But I know that with passages like this, it's going to take weeks until it settles. . . .

Despite this Stage 2a activity in Session 8, the main focus of practice had shifted. As Gabriela said, the fingerings had to settle and meanwhile her focus shifted to a new goal.

Stage 2b: The Gray Stage (Sessions 7–16)

The next goal is to develop automaticity. The gray stage is the period when automaticity is developing, but is not yet fully reliable.

The gray stage is, in some ways, the hardest. It is frustrating. Your memory is starting to be accurate but the playing is not so good yet. You don't yet have good coordination between mind and fingers. It is a matter of control, of whether you can actually tell your hands what to do or whether your hands are ahead and you come along behind and just check on what they did. You want to be in control, to be out in front. But your fingers (motor memory) can go much faster. The conceptual representation is much slower.

For me, the greatest struggle at this stage is to speed up conceptual memory to close to performance tempo. Because the motor memory is not completely developed you need a lot more conceptual control at this stage than you will later. You have to anticipate the mistakes your fingers will make and prevent them from making them. Rather than saying, "Okay, fingers do your job and I'll check and see that you do", you say, "I'll tell you what to do". But your brain just doesn't work that fast. Your fingers can go much faster.

The learning of the *Presto* was going more slowly than expected. When she returned to it at the beginning of Session 7, at the beginning of the gray stage, Gabriela noted how much easier the first movement had been to learn.

Now, as far as number of pages [in the score], we're talking the same amount, seven pages. And for some reason this [the first movement] was just about a million times easier to learn. I have a couple of suspicions [about why]. [First], it is much easier as it is. . . [Second], I also allowed myself to sit down and stay for longer periods of time at the piano than I did with [the *Presto*]. I had a little more time. I really do prefer to dig into my practicing and work longer sessions.

Asked about this comment during an interview, Gabriela explained that concentrated practice:

Gives it a better chance to be stored, first of all, in muscle memory, where things become second nature. . . . Neuhaus, a Russian pianist, . . . compared [spreading out practice too widely] to trying to cook a meal. If you put the kettle on the stove, and, just when you are about to bring it to a boil, you have to go off and do something else, you will never get the meal cooked. [In learning the *Presto*], I actually let my soup get completely cold before I went back to it. With my students I give them simple advice. I tell them, "Three times you have to practice in [close] succession to get any kind of result."

Gabriela also explained in this interview why she had been unable to follow her own advice:

I was playing a recital . . . [which] is much higher priority. It was Christmas and New Year's. . . . That is one of the greatest problems of all performing and teaching pianists. You have to switch so often from doing completely different things. It takes a lot of energy just to switch. I knew that I was making it difficult for myself.

Asked if she considered postponing the work until she had more time, Gabriela replied:

> No, I had made a bargain with myself, that I had to have it learned by the first of the year. So I was just fitting it in the best I could. . . . And, as you know, at some point I got on with it.

She did get on with it in Session 8, which, at 1 hour and 47 minutes, was the longest of the entire learning process.

> Today, I am going to really try to get this wrapped up. I am really frustrated because I have the first movement memorized and I spent just a fraction of the time on it. I . . . think I need to sit down and stay till I really accomplish something, not wasting my time, so here we go!"

The longer session had the desired effect. After 40 minutes, Gabriela was able to play through the entire piece from memory. The performance was far from fluent—there were several interruptions when she had to back up and repeat a passage, and at least twice she had to look at the score, which was still open in front of her. (We will have more to say about this memory run in chap. 9.) Yet she got through it, commenting as she finished:

> That was memorized, as horrible as it sounds. At least I know what I am doing. I still have a couple of deep gaps in memory, but. . . .

This session also saw the first mention of playing sections from memory:

> This page with the fugue. . . . I am going to try to play it from beginning to end a couple of times, then I might even try to play it from memory.

Memory at this point is largely motor memory.

> I reach a level of performance that is relatively "sufficient." It's pretty much in tempo. The sound is not very good, but I know that I am trying to play everything out quite roughly because I know that the hand has a better memory if it's exercised well. I'll play it by memory and try to accept the fact that the level [of playing] is going to drop dramatically because I cannot concentrate on more than trying to figure out the notes and see where the holes are in memory (Session 8).

Having sacrificed musicality in Session 8 to test and develop her memory, in Session 9 Gabriela began to pay more attention to interpretation. By the end of the session, she appeared to reach a turning point.

> It's getting there. It's fun to see some music finally coming out of it, because until now it's just been pulling teeth and torture.

None too soon. The date was December 28, and there were only 3 days left to fulfill the bargain she had made with herself to have it learned by the New Year. However, she was not able to get back to the *Presto* again until New Year's Eve, when she explained:

> I was so frustrated because I wanted to practice, just touch up a few places, and I couldn't start the video at any time because I didn't have the continuous time. . . .

The main focus of the 45-minute practice session was again on interpretation. "Mostly, I am working on phrasing." By this time, the first learning period was almost over. The following day, New Year's Day, at the beginning of Session 11, Gabriela noted:

> I'm just running through the concerto. From now on it's just going to be . . . maintenance work. I won't have much time to spend on it. I'll just run through it a couple of times and try to fix whatever goes wrong.

The goal of being able to play the piece at a sufficient level by the first of the year had apparently been met.

That her practice was still in the gray stage at this point is indicated by a remark made a week later in the final session of the first learning period:

> It still gives me palpitations to play through it, because I don't feel safe and comfortable. I feel like I really have to concentrate and control. But, . . . as long as you do that, you actually make it more difficult for motor memory and for the automaticity of memory to work, and you should not mess with that. So, I feel like you're between a rock and a hard place. It just is not to the point where it's perfectly automatic. . . . And, in the meantime, the more I try to control it, the more I sometimes interfere with things that are well set up (Session 12).

One could not ask for a clearer expression of the gray stage difficulties of integrating automatic and conscious control.

At the end of this session, Gabriela ran through the last movement one more time and then proposed to test her memory before putting the piece aside for several weeks. She played through it twice from memory. The first time she got stuck and had to open the score, but the second time she sailed right through with minimal hesitation. She summed up her progress:

> Well, that's not awful, but, I feel like . . . the memory process is just pretty much 60% done, and there is a lot of work to be done, mostly on being able to switch to a different section.

If Gabriela had continued to practice instead of taking a break, she probably would have moved to the next stage of putting it together at this point. As it was, there was a hiatus of 3 months. When she came back to it, she would need to recover the ground she had lost before moving on. In Session 12, Gabriela explained the reason for the break:

> Early on in the learning process, having too long breaks can be devastating, but later on, when the piece starts to feel comfortable, it actually helps very much to set it aside because that forces you to relearn it. Every time you relearn something you really solidify memory. So, it would be good for me to not look at this [piece] . . . it is good to set [it] aside for a few weeks [or] months . . . and then start it all brand new again and look at it like you've never seen it. Each time you do [this], count on forgetting some. It pretty much depends on how well your motor memory is set.

At the beginning of the second learning period, Gabriela talked about how she was going to relearn it:

> There are two ways to go about relearning or rereading a piece. This [way I am going to use now] is the . . . more painful one, which is reading. Because you are not relying on motor memory at all. The other way is to just close the music and try to just get through [it] and not worry too much. Most of the time, it's just anxiety and inhibition that will stop this from working and you will see a big difference [when you get to] the second turn playing it. [The second turn] is just going to be much more fluent. You just have to get through that first time (Session 13).

Sessions 13 and 14 were isolated, occurring 8 weeks after Session 12 and 6 weeks before the main body of learning period 2. Session 13 took place 2 days after the performance of *Clair de Lune*, but then the *Presto* was set aside again while Gabriela prepared for her Carnegie Hall debut and then rested her hand after spraining it in a fall on the ice.

Two events provided the impetus for returning to the *Presto* at this time. One was the sprained hand, which forced Gabriela to consider substituting the *Italian Concerto* for Busoni's transcription of Bach's Chaconne in D minor in her next recital. The *Italian Concerto* would be easier on the injured hand. The other was the approaching end of the concert season. The next recital would be Gabriela's only opportunity to play the *Italian Concerto* for an audience before the recording session in September. Preparation took place over a 14-day period during which she practiced the *Presto* an additional 11 times. Sessions were generally shorter than in the first learning period and became progressively so as the recital date approached.

We have less information about practice during the second learning period because many of Gabriela's comments were inaudible for these sessions due to the microphone malfunction. This was particularly true of Sessions 14 to 16, and their inclusion in the gray stage is based primarily on the clear evidence that the next stage of putting it together began in Session 17. Consistent with the inclusion of Sessions 14 to 16 in the gray stage is Gabriela's retrospective report that it took her at least three or four sessions to relearn the piece to the level that it had been at the end of the first learning period, and the absence of sharp differences between these sessions and Sessions 11 to 12.

However, there are indications that Gabriela was getting ready to move to the next stage of putting it together. In Session 14, she began using a miniaturized photocopy of the score with the pages attached to each other concertina style, which allowed her to play through the whole piece without turning pages. At the same time, she began paying more attention to switches—places where different repetitions of the same theme diverge from one another (see chap. 8). Getting the switches sorted out is a necessary precursor for putting the pieces together.

Stage 3a: Putting It Together (Session 17)

Once the playing of the individual sections is fluent, it is time to put aside the music, create a mental map for the whole piece, and learn to play from memory. Having a schema for the piece makes it possible to play from memory by providing a retrieval scheme that allows the pianist to keep track of where she is and avoid taking wrong turns. The schema specifies the sequence of themes and pinpoints the switches. Getting the retrieval scheme to function effectively at performance tempo was a challenge:

> Another important aspect of this stage of practice is learning not to get lost in the transitions from one section to another. In a slow piece or a piece with a simple structure this is not a big issue. There is plenty of time to think about

what is coming up next and the structure is simple. The possibilities for taking a wrong turn are limited. The piece that we studied was a different matter. First of all, the piece is very fast, and there are no sustained notes or pauses where you can collect your thoughts. If you do not know where you are going, you are sure to get lost. This is because the A theme keeps returning, a little different each time. One variant puts you on the track for the second return of the A theme. A slightly different variation puts you at the end of the piece before you know what has happened. You are like a train coming up to a set of points which switch the train from one track to another. If you set the points one way, you go in one direction; if you set them the other way, you go in the other direction. You have to throw the switch before you get there, or you are liable to wreck the train.

Putting it together occurred in Session 17, in which the practice was clearly different from what had gone before. It was the first and only session devoted entirely to learning to play from memory. Gabriela had played from memory in Session 8 at the cost of the musical integrity of the piece and in Session 12 just to show that she could do it. Now playing from memory was the main goal. As she explained at the beginning of the session, "I want to play this piece in ten days in Arkansas."

The main task in Session 17 was "learning not to get lost in the transitions from one section to another." Transitions and switches were the focus of the first half hour of the session as Gabriela worked with the score, carefully comparing the different returns of the A and B themes. For example, after comparing the various repetitions of the A theme, she summarized her conclusions:

Okay, so . . . this is our second ending, third ending actually. One was [plays]. Oh, sorry [plays]. The second one is right at the end [of the segment] that I practiced [plays]. And this is the third, a different key.

With the details of the transitions and switches clearly in mind, Gabriela was now ready to put the piece together. She eased into it in stages, running through it with her miniaturized score folded so that she could only see some of the pages. Then she closed the score altogether and played entirely from memory. The first run without the score was much more successful than the previous effort in Session 12. Gabriela explained the difference:

The last time I played from memory, if you remember . . . I was relying very much on motor memory . . . I had very few reference places, where I knew exactly what I was doing. I had a lot, but compared to now it was much less.

So, now I think, even though I made a few mistakes, I know what the mistake was, and how to fix it.

After successfully running through the piece twice without the score, Gabriela was ready to play it for an audience and called out to ask her husband, Dan Spalding, to listen. She played it again, but not as well. "That was really bad. I fell into almost every trap on the way." The next run went better until toward the end. Gabriela concluded that she had run out of steam. It was time to stop.

Session 17 had accomplished a transition to a new stage. Gabriela could now play reliably from memory. She had put together a schema for the overall structure of the piece that could be used to guide its recall from long-term memory. The retrieval scheme provided the reference places or retrieval cues needed to monitor the progress of the motor program. The motor program was by now largely automatic, but conscious attention was still needed to retrieve the various chunks or sections from memory and initiate their execution.

Stage 3b: First Polishing (Sessions 18–24)

Having a mental schema for the whole piece and being able to play it through from memory makes it possible to adjust the balance and interrelations of the various sections. This, in turn, suggests further musical ideas that lead to further refinements of the performance. This process of polishing is never really finished and can be redone over and over:

> The main goal of the polishing stage is to settle the piece in to your memory at a high level of performance and with a definite emotional shape to it. It is really a matter of routine rehearsal rather than practice.
>
> Another goal is to build up your confidence for the trouble spots. Almost every piece, especially technically challenging pieces, have their pitfalls, places that could be problems or places that you are just afraid of. During the last stage you want to enter a period in which you a have a really good percentage of success. It's like ice skaters with their triple axels and lutzes. You have to try and get them solid and consistent for several weeks before and build up confidence.
>
> A third goal is to make sure that the emotional architecture of the piece stands out clearly, and that the piece flows well. You make sure that nothing is overdone, that you do not overplay; that you don't shoot your climaxes by getting there too early, giving it away; that you don't plan it so that your greatest climax comes too early, so that the rest of the piece is an anticlimax. When you have a whole recital, you have to do the same thing for the whole recital, making sure it flows well.

A fourth goal is checking your memory. You have to check your memory cues to make sure of your reactions to them. Memory has to be very secure because you have to be ready for the unexpected in performance. No two performances are alike. You never know about the piano, whether you will like it or hate it, or whether the audience is going to be warm or cold. During a performance you have to deal with factors that you cannot know about before hand. It may be little kids wriggling about in the first row or some problem with the piano. Whatever the problem, the show must go on. You have to make sure that you don't fall apart."

Polishing in Sessions 18 to 24 was marked by two new activities: practice performances and slow practice. We already mentioned the first practice performance for Dan at the end of Session 17. The purpose was to become accustomed to the added pressure of an audience. As Gabriela said at the beginning of Session 19, "I am going to play this for Dan. Put a little bit of pressure on." Dan was called on to listen to the piece again in Sessions 20 and 22. The final practice audience was a piano student (Roger and Mary's son, Ben), for whom Gabriela played the whole concerto in Session 23.

Extended slow practice occurred for the first time in Session 18 and occurred in every session from 19 to 24. Slow practice develops conceptual memory. By decreasing the efficiency of motor memory, it forces musicians to think about what they are playing. In these sessions, Gabriela was thinking about her expressive goals for the piece and also about fingerings and patterns of notes—things that had not been actively practiced for some time (see chap. 8). This was the process of remapping described in chapter 3, in which the artistic and inspirational elements are brought to the fore, allowing the problems to recede into the background. In chapter 9, we show that in these sessions Gabriela was training herself to focus on expressive goals, making sure that the thought of these was sufficient to elicit all of the fingerings and complex actions that had become automatic during the many sessions of gray stage practice.

Another part of polishing was the addition of further interpretive refinements that had to be worked into the performance. At one point, Dan's opinion was solicited:

I want to ask you something. I . . . did not make up my mind, but I kind of, I think it is a double theme. It is really a polyphonic theme. You know, it's not theme and accompaniment (Session 20).

Performing the piece in public after Session 24 was risky. Gabriela did not fully trust her memory yet; for the public performance, she had the score out on the piano "as an insurance policy." This was highly unusual. Gabriela has performed with a score on only a handful of occasions and is not accustomed to it. The score is one more thing to think about and can be a serious distraction. She did not expect to need it, but nevertheless the intricacies of the *Presto* are such that she felt that the possibility of a memory failure was too great to risk playing without it.

Stage 3b: Repolishing (Sessions 26–30)

We might say that the *Presto* had been learned at this point. However, Gabriela saw it as still under development for the recording session, 4 months away, and continued to record her practice. Because the polishing stage lasted for such a long time, we have subdivided it into three parts: first polishing, repolishing, and increasing the tempo. Repolishing began after an interval of 8 weeks with three isolated sessions (25–27), which were occasioned by a meeting among the authors to discuss the progress of the research. Gabriela played the *Presto* through from memory to see how well she could remember it and then practiced it in two short sessions on successive days.

Practice sessions were much more spread out during the third learning period. There was a 2-week interval before Gabriela returned to the *Presto* again in Session 28 and another week before Session 29. Each time memory needed some refreshing. At the beginning of Session 28, "I have to go and work out a couple of places that need refreshing." In Session 29,

> I'm going to put out all the music in my nice handy-dandy Xerox version and I'm going to play it five or six times, medium to moderately slow. Definitely under tempo and with a very nice rich tone and just clean it up a little, and then try to remember all the details that were there before and try to repeat different ones and then try to work some more on details.

Once memory for the details had been refreshed, there was "cleaning up" work to be done. Again in Session 30, "I cleaned up the right hand and I am very happy with that." Some spots involved technical problems.

> There are a couple of technical problems that I am not happy with and two of them are the . . . big leaps in left hand in bar 67 and bar 153. I'll have to work on those.

Most of Gabriela's attention, however, was on interpretation:

I want it to be exciting and very full of stuff, but I don't know how much somebody can hear. See what I would like is sort of a stereo effect here. . . . You know, one [part] comes in and one comes out, but I'm not sure at that speed if anyone can catch that (Session 28).

In Session 30, she was ". . . trying to bring out the left hand there as you see."

By the end of this session, Gabriela had done all that was possible in this direction and concluded, "It's really a matter of endurance from now on."

But still she was not satisfied. The *Presto* was too bland. It lacked the excitement and dramatic impact to bring the concerto to a satisfactory conclusion. Despite the possibility that a faster tempo might make it impossible for a listener to hear some of the refinements of the interpretation, increasing the tempo was the solution:

I don't know how much somebody can hear . . . I'm not sure at that speed if anyone can catch that.

Stage 3b: Increasing the Tempo (Sessions 31–44)

The decision to change the tempo was announced in Session 31. "I talked to Dan yesterday. He said I should play it even faster." In reaching her decision, Gabriela had also consulted a pianist colleague, Ena Bronstein, but the decision had been foreshadowed in an exchange with Dan about tempo 3 months earlier in Session 20. Gabriela had mused, "I think I am playing it too fast. . . . "

Dan, helpfully noncommittal, said "Think so."

Gabriela said, "Oh, I'm sure . . . It's nerve-racking. But that's the fun. It has to be. If you can do all the things [at] this tempo . . . That would be pretty exciting."

That was Session 20 and they were talking about a tempo of 132 beats per minute. At the beginning of Session 31, Gabriela tried a new, faster tempo and concluded that it was "excellent." Putting the metronome on it, she determined that the new tempo was 132—the same tempo she had liked in Session 20.

Bringing the *Presto* up to the new tempo took 11 more sessions spread out over 5 weeks. The long haul began in earnest with a marathon 1¾-hour session, the second longest of the whole learning process. Session 32 introduced a new form of practice that became a feature in the weeks that followed. Gabriela worked on the fugue (Section D) with the metronome, beginning at a slow tempo and increasing it one notch after every two repetitions. She was not happy about this.

Well, I don't have any choice. I do have to do this and it's miserable work. . . .
Metronome's going to hate this too. It's terrible.

The metronome was used again in the same incremental way in three more sessions.

By Session 35, the new tempo was becoming more comfortable. Gabriela noted, "Every time I slow down, just a little bit, it seems like it is so much easier." In the following sessions, she increased her target tempo to 138, giving herself some leeway to slow down eventually to the initial target of 132. In Sessions 40 and 42, she tested the stability of the tempo using the metronome. "The metronome seems to have helped because it seems to me it's much more stable."

It was nearly there. In Session 41, she concluded, "There isn't that much more that I can do," and at the beginning of Session 43, "I'm running through my program fixing little things and just basically once or twice through every thing." But it did not go well. "I can't believe [I am still having trouble with this]." After some more work with the metronome, "I don't like it. It's irritating, maddening, hate it."

Finally in Session 44, the trial performance went off without problems. The learning process was finally over. Gabriela stopped taping her practice, turning on the video camera again in Sessions 49 and 50 only to record a good performance for Roger to use with his talks about the research.

Stage 4: Maintenance (Sessions 45–57)

Once a piece is learned, it has to be maintained at a high level of readiness until the day of the performance. Sessions 45 to 57 were devoted to maintenance.

Knowing when a piece is ready for performance can be difficult. Often, of course, you are working against a deadline. You work differently against a deadline than when you can take a more leisurely approach. A deadline is not necessarily bad. It pushes you.

Some performers, for example Pablo Casals, would not perform a piece in public until they had worked on it for two years. On the other hand there is Christina Kiss who embarked on this huge endeavor of performing the complete Liszt, an enormous undertaking. She will prepare something fairly fast, in just a few months, and play it once in recital. She plays four or five recitals a year, each one a different program. The preparation in these two cases has to be different. The goals are totally different. Casals wants to give the ultimate performance. He wants to make sure that he has put the piece through every test and that it is exactly as he wants it. Kiss's task is different, to present in New York for the first time the entire Liszt opus. Her accomplishment is perhaps even more impressive than Casals, but I am sure she is not giving her ultimate performance of these pieces.

I would like to be closer to Casals. I practice so much because I want to get close to my ultimate performance. Not that this is a fixed thing. Every pianist knows that almost every time you relearn a piece you find new things that you missed the first time, even after ten or fifteen years and playing it dozens of times. There is always room for another, more interesting interpretation. That is partly why some performers record a piece more than once and why they don't like to listen to old recordings. It bothers them that they have accomplished more with the piece since they recorded it. But even knowing this, you try to get close to the "truth" of a piece; the truth for you at that time.

Even after a one or two week break from a piece your understanding of it changes dramatically. That also tells you that there is something to be said for not practicing. There are pianists, Glenn Gould for example, who would not play a piece for two weeks before performance. I can understand that. Sometimes when I relearn a piece and it has not been forgotten too completely, I sit down and play it, and I feel that first performance is more fresh and more interesting than almost anything I will be able to do in three weeks of practicing it. I don't know how to capture that freshness and that feeling of newness. It is a struggle to strike this balance and to know when a piece is ready.

There are some pianists, not very many, who have such an extraordinary ear and such an extraordinary talent, and such extraordinary confidence, that they can perform without much preparation, without taking the trouble to reinforce their backup systems. For example, Martha Argerich is said to have had an extraordinary superstition in her youngest years that if she played a piece from beginning to end once, it would not be good in concert. So she never played it through from beginning to end, except in performance. I don't think she does that any more. But she is one of those extraordinary talents.

Pianists divide more or less evenly on whether and how much and what you should practice on the day of a performance. Some work through the pieces dutifully. Some don't touch those works that day. Most people won't really play through anything on the day of a performance. Part of the reason for this is the fear that if anything does go wrong it is going to wreck your performance at night. Others think that if something goes wrong, I had better fix it before I go in.

In the days immediately before the recording session, Gabriela continued to run through her program, playing pieces two or three times each. For the *Presto*, the last of these sessions occurred the morning of the day the recording was made. During the recording session, Gabriela played the *Presto* twice, both flawless performances.

EFFECTS OF OBSERVATION ON PRACTICE

Did taping her practice alter Gabriela's learning process? Yes, although only as one of myriad factors that influenced when and how she practiced. We have seen that the need to record her practice made it harder to fit the *Presto* into her practice schedule in the initial sessions. It was inconvenient to have to turn on the video recorder, which was in a different room from the piano. Also, she felt self-conscious about the camera. She first referred to this at the beginning of Session 7, when she mentioned that she had found the first movement much easier to learn. Not only was it less complex,

> It is a little bit inconvenient to have to turn the [videotape] machine on, because sometimes I [would like to] just sit down and touch something up, but [the need to record] forces me to be very structured and be dressed appropriately.

She returned to the same point at the beginning of Session 9:

> "I've been wondering how much the camera is inhibiting me, because really, this is not something that many people would be happy about. It's quite a personal affair, to work on a piece. It's not that I don't feel comfortable in front of the camera. [But] it's just like having your dirty laundry in plain view of people. . . . I can't get over how different the two movements [the first and third] have been in the way I've learned them. You have seen, I played for you the first movement after only two and a half days of practice and those weren't six hour days. They were just small sessions. . . . I still think it [the Presto] is a very difficult movement."

In Session 10, Gabriela reported that the same thing had happened again:

> Yesterday I was so frustrated because I wanted to practice, just touch up a few places. And I couldn't start the video at any time because I didn't have the continuous time, plus I wasn't dressed for the occasion. I love to practice in my robe and soft things that are comfortable.

So recording made Gabriela avoid short practice sessions, resulting in longer intervals between sessions than she would have liked, slowing down the learning process.

PRACTICE RECORDS

To understand more concretely what was going on in each session, we devised a visual representation of the practice record. An example is shown in Figure 6.2. The score appears on the horizontal axis at the bottom of the figure. Below the score, bar numbers are indicated along with the sections and subsections. The example shows practice of Section C, which consists of three subsections, Ca, Ca', and Cb. (Sections and subsections are referred to collectively as *sections*, and Ca and Ca' are referred to as the Ca *section*.) The vertical axis represents the practice segments, starting at the bottom of the figure with the first segment and ending at the top of the figure with the last. Each line of the record represents the playing of one practice segment (i.e., a sequence of notes played without stopping). Each time the playing stopped, the record begins again on the next line up. Figure 6.2 shows the portion of Session 4 during which Gabriela worked on Section C for the first time. The record of practice starts at the bottom left with two segments that start at the beginning of Section Ca. The first segment stops at the end of Ca. She then returned to the beginning of Ca, played through it again and on into the Cb section, stopping six notes into Cb. She then went back to the beginning of Cb where the next several segments start; and so on. The 150-plus segments in the figure represent approximately 15 minutes of practice.

Creating the practice records for these figures was slow work. It would have been impossible without the enthusiastic help of hard-working and dedicated student assistants who listened repeatedly to each session and recorded where each practice segment started and stopped. It was necessary to make some compromises. Gabriela worked extremely fast. In the initial sessions, there were many "stutters" where she repeated a note as she organized her thoughts about how to continue. Early on we adopted the stutter rule. Repetitions of a single beat were not recorded unless they occurred more than three times.

The computer-generated representation in Figure 6.2 is a far cry from our first efforts at creating practice records, which were much cruder. As the first videotapes of the early practice sessions arrived by mail, Roger and his students made reduced sized copies of the score and attached them to the bottom of large sheets of graph paper, drawing in each practice segment by hand. Soon we had enormous sheets of paper wrapped around three walls of an office. It was time to rethink this approach. Eventually, with some programming help from Roger and Mary's son, Ben, we managed to shrink things down to a more manageable size (Fig. 6.2).

As Gabriela looked at the first practice records, during the interval after Session 12, she realized that they did not display what is, for her, the most

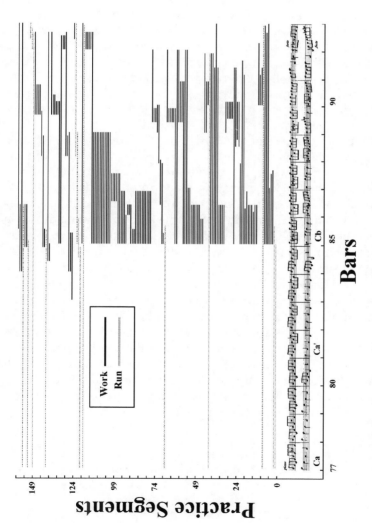

FIG. 6.2 Practice record for the first time the pianist worked on Section C, showing where the pianist started and stopped. The record reads from bottom right with each line representing the uninterrupted playing of the music shown on the horizontal axis. Each time playing stopped and restarted, the record begins again on the next line up. Practice was organized by sections and Section Cb was practiced more than Section Ca. From "A comparison of practice and self-report as sources of information about the goals of expert practice," by R. Chaffin and G. Imreh, 2001, *Psychology of Music, 29,* p. 47. Copyright 2001 by the Society for Research in Psychology of Music and Music Education. Adapted with permission.

117

beautiful part of practice—when she puts together her work on different sections and runs through a larger segment of the piece, seeing how things fit together. We call this type of practice *runs* and distinguish it from *work*. Work involves playing the same short passage repeatedly to solve particular problems, establish muscle memory, develop fluency, and make the playing of the passage more secure. Runs are longer practice segments. For the *Presto*, runs were defined as practice segments extending over two or more complete sections with minimal interruption.[4] They have three main functions. One is to test and locate problems that require work (Miklaszewski, 1989). For example, runs test memory for difficult passages. A feature that can be managed easily enough when played as part of a short segment may not be secure when encountered in context. A second purpose is to practice transitions between sections. Finally, runs allow interpretive and expressive decisions to be evaluated in the broader musical context of surrounding sections or the entire piece.

Work is represented in Figure 6.2 by dark lines, runs by gray lines. Almost all the practice on the two Ca sections was in the form of runs because the two sections were played without interruption, whereas most of the practice on the Cb section was in the form of work. Gabriela first played through the Ca section as part of a run that started in an earlier section (not shown in the figure) until she came to the beginning of the Cb section, where she stopped. The practice of the Cb section was then mostly work interspersed occasionally with runs in which Cb is connected with Ca.

The figure illustrates four important features of the practice. First, like the practice of Miklaszewski's (1989) pianist, it is divided into work on short passages separated by longer runs. This reflects the problem-oriented nature of the practice. Everything was done with a specific goal in mind. Chapter 8 shows the effectiveness of this approach in disposing of one class of problems after another. For now, the work on Section C provides a good example. The work shown in Figure 6.2, from Session 4, largely solved the problems of this section so that they did not need to be revisited. Ironically, when Roger later pointed this out to Gabriela, she was spooked. The following day, in Session 29, she commented,

> I messed up . . . around [bar] 85 [the beginning of Cb]. I was thinking about what you told me yesterday, that I never had to rework that section. It bothered me. . . .

The second feature to note in the practice record is that the Ca sections received much less practice (25 segments) than Cb (162 segments). This is because Cb was more difficult. In chapter 8, we see why. Cb involved more fingering decisions and technical difficulties.

Third, practice segments tended to start at the beginnings of sections. They start in many different places, but the beginnings of Ca and Cb have a special importance. The significance of this use of the formal structure to organize practice is explored in chapter 9 as part of our discussion of memorization.

A fourth important feature of practice is apparent when Figure 6.2 is compared with Figure 6.3, which shows the only other time Gabriela devoted substantial work to Section C in Session 9. The difference between Sections Ca and Cb in the amount of practice they received is much reduced compared to Session 4. Section Cb was getting easier. The effect of practice was to reduce differences between easier and harder passages. Eventually the difference was eliminated altogether. By the fourth time Gabriela worked on this passage, in Session 13, the entire C section was practiced as a whole, and the Ca and Cb subsections were treated identically.

QUANTITATIVE MEASURES OF PRACTICE

The different patterns of practice seen in Figures 6.2 and 6.3 are now described in terms of three quantitative measures: length of the practice segments (segment length), number of practice segments (number of segments), and number of times each bar is played (repetitions per bar).[5] Each of these measures was computed separately for runs and work, allowing a comparison of the amount of playing devoted to the two types of practice (percentage of practice devoted to runs).

Four more measures examined temporal aspects of the practice. The duration of the practice sessions has already been summarized in Table 6.1. Here a slightly different version of the same measure is used: Time spent in activities other than playing was subtracted from the session duration to give a measure of the actual playing time in a session. A second important temporal aspect of practice is tempo, which was measured as the average tempo used in a session (mean target tempo). To examine how much playing time was actually expended in playing up to tempo, we measured the practice rate by taking all the music played in an entire session (expressed as the number of beats) and dividing it by the playing time for the session. The practice rate is thus the average number of beats played per minute over the course of a session. If playing is largely up to tempo, and if there are few pauses and hesitations, then the rate of practice would

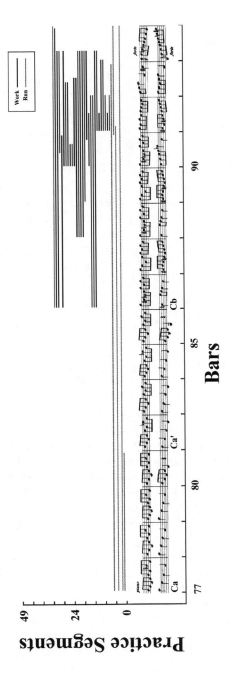

FIG. 6.3 Practice record for the second time the pianist worked on Section C. Differences between the Ca and Cb sections were much reduced. From "A comparison of practice and self-report as sources of information about the goals of expert practice," by R. Chaffin and G. Imreh, 2001, *Psychology of Music, 29*, p. 47. Copyright 2001 by the Society for Research in Psychology of Music and Music Education. Adapted with permission.

be close to the mean target tempo. To the extent that the rate of playing falls below the target tempo or is interrupted by hesitations and pauses, the rate of practice is less than the mean target tempo. This ratio was expressed as the rate/tempo ratio—the ratio of the practice rate to the mean target tempo.

The large number of practice sessions makes it impractical to give values on all these measures for individual sessions. Instead, sessions are grouped into sets of adjacent sessions addressing similar goals. The main criterion used to determine groupings into sets was Gabriela's comments during the practice sessions, but the measures and analyses described here and in the following chapters were also considered. The resulting organization consists of four sets of sessions for each learning period. (Period 1: Sessions 1–6, 7–8, 9–10, and 11–12; Period 2: Sessions 13, 14–16, 17, 20–24; and Period 3: Sessions 26–27, 28–30, 31–44, 45–57).[6] A comparison of these session sets indicates how practice changed over the learning process.[7]

Segment Length

Figure 6.4 shows the length of practice segments separately for runs and work. The length of runs generally increased as learning progressed, whereas the length of work segments showed no overall increase. The length of runs more than doubled during the first learning period. At the beginning of Period 2, in Session 13, runs were about the same length as at the end of Period 1, and again they more than doubled by the end. Session 17 was an exception to the pattern of linear increase; in it runs were longer than in any other session. This was when Gabriela put the piece together, learning to play from memory. The latter part of the session consisted solely of runs through the entire piece without the score, whereas in other sessions the piece was generally played from start to finish only once or twice.

The third learning period recapitulated the second (again with the exception of Session 17). At the start, the length of runs dropped to what they had been at the start of the second period and climbed back up to the same endpoint. The second learning period built on what had been accomplished during the first; the third period recapitulated the second except that the putting it together stage in Session 17 was absent.

Changes in segment length developed differently for work and runs, supporting the idea that they are distinct types of practice. In Period 1, work increased steadily in length, but the changes were much smaller than for runs. Gabriela was working on short passages, making basic decisions about fingering, articulation, and phrasing, and establishing the motor and auditory memories necessary to implement them. As she mastered each

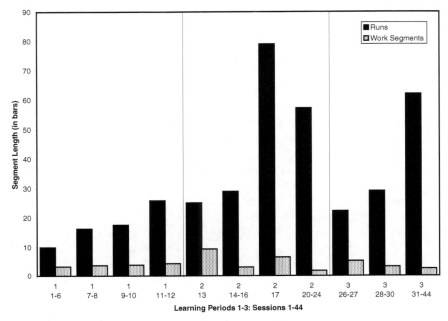

FIG. 6.4   Mean length (in bars) of run and work segments in each session set.

small passage, she connected it to its neighbors and the work segments lengthened. The process can be seen in the practice on Section C in Figures 6.2 and 6.3.

In Periods 2 and 3, in contrast, the direction of change went the other way. Work segments were longest at the beginning of each learning period and became shorter as learning progressed. As the number of problems needing work was reduced, work segments increasingly focused on one problem at a time and were limited to its immediate context. Again, Session 17 was an exception to the general pattern—another indication that the goals for this session were different from other sessions.

Number of Run and Work Segments

Figure 6.5 shows the number of practice segments per session for runs and work. The number of segments generally decreased across the three learning periods and across session sets within learning periods primarily because of the decrease in the length of practice sessions already noted (see

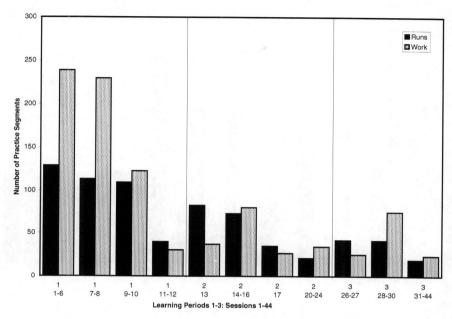

FIG. 6.5 Mean number of practice segments (separately for runs and work) in a single session, by session sets.

Table 6.1). The main exception to this pattern was in Period 3, when there were more practice segments in Sessions 28 to 30 than in Sessions 26 to 27.[8]

Repetitions per Bar

Although the number and length of practice segments capture important characteristics of practice sessions, neither alone provides a direct measure of the amount of practice in a session. This is best measured by the product of the two measures, which gives the total number of bars played in the session. Dividing the total number of bars played in a session by the number of bars in the piece gives the number of repetitions per bar.[9] The number of times a bar is repeated is the amount of practice it received, and the mean for all bars is the average amount of practice accomplished in a session.

Figure 6.6 shows the mean number of repetitions per bar for runs and work. If we think of runs and work together as a measure of the amount of

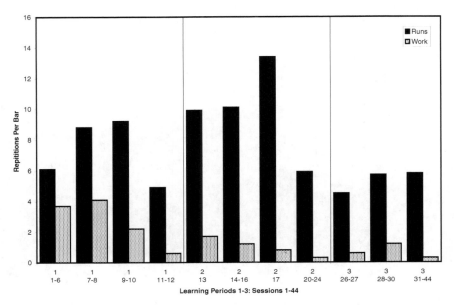

FIG. 6.6   Mean number of repetitions of each bar in a single session (separately for runs and work), by session sets.

practice in a session, then the amount of practice per session was approximately the same in the first two learning periods but lower in the third. It was also lower in the last session set of Periods 1 and 2 than in earlier ones. For most of Periods 1 and 2, each bar was played 10 to 13 times in each session. At the ends of these periods and in Period 3, each bar was played 5 to 6 times—half as often. The differences in the amount of practice are due to the shorter length of practice sessions at the end of Periods 1 and 2 and in Period 3. The number of repetitions per bar is determined jointly by the playing time in a session and the rate of practice.[10]

The percentage of repetitions that were part of a run rather than part of a work segment provides a measure of the percentage of practice devoted to runs (Fig. 6.7).[11] The first thing to note is that the values are all greater than 50%. The greater length of runs means that more bars were played during runs than during work, even in Sessions 1 to 6, where work accounted for well over half of the practice segments.[12]

The second thing to notice is the increase in the proportion of practice devoted to runs across learning periods and within each learning period. The percentage of repetitions that were part of a run started out at 60%,

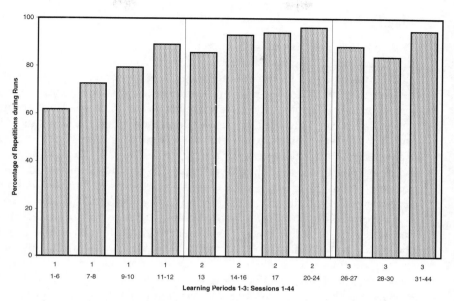

FIG. 6.7 Percentage of practice (repetitions of each bar) devoted to runs in each session set.

increasing steadily to almost 90% by the end of the first learning period. The percentage decreased slightly at the beginning of Periods 2 and 3, before increasing to a maximum of 96% during the polishing for the first performance and 94% while increasing the tempo in Sessions 31 to 44. These increases suggest that work was directed at solving problems and that the number of problems in need of solution decreased with practice.

It is important to note, however, that work never disappeared entirely. Even at the ends of Periods 2 and 3, work still accounted for 5% of practice. In terms of number of practice segments, of course, the proportion was much higher. In Session 20 to 24 and 31 to 44, work accounted for slightly more than 20% of practice segments. Work remained a significant part of practice even when the great majority of practice was devoted to runs. Sessions 28 to 30 provide a case in point. The percentage of runs was lower than in the rest of Period 3 and lower than in most of Period 2. In these sessions, Gabriela was refining her interpretation, working on bringing out themes and syncopations (see chap. 8). The decrease in the proportion of practice devoted to runs in these sessions reflects the work involved in establishing the new phrasing and dynamic effects which involved the repetition of short passages.

Playing Time

The playing time in a session is the amount of time spent actually practicing, excluding both extended interruptions and the time needed to sit down and begin playing after turning on the camera. Interruptions were not frequent, but they did happen from time to time. For example, on one occasion Gabriela compared different editions of the score. At other times, she talked at length to the camera and occasionally left the piano to attend to other matters. The duration of these extended interruptions was subtracted from the total session duration given in Table 6.1 to provide a more accurate measure of the time actually spent in practice. Interruptions were excluded from the measure of playing time if they lasted for more than 30 seconds. Pauses of less than 30 seconds were included because most of them were clearly part of the work of practicing. Most lasted for less than 5 seconds while the pianist wrote on the score, spoke to the camera, or sat in thought. (The amount of time spent in these activities was surprisingly large.)

Playing time decreased from an average of an hour per session in the first learning period to half an hour in the third (see Fig. 6.8). Playing time was generally longer at the beginning of a new stage or when work began on a new practice goal. The first six sessions were each about an hour long, but this was not long enough. At the beginning of Session 7, Gabriela attributed her slow progress on the *Presto* to not having time for longer sessions. Comparing it with her more rapid mastery of the first movement, she concluded:

> I allowed myself to sit down and stay at the piano for longer periods of time [for the first movement] than I did with the last movement [the *Presto*] . . . I had a little more time. I really do prefer to dig into my practicing and work longer sessions.

When she was finally able to take more time in Session 8, which at 1¾ hours was the longest session of the entire learning process, it did the trick and she was able to play through the entire piece from memory for the first time. The last two sessions in Period 1 were shorter than the others. As Gabriela noted at the beginning of Session 11,

> It's going to be a short session. . . . It's going to be . . . maintenance work. I'll just run through it a couple of times and try to fix whatever goes wrong.

In Period 2, two sessions were much longer than the others—Session 13 and Session 17. In Session 13, Gabriela was reviving her memory after a 2-

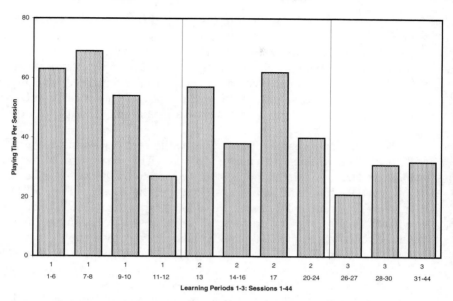

FIG. 6.8 Playing time: Time spent in playing (min) during a single session, by session sets.

month interval. In Session 17, she put the piece together and played it through repeatedly without the score. In Period 3, sessions were generally shorter. The one exception was Session 32, which lasted 1½ hours and began the work of increasing the tempo to the new level decided in Session 31. (This exception does not appear in the figure because Session 32 is averaged in with the 14 other sessions in the set.) Generally, sessions in which work on a new goal began were longer and were followed by shorter sessions in which the skill was consolidated.

Tempo

To obtain a measure of the average tempo in each session, tempo was measured 10 times at roughly evenly spaced intervals by adjusting an electronic metronome until it corresponded to the tempo of the playing. The mean of these values represents the target tempo at which Gabriela was aiming to play during the session. Figure 6.9 shows the mean target tempo per session as well as the maximum and minimum target tempo measured during each session set.[13]

Even the maximum and minimum tempi do not give a complete picture of the range of tempi that actually occurred. Often, the tempo varied continuously as Gabriela slowed down to think about what came next, and then speeded up again. To deal with this moment-to-moment variability, we set the metronome to match the tempo that reappeared repeatedly in between slower passages. The slower tempi were not measured because they occurred too briefly and because hesitations and pauses do not have a tempo.

The mean target tempo increased steadily across sessions, beginning at 82 beats per minute and ending with 114. The maximum target tempo increased from 112 in the first learning period to 120 in the second to 148 in the third. Within learning periods, however, the maximum tempo did not increase systematically across sessions except during the third period, when Sessions 31 to 44 were devoted to increasing it. The minimum target tempo, in contrast, did not change systematically over the learning process, but remained within a narrow range of 64 to 88. In Sessions 20 to 24 and 31 to 44, there were prolonged periods of deliberate slow practice, and the minimum tempo in these sessions reflects of this kind of practice. It is interesting to note, therefore, that a similar minimum tempo occurred in all the other session sets even though these did not contain episodes that could clearly be labeled as *slow practice*. Apparently short episodes of slow practice were interspersed throughout the learning process.

Gabriela's first choice of a tempo for performance was 120 beats per minute. At the beginning of Session 24, she played the piece through several times at this tempo. Because her first public performance was the following day, we may assume that this was the tempo she intended to use. (Unfortunately, we do not have a tape of the performance.) It is interesting that this same tempo occurred in Session 8 during the first fluent run through the entire piece and again in Session 17, when she was first practicing playing from memory. It appears that 120 was the goal all the way through, although there was relatively little practice actually at this tempo.

In Session 31, Gabriela announced that she had decided to "play it even faster" and chose 132 beats per minute as "pretty exciting . . . an excellent tempo." As already noted, this was not an entirely new idea. The same tempo had been tried out in Session 20, and also used briefly in Session 26. Yet the new tempo presented problems, particularly for the fugue (Section D). The solution was slow practice. The following day, Gabriela brought the fugue up to the new tempo in a marathon session. She began work with the metronome at 66. Playing the passage twice at each metronome setting, she increased the tempo one notch at a time, finishing at 138.

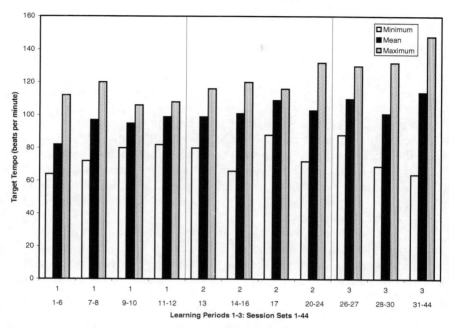

FIG. 6.9 Mean, maximum, and minimum target tempo (beats/min) in each session set.

Gabriela continued to work with the metronome until the last taped session, using tempi both slower and faster than her goal of 132, with an average of 114. She experimented with faster tempi, working up one step at a time, in Session 37—from 136 to 148—but settled on 138 as the maximum. This was the tempo used in Sessions 49 and 50 when she played through the piece several times to record a performance on videotape. On the CD recording, however, the tempo is back to 132, the tempo originally selected in Session 31.

If the target tempo in Sessions 31 to 44 was between 132 and 148, why was the mean target tempo in these sessions only 114? Similarly, if the target tempo while polishing for the first performance was 120, why was the mean target tempo for these sessions only 103? The answer is slow practice, which Gabriela first used for extended, repeated runs in Sessions 19 to 24 and then again in Sessions 32, 38, and 39. In polishing for performance, slow practice rehearses and strengthens memory retrieval cues that guide performance.

Measures of Effort and Fluency

Practice Rate. The predominant impression of all the practice sessions was one of continuous, urgent activity. We wanted to document this intensity and urgency by showing that almost every moment of playing time was filled. To this end, we computed the practice rate by dividing the number of beats played in a session (number of repetitions per bar x 210 bars x 2 beats per bar) by the playing time. The practice rate is thus the average number of beats actually played per minute across the course of the whole session. We expected the practice rate to be lower than but fairly close to the mean target tempo for the session—perhaps around 100 beats per minute, indicating that Gabriela spent almost all of her practice time actually playing. This is the impression one gets from watching the tapes of the practice sessions.

We were somewhat taken aback to find that the numbers did not support this impression at all. The average practice rate is shown in Figure 6.10. Across all sessions, the rate was a mere 24 beats per minute, fluctuating between 18 and 30 beats per minute. The practice rate was three to five times lower than the average tempo for a session. On reflection, it is clear that two factors are responsible for this—short pauses and playing below the target tempo. Although we had excluded long interruptions during practice sessions from our measure of playing time, this still left the much more numerous short pauses. These momentary gaps, mostly 1 to 3 seconds in length, occurred when Gabriela paused to think, talk to the camera, or, in the early sessions, annotate the score.

The other source of the low practice rate was playing below the target tempo. As mentioned earlier, Gabriela rarely played at a steady tempo except when doing long runs up to speed. The rest of the time the tempo varied continuously. A short passage would often be played first slowly and then repeated at varied and increasing tempi until it reached or exceeded the target tempo. The tempo of longer passages also varied continuously. For example, at the beginning of Session 12, she played through the whole piece from beginning to end. The target tempo of 112 appeared repeatedly, but was frequently interspersed with much slower tempi as Gabriela slowed down to avoid making a mistake or mentally review what came next. These slower tempi are not reflected in the measurement of the target tempo because each persisted for only a few seconds, changing from one bar to the next. (We look at the source of these hesitations in chap. 9.)

These considerations suggested that we should think of practice rate as a measure of fluency. The rate of practice reflects the slowdowns, hesitations, and interruptions to the fluent progress of the music. If practice rate is a

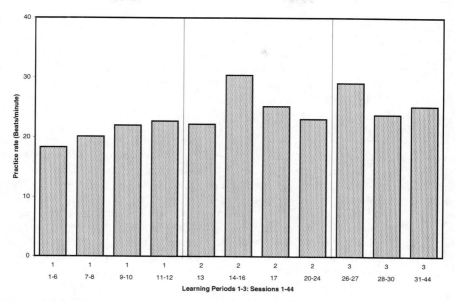

FIG. 6.10 Mean rate of practice (beats/min) in each session set.

measure of fluency, then we would expect it to increase across sessions. The ability to play fluently must certainly have increased with practice. Several of the changes that we have already noted point in this direction. Mean target tempo increased across sessions, as did the length of run segments and the percentage of repetitions that were part of a run. In addition, pauses to annotate the score and make comments occurred less in the later sessions. All of these things would be expected to result in higher rates of practice in later sessions.

With so many factors converging to produce an increase in the practice rate, it was surprising to find that it did not show a steady increase across sessions. Practice rate does appear to increase initially through Sessions 14 to 16, but then it drops sharply and at the ends of Periods 2 and 3 was no higher than at the end of Period 1. Statistical tests show that the differences were just random fluctuations rather than representing any real change.[14]

What is going on? We know that the mean target tempo increased. The last set of sessions was 30 beats per minute faster than the first set. How could this not result in an increase in the rate of practice? Part of the answer is the use of slow practice in later sessions (20–24 and 31–44). The other part of the answer is that use of highly variable tempi persisted. Even when the piece was well learned, Gabriela's playing continued to be interspersed with hesitations and slowdowns. Why? What was she doing?[15] The answer, which came as a big surprise to some of us, was that she was thinking. Sometimes she slowed down to make sure she did not make a mistake at some spot that had been giving her trouble. Sometimes she paused to mentally rehearse what came next before playing it. Sometimes she even tried to trip herself up:

> Sometimes I purposefully try to short circuit my playing in order to double check my back-up systems. I try to make it uncomfortable. For example, I might think about a mistake to make myself concerned to see if this short circuits my playing. Another time I might use the opposite approach and think, "I can handle this," and make myself feel confident. Playing for someone [a practice audience] is another way of doing the same thing. It puts the pressure on. I know it will make me crack up, but I don't know exactly where. Then when I see where the problems are, I know what I have to work on. In our study, playing for the video camera had the same effect. You can see this when I played from memory in session 12. The first time through I was very nervous and I had all kinds of problems. The second time I was much more relaxed and it went much more smoothly.

So we return to the idea of practice rate as an index of effort, but now we must think of low practice rates as more effortful than high rates instead of the other way around. A low practice rate means that the pianist is continually slowing down to think about what she is doing instead of simply playing fluently and easily. The average practice rate ranged from 18 to 30 beats per minute, approximately four times slower than the average target tempo and three times slower than the minimum target tempi we sampled. Watching the tapes, one has the impression that the piece is being played continuously and at a fast tempo. In fact, most of the time is taken up with pauses and hesitations. It is this, as much as the continuous playing, that is responsible for the overall impression of constant hurry, effort, and striving.

It would not be surprising to find this kind of halting performance in the case of work, which naturally consists of short segments and frequent interruptions. What we have learned from looking at the rate of practice is that the same thing happens during runs. The goal of a run is not simply to provide a fluent, concertlike performance. More often the fluent progress of the playing was deliberately disrupted so that Gabriela could test herself under the kind of adverse conditions she might encounter if things went badly during a performance.

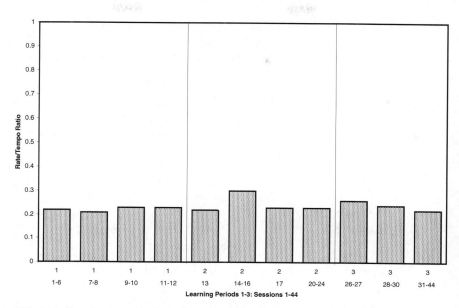

FIG. 6.11   Rate/tempo ratio (rate of practice/mean target tempo) in each session set.

Rate/Tempo Ratio.   To see how much practice is taken up with hesitations and pauses, we need to look at how much the practice rate falls short of the target tempo. The difference is a measure of how far playing departed from the smooth, fluent ideal. The relationship between the target tempo for a session and the practice rate is provided by the rate/tempo ratio (Fig. 6.11). The rate/tempo ratio was low—.23—and the small fluctuations between .21 and .30 were no greater than would be expected by chance.

Let us try some different ways of understanding what a rate/tempo ratio of .23 means. If Gabriela had played at the target tempo consistently, a one-hour session would have been over in 15 minutes. Alternatively, if she had played at the target tempo for an hour, she would have played four times as much music as she did. Like practice rate, the rate/tempo ratio can be seen as a measure of effort at least after playing has become automatic. Lower ratios reflect higher levels of effort. Playing up to the target tempo, without hesitation or slowing down, is easier and more satisfying than playing while continually hesitating, pausing, and slowing down. On this way of looking at it, a ratio of .23 indicates a high level of effort. Three quarters of practice time was spent not in playing, but in thinking—thinking about what was being played, what had been played, or what was about to be played. This suggests that the consistency of the rate/tempo ratio across sessions may represent an upper limit on the amount of effort Gabriela was able to sustain or the amount of disruption she could tolerate while still practicing efficiently.

This conclusion solves a puzzle about Gabriela's practice. Piano pedagogues emphasize the importance of slow practice. If you can play a passage correctly at a slow tempo, then bringing it up to tempo is easy. Yet slow practice appeared to be absent from most of Gabriela's early practice sessions. Only in Sessions 19 to 24, 32, 38, and 39 did she systematically play large sections of the piece at a much reduced tempo. The practice rate of 24 beats per minute suggests a different story. Gabriela was doing a lot of slow practice, but for short passages. Slow practice was intermixed with practice up to tempo. She rarely played at a slow tempo for long, but she did so frequently. When slow practice was needed, she slowed down. When it was not, she speeded up.

When this feature of her practice was pointed out to her, Gabriela was pleased. She knew that other pianists rely heavily on slow practice, and her teachers had always emphasized its importance. Although she believed that her style of practice worked for her, she had wondered whether she should be doing more of it. She explained that in practicing the *Presto*, she would slow down at passages where there were difficulties so that she could be sure that, "My head was in front of my hands. I wanted to be sure that I could play the difficult passages consciously."

To summarize this complicated tale: We began by looking for a measure that would reflect the concentrated effort and continuous, relentless activity apparent in the practice tapes. Initially, we thought that the high level of effort would be reflected in high rates of practice, but we had overlooked the enormous amount of playing below the target tempo. As a result, we were surprised by how low the practice rate turned out to be—about one quarter of the target tempo. It might seem that Gabriela was taking it easy, spending three quarters of each practice session doing nothing—just day dreaming or resting. Yet the videotapes showed that nothing could be further from the truth. So we had to turn our initial thinking on its head. Instead of effortful practice being indicated by a high practice rate, it is reflected by a low practice rate and low rate/tempo ratios. Practice that is full of pauses and hesitations is effortful. We still see practice rate as a measure of concentration and effort, but at least for this pianist and this piece low rates indicated a high level of effort.

Initially we were puzzled by the fact that neither the practice rate nor the rate/tempo ratio changed across sessions. We knew that tempo and segment length increased across sessions, and it seemed that these changes should lead to an increase in the rate of practice. However, seeing the practice rate and the ratio as measures of effort makes sense of the lack of change. Effort remained constant. Gabriela was not practicing just for the pleasure of playing the piece through and hearing how nice it sounded. She was working on it and continued to work to the very end.

It seems likely that the high level of effort reflected in the rate/tempo ratios is one of the characteristics of effective practice that we set out to find. Based on what we learned in chapter 5 about the nature of deliberate practice, it is perhaps not surprising that an expert's practice would involve continual monitoring and rapid changes of strategy. What is surprising is that so much more time is spent on the mental processes involved in making these judgments and decisions than in actually playing the notes. Although several of the pianists in chapter 3 talked about the importance of mental rehearsal, we did not expect to find that even practice at the keyboard was more mental than physical.

SUMMARY

In this chapter we provided an overview of the learning process. The complex structure, rapid pace, and *moto perpetuo* style of the *Presto* meant that 29 hours of practice over 10 months was required before Gabriela was satisfied that it was ready for recording, followed by another 4 hours while it was maintained in readiness until the performance. Practice was divided into three learning periods separated by periods of 2 to 3 months. Practice sessions became shorter as learning progressed, being longer in the first learning period, at the beginning of each period, and when a new skill, such as playing from memory, was first acquired. The initial learning took 11 hours, after which Gabriela pronounced the *Presto* to be about 60% learned. This proved to be about right so far as the first performance was concerned. It took place after another 8 hours of practice. Yet for the recording, Gabriela wanted a lot more—more excitement, more expression. Another 10 hours of polishing were needed before she felt ready to perform it the way she wanted, with 4 more hours of maintenance practice bringing the total practice time to 33 hours.

Gabriela settled on a tempo of 120 early on and appears to have used this for her first performance. During Period 3, however, she decided that this tempo was not fast enough. It did not provide the headlong sense of excitement and momentum that she thought Bach had in mind when he scored this piece in 2/2 time and marked it "Presto." She chose 132 as the new tempo, and this was the tempo eventually used in the recording. In practice, however, she regularly set faster tempi, generally around 138, but sometimes even higher. To bring her playing up to speed, Gabriela made frequent use of slow practice, gradually increasing the tempo up to and beyond the target. She also used slow practice to check conceptual memory in polishing for performance.

The initial practice of Section C (Figs. 6.2 and 6.3) provides a representative picture of several important characteristics of the practice. There were periods of intensive work on a short passage interspersed with longer runs fitting several sections together. In addition to ironing out the joints between chunks, runs served to evaluate the success of the most recent work and identify other problems needing work. More difficult passages, such as Section Cb, were practiced more than easier sections, like Ca. With practice, the differences between easier and harder passages decreased until they disappeared altogether. Runs became longer, and their proportion increased. Runs accounted for the majority of bars played in every session, even at the beginning of the learning process. This proportion increased across sessions so that, by the end, runs accounted for about 95% of all the bars played. However, work did not disappear altogether, even in the final stages of polishing.

Two important features of the practice apparent in Figures 6.2 and 6.3 were not explored here, but are left for later chapters. First, more practice was devoted to the more complex Cb section than to the simpler Ca sections. In chapter 8, we examine the effects of different kinds of complexity on practice. Second, section boundaries served as starting and stopping places for practice segments. The use of section boundaries to organize practice suggests that the formal structure may have served as a retrieval scheme as suggested in chapter 4. We return to this idea when we discuss memorization in chapter 9.

Gabriela's practice was continuous, intense, and relentless. This was reflected in the low rates of practice and low rate/tempo ratios, which did not change across the learning process. Playing was continually interrupted by short pauses and hesitations, and this was as true for later sessions when the piece could be performed fluently as for early sessions before fluency had been achieved. Three quarters of practice time appears to have been spent in thinking rather than playing. This intense mental effort may be one of the characteristics that make the practice of an expert so effective.

ENDNOTES

1. On the CD cover the piece is listed as lasting 3:14. The shorter duration listed here is based on measurements of bar duration described in chapter 9.

2. The symmetrical repetition of the B and C themes around the D theme represented in Figure 6.1 was not explicitly represented in Gabriela's initial description of the formal structure which consisted of the labeling of sections, subsections, subsubsections, and switches in a four-level scheme. Switches were listed in this initial description of the formal structure, but their significance was not appreciated at the time by Roger. When he did begin to understand their importance, approximately 3 years later, he asked Gabriela to mark them on the score, not realizing that he already had the information. Gabriela did so, and it was this second report that was used in the analyses reported in chapters 8 and 9.

3. The amount of practice given here differs slightly from that reported by in Chaffin and Imreh (1997). Lower estimates were used here for the duration of the sessions that were not taped (Sessions 23, 45–48, and 51–57). Also, one session in which a new tape was started midsession was treated as two different sessions in the earlier report.

4. A series of shorter segments extending over two sections was also regarded as a run if it appeared that the run was simply interrupted by the need to correct a few notes. Series of overlapping shorter segments that extend over more than two sections were regarded as segments of a run unless they included three successive repetitions of a note or sequence of notes, in which case the repetition was classified as work. All practice segments that did not meet the criteria for being part of a run were classified as work.

5. When a practice segment started or stopped in the middle of a bar, the bar was counted if more than a single beat of the bar—that is, more than half the bar—was played. Segments of a single beat or less were not included unless they were repeated more than three times in succession (the "stutter rule").

6. No quantitative data are reported for Sessions 45 to 57. Most of these sessions were not recorded because learning had been completed and maintenance practice simply consisted of two or three runs through from beginning to end. Sessions 49 and 50 were recorded to obtain a record of a finished performance. Because there was some practice in these sessions, these data are included with those for Sessions 31 to 44. However, this session set is referred to as Sessions 31 to 44 because sessions after 44 were devoted primarily to maintenance. To obtain means for session sets, means were first computed for each session and the session set means computed from those means.

7. Statistical comparisons using two- or one-way ANOVA's followed by post-hoc comparisons showed reliable differences for all the measures involving segment length and frequency between at least two of the learning periods and at least two of the session sets. Mean target tempo also showed reliable differences, but practice rate and the rate/tempo ratio did not.

8. The difference in number of run and work segments in Sessions 26 to 27 and 28 to 30 was statistically reliable.

9. More precisely, the total number of bars played in a session was divided by the number of bars in the piece played at least once in the session. Every bar of the *Presto* was played at least once in every session but one after the section-by-section stage of the learning process.

10. This was confirmed by a multiple regression analysis in which playing time and practice rate together accounted for 85% of the variability in the number of times each bar was repeated ($R^2 = .85$).

11. The percentage of repetitions that occurred as part of a run = (((runs/(runs+work))*100).

12. The percentage based on the number of run and work segments is not presented here.

13. When the Franz electronic metronome used for these measurements was calibrated against a stop watch, measured tempi were slower than true tempi by 3.4% at 120 beats per minute and 8.0% at 60 beats per minute—about one marking on the metronome scale. The measures reported in the text and figure in this chapter have *not* been

adjusted, however, because the metronome used by Gabriela appears to have been subject to a similar measurement error. In Session 31, Gabriela reported that the new, faster tempo she had chosen was 132 on the metronome she was using. Measurements of bar duration at this tempo (described in chap. 9) indicated that the actual tempo was 139 beats per minute, 5.3% faster than the tempo indicated by the metronome. To maintain consistency with this reported tempo, the measurements of tempo reported here have not been adjusted. Most metronomes are probably subject to a similar level of error of measurement. The tempi reported here probably underestimate the true values by 3% to 8%.

14. The one-way ANOVA's for rate of practice and rate/tempo ratio were not significant ($p > .05$).

15. Commenting to the camera added to the pauses in practice, and so the rate of practice might have been decreased by the presence of the camera. Three considerations suggest that comments had little impact on the rate of practice and should not alter the conclusion here. First, the rate of practice was equally low in sessions where there were few comments (11--12, 20--22, and 31--44; see Table 7.2) and in sessions where there were the most comments (1-6). Second, the rate of commenting was never very high, ranging from one comment every 2 minutes in Sessions 1 to 6 to one every 5 minutes in Sessions 31 to 44. Because comments were typically short, taking 1 to 3 seconds, this rough estimate suggests the proportion of time taken up in commenting ranged from 1% to 3%. These small values do little to make up the 77% of practice time that has to be accounted for. Third, making comments requires thought and mental effort so that even if commenting did affect the practice rate, the observed rate still represents a lot of mental effort.

SEVEN

In the Words of the Artist

Roger Chaffin and Gabriela Imreh

A s she practiced, Gabriela commented from time to time on what she was doing. Our description of the learning process depends heavily on these comments. Although describing the pianist's activity at the keyboard provides important information about what went on in the practice sessions, it does not tell us what she was trying to accomplish. For this, the comments are much more helpful. In the next chapter, we return to the activity at the keyboard and link it more directly to its goals. First, let us see what can be learned about those goals from the pianist's account of her own activity.

Gabriela talked about what she was doing as much as she could without interfering with her work. Particularly in the early sessions, she made frequent comments. Most were short, made during brief pauses between practice segments. Some are cryptic, but many provide a clear and detailed account of goals and strategies. From time to time, Gabriela stopped practicing to provide a longer explanation of some point she felt was significant. At the end of three sessions (12, 17, and 24), she gave particularly detailed descriptions of what she had been working on, going through the score identifying features of the music that currently needed her attention.

TABULATION OF THE COMMENTS

Gabriela's comments were transcribed and the frequency of 20 different topics counted. The topics, shown in Table 7.1 with examples, were organized into four broad groups. Comments about basic issues (fingering, technical difficulties, and familiar patterns) dealt with those features of the piece that a pianist must pay attention to simply to play through it. Comments about interpretation (phrasing, tempo, dynamics, and miscellaneous) dealt with decisions that shaped the musical character of the piece. Comments about performance (memory, musical structure, use of the score, and attention) concerned issues involved in performing from memory. Comments about metacognitive issues dealt with progress or lack of it (evaluation, affect, learning process), reflections about the research (research), and strategies (plans, slow practice, use of metronome, fatigue, evaluation of edition of the music).

The first three of these groupings were initially developed by Gabriela when describing the decisions she made during practice and the features of the piece she attended to in performance. Details of this description are given in the next chapter, where it is used to identify the aspects of the piece that received the most practice at each stage of the learning process. In this chapter, we use a similar framework to determine which aspects of the piece received the most comments. This makes it possible to see whether the topics commented on most were also the ones that were practiced most (Chaffin & Imreh, 2001).

The number of comments on each topic was counted for each of the 37 practice sessions for which the comments were audible, and sessions were combined into sets. Comments from Session 24 are reported separately because they came at the end of the session when Gabriela went through the score describing in detail her interpretation of the piece and the features she still needed to attend to in performing it. This lengthy description was unlike the short comments made during practice and was tabulated separately.[1]

THE SHIFT FROM BASIC TO INTERPRETIVE TOPICS

The pianist's concerns changed across the learning process. The main direction of the change can be seen in Figure 7.1, which shows the percentage of comments about basic, interpretive, performance, and metacognitive issues in each learning period. Comments about basic issues

TABLE 7.1
Categories Used in Content Analysis of Comments Made During Practice

Topics	Examples
Basic	
Fingering	These are very weak fingers.
Technical	It sounds absolutely insane because of the large stretch.
Patterns	I have no idea where this motif is going. It just goes all over the place.
Interpretation	
Phrasing	I'm trying to emphasize this syncopation.
Tempo	At least there's no tempo problems.
Dynamics/pedal	That gives me room for a nice crescendo.
Miscellaneous	It's really a polphonic theme . . . not theme and accompaniment.
Performance	
Memory	There's nothing else like it, so there is nothing to short circuit it.
Musical structure	I have to check every transition because every time it is something different.
Use of score	I'll try to play the first two pages from memory.
Attention	I really have to concentrate to get through it in one piece.
Metacognitive	
Evaluation	I am still not happy with it.
Affect	It is miserable work.
Learning process	I never had to rework that section.
Research	It's a little bit inconvenient to turn the machine on.
Plans + strategy	What I am going to do today is just touch it up.
Slow practice	I am going to play it . . . definitely under tempo.
Metronome	The metronome seems to have helped.
Fatigue	I'm going to stop because I am very tired.
Editor	I am going to look at another edition because I want to know if I have options.

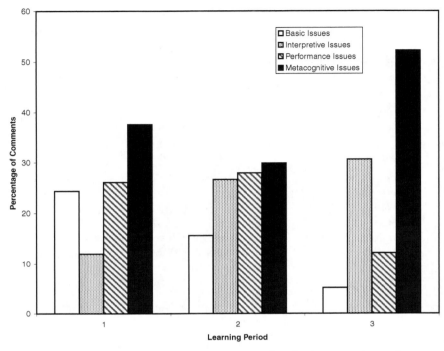

FIG. 7.1   Percentage of comments made during practice about basic, interpretive, performance, and metacognitive issues in each learning period.

decreased over the three learning periods, whereas comments about interpretation increased steadily. Comments about performance issues were frequent in the first two learning periods and decreased in the third. Comments about metacognitive issues were the most frequent throughout and increased substantially in the third period.

Table 7.2 shows the frequency of the individual topics for each session set. In the following sections, we use Gabriela's comments, organized in terms of the four main categories, to provide a more detailed picture of the learning process.

Basic Issues

Comments about the basic topics of fingering, technical difficulties, and familiar patterns were concentrated in the section by section stage (Sessions 1–6) as the pianist was working her way through the piece for the first time (see Table 7.2). Comments on these topics then decreased sharply, consistent with the idea that these basic topics have to be addressed only at the outset. Interestingly, however, a few fingering and technical difficulties were mentioned as still needing attention right before the first performance in Session 24, suggesting that they were functioning as performance cues (see chaps. 8 and 9).

Fingering and Technical Difficulties. Fingerings are a very personal choice depending on the size of the hand and the influence of one's school of piano playing. The choice of which finger to use for a note is constrained by a variety of technical, interpretive, and expressive factors, as well as performance considerations, such as the need to attend to other aspects of the music at a particular point in time and pragmatic factors such as ease of memorization. Fingering was the subject of the majority of the pianist's comments in Sessions 1 to 6 as she worked through the piece, a section at a time, trying out fingerings and writing decisions on the score.

A pianist's training includes learning fingerings for standard patterns of notes (e.g., scales, arpeggios, and diatonic triads). Fingerings for these standard patterns are relatively automatic for a skilled pianist (Sloboda, Clarke, Parncutt, & Raekallio (1998). In Session 1, Gabriela expressed a preference for a standard fingering, explaining that,

> I am going to change this fingering [the editors'], because it's obviously useless. I'm going to count on a straight F major fingering as opposed to what they [the editors] do . . . [because] I'd have to learn something brand new.

In the edition Gabriela used, the editor, Kurt Soldan, had indicated fingerings (see Appendix 1), and part of the decision-making about fingering involved evaluating his suggestions. She rapidly formed a good opinion of his work. During Session 1, she turned to the cover page to see who the editor was and then repeated a suggested fingering with the comment,

> Some of these ideas are really good. For instance, this is really intriguing and it's quite unusual, but it might work like a charm.

Later in Session 5, she regretted giving the editor's suggestions so much weight: "I have to rework this . . . I learned it all wrong . . . I took for granted what was written, and it can be done so much better."

TABLE 7.2

Frequency of Comments by Topic and Session Set With Percentages for the Major Categories

Topic	Practice Session Sets									
	1-6	7-8	9-10	11-12	13	17	20-22	24	28-30	31-44
Basic										
Fingering	32	3	1	0	2	1	0	12	0	0
Technical	7	0	2	0	0	0	0	7	2	4
Patterns	10	1	1	0	0	1	0	1	2	0
Total Basic	49	4	4	0	2	2	0	20	4	4
%	38	14	10	0	20	7	0	23	12	3
Interpretation										
Phrasing	4	1	6	0	1	0	0	11	3	4
Tempo	4	1	2	0	0	0	2	2	1	20
Dynamics	2	0	0	0	0	0	0	14	0	2
Miscellaneous	2	0	6	0	0	0	5	6	5	13
Total Interpretation	12	2	14	0	1	0	7	33	9	39
%	8	7	34	0	10	0	27	37	26	32

Performance

Memory	14	5	0	3	1	4	2	3	5	2
Attention	7	2	0	1	1	1	1	10	1	3
Structure	19	0	3	6	1	8	0	7	0	2
Score	0	1	0	0	0	4	0	0	2	4
Total Performance	40	8	3	10	3	17	3	20	8	11
%	28	29	7	50	30	57	11	23	23	10

Metacognitive

Evaluation	25	5	13	3	3	4	9	4	5	15
Affect	5	2	1	1	0	3	3	3	0	5
Learning Process	2	4	2	2	1	2	0	1	0	4
Research Process	2	1	2	0	0	1	0	4	3	1
Plans + strategy	9	2	2	4	0	0	3	3	3	18
Slow-practice	0	0	0	0	0	0	0	0	1	7
Metronome	0	0	0	0	0	0	1	0	0	14
Fatigue	1	0	0	0	0	0	0	0	1	3
Editor	0	0	0	0	0	1	0	0	0	2
Metacognitive	44	14	20	10	4	11	16	15	13	69
%	30	50	49	50	40	37	61	17	38	56

Technical considerations were one basis for fingering decisions: "Just trying to see if the fingerings match together. Here it looks like a problem with right and left hand. [PLAYS]. The two hands don't seem to bother each other" (Session 1). Also, "See, in the fingering here there are too many turns. . . . So I'm eliminating them all in this one group. I hope it's going to help. [PLAYS]. It works" (Session 4). Decisions about fingering were also based on interpretive and expressive considerations: "The reason he [the editor] does this is because these are very weak fingers, so he's . . . using stronger fingers so we might have more clarity" (Session 2), and "It's a crazy, very uncomfortable fingering, but it's going to sound better and I can get away with it if I replace . . ." (Session 4).

Another constraint in selecting fingerings was ease of memorization. Gabriela was looking for repeated patterns and, whenever possible, used the same fingering for a pattern each time it appeared. In Session 1, she noted that she was trying, "To keep the fingering as symmetrical as possible, which helps most with my memory." Absence of a familiar pattern made memorization more difficult: "What I don't like about this fingering is [that] it breaks the pattern completely. The hand is not able to have [a] . . . solid referral point."

Settling fingerings is the first priority when learning a new piece. Motor memory begins to develop immediately so that changing a fingering produces interference between the old and new fingerings and takes a lot longer to learn than the original choice. To avoid this interference, a pianist must try to anticipate how she will want to perform the music when she is able to play fluently and up to speed. Even in the initial sessions, before she could play fluently, Gabriela had to anticipate her interpretive and expressive goals so that her choice of fingerings would not constrain her. Thinking about this in Session 4, she noted,

> I sometimes do change [fingerings] much later in the [learning] process. [Just] because everything is working [in] slow time, of course, [does not mean it will work at a faster tempo]. Certain things just turn out not to work at all.

There were also comments about technical difficulties that did not involve explicit discussion of fingering choices:

> Right here it's purely a technical problem. I am having trouble because I am trying to phrase similar notes differently. I am trying to play A sharp and I am not very successful at it. (Session 4)
>   The right hand is fairly easy . . . [but the same motif] is exactly what bothers the left hand. The weak fingers stop this nice rotation, so I'm trying to

transmit some strength from the right hand. It's like if I explain to both hands that they have the same thing to do, maybe it's going to help. (Session 5)

You know occasionally, although there is not any obvious technical difficulty, there is [a problem]. To hit that G is one. For some reason I keep overshooting it. (Session 9)

Patterns. A pianist's selection of fingerings begins with the recognition of familiar patterns of notes for which standard fingerings are automatically available (Sloboda et al., 1998). Most of these went unremarked, but Gabriela noted in Session 1: "The sequence is [PLAYS]. See how simply they settle in."

However, unpredictability is characteristic of Bach's music, and the *Presto* is no exception. Bach's unpredictability is due partly to his repetition of themes and patterns in new variations and partly to his historical position at the beginning of the development of piano technique. As a member of the first generation to compose for the pianoforte, Bach did not have the benefit of the developments in piano technique that came from the work of the great pianist-composers like Beethoven, Chopin, and Liszt. These later composers established the characteristic patterns of pianistic composition so familiar to us today. In Bach's time, these familiar patterns had yet to be invented, so the patterns he used seem unpredictable to us today.

These differences are reflected in the way the different composers worked—Bach on paper (so far as we know), Chopin and Liszt at the piano—and in the music—Bach's music comes from the head, Chopin and Liszt's from the hand. Gabriela remarked on these differences:

> If you listen to these . . . , it's not like a Chopin nocturne where you can pretty much predict what is going to happen. Everything is new. Almost every bar [there] is something that has almost nothing to do with the idea before. . . . [Here there is a] scale . . . and then . . . that's something new, [that has] absolutely nothing to do [with what went before]. (Session 1)

Gabriela noted the impact of this lack of predictability on motor memory:

> A problem is that none of the hands can go on automatic pilot, which, to be honest, I've gotten used to [in playing a lot of Romantic repertoire]. . . . For instance, here I have to . . . watch for that. I may actually change the fingering back [to the standard fingering] because it seems to take too much of my concentration. (Session 1)

She also noted the importance of predictability for auditory memory. "I have no idea where this motif [is going]. It just goes all over the place. This is one of those places . . . where audio memory does not help whatsoever" (Session 1).

Interpretive Issues

Comments about interpretation occurred mostly at the beginning and end of the learning process (see Table 7.2). There were some comments about each aspect of interpretation in the practice by sections stage (Sessions 1–6) and early in the gray stage (Sessions 9–10). After this, there were almost none for the remainder of the gray stage or during the putting it together stage in Session 17. Not until the polishing for the first performance (Sessions 20–23) do comments about tempo and general interpretive issues reappear, and even then the number is small. However, Gabriela must have been thinking about interpretation because it is the main focus of her description of how she plans to perform the piece at the end of Session 24. After this, interpretation continued as the most frequent topic of comment during the third learning period. In the final session set (31–44), interpretation was mentioned more frequently than at any other time.

Interpretation of Bach's music is a controversial subject for musicians. Interpretive options are generally considered to be more restricted for Baroque than for Romantic music. Baroque composers were more content to follow convention, whereas the Romantics valued unconventionality. Also, the dynamic limitations of Baroque-era keyboard instruments (e.g., the harpsichord and clavichord) are assumed to have placed limitations on the use of dynamic variation in the performance practices of the period. There were, however, still plenty of interpretive decisions to be made.

Phrasing and Dynamics. We have already noted that decisions about fingering were based, in part, on interpretive and expressive considerations. Other comments in Sessions 1 to 6 also indicate that Gabriela was thinking about interpretation in the initial section by section stage: "I've been dying to try that, to put the forte in on that" (Session 4).

Most of the comments about phrasing and dynamics in Sessions 1 to 6 explained how trying to implement a particular interpretive decision made a passage difficult to play:

> Actually, I want to put the accent here . . . and that's much harder to do. (Session 4)

The reason I stumbled is when I wanted to do something interesting. You see how here it has a feeling of four quarter notes. . . . It feels like the bar divides up in two, and actually it gives it a lot of energy, so I want to do that and emphasize it. (Session 4)

Comments like this suggest that decisions about phrasing only attracted comment when they resulted in technical difficulties or a nonstandard interpretation of the music. Because she had played so much Bach, Gabriela may have made many interpretive decisions automatically by analogy with pieces she already had in her repertoire.

Other than general evaluative remarks, interpretation became the most frequent topic of comment in Sessions 9 and 10. Most were about phrasing. For example, "Okay, I was thinking about bringing out all the long notes." Comments continued to be directed at the difficulties that phrasing caused: "Every time I try to bring out the left hand . . . I screw up." But aesthetic effects are also mentioned: "Oh, that is a beautiful discovery. I am going to keep it like that, and I haven't heard it like that with other people, [PLAYS]. To bring out the long notes."

In Session 10, Gabriela noted that phrasing was her central concern:

Mostly, I'm working on phrasing. I'm playing some things very short . . . and some things very long and precise, and its really three plans [voices] or four that you have to control at the same time, as you see [PLAYS]. See that's why . . . I'm having more trouble with that bar, because there [are] three things happening. I'm trying to teach myself to detach those notes. Trying to emphasize this syncopation.

After 5 minutes more work, "I have to work in one accent that I haven't got. . . . " Later in the same session, "It's terrible because I feel like I should hold the E, and that breaks completely the whole rhythm."

The work on phrasing continued at the start of the second learning period. In session 13, Gabriela commented, "I am trying to bring out [the] soprano, the top. . . . It's just an experiment to make it more enjoyable." Unfortunately, except for Session 17, which contained no comments on interpretation, the commentary was largely inaudible from Session 15 to Session 23.

Session 24 was the last practice session before Gabriela performed the piece in public. She was leaving to fly to Arkansas later the same day. Her goal was to "Just touch it up." At the end of the session, she described what she had been working on: "I'm trying to work a lot more on touches, sound quality, and differences in dynamics that are also differences in tone and color." She then went through the piece, bar by bar, describing what she was trying to accomplish at each point. Fingering and technical difficulties were mentioned, but the main focus was on phrasing and interpretation:

> In bars 8, 9, 10 and on I'm trying to lighten the sound up . . . and bring out the left hand. Just every other note, forcing it a little bit out. I'm also trying to make the theme a bit more robust with a little pedal on the ending once in a while.

There was also a focus on dynamics: "The dynamic changes I already worked in at [bar] number 17. Remember, I'm doing an echo, and I think it works very well in bar 19. And then back to forte in bar 20." There were comments about tempo: "And I slow down a little bit at the ending of 23 . . . just to emphasize the end of the first musical section," and about expression: "I'm trying to bring [the theme] out in a more lyrical way in bar 52–53 and maybe not quite so short." The pianist's concerns with interpretation were also evident in some of her comments about technical difficulties: "I try to put the accents in; it's very hard."

Gabriela was also attending to relations between different repetitions of the same theme, making sure to give each its own distinct character.

> [Bar] 155 [is] again very light pianissimo. This time, though, I'm doing different dynamics from the similar section on 77. . . . Here I do a crescendo. It reverses again, and I'm trying to emphasize how the whole section expands in two directions. It's quite exciting, and I still have to think here.

The focus on interpretation continued in the third learning period. Comments in Sessions 28 to 30 were primarily concerned with phrasing and dynamics:

> It sounds a bit busy. I am trying to thin it out. (Session 28)

> I'm making some more musical decisions. . . . There are a few themes that I want to bring up, especially when they come in left hand like [bar] 93, and also when it comes in the middle of the fugue. I want to bring it out. (Session 28)

> I was trying to bring out the eighth notes in that line. (Session 31)

> I'm going to bring out these lines. . . . That's the first one. There's one here that's much more interesting because the voices move a little bit on that. That's [bars] 72 through 73 and on. And then, yes, let's see. . . . (Session 33)

> I read . . . that Bach wasn't much of an echo dynamics fan, but this is one of the few places where he actually wrote some in. And I [found] out more in

[this piece] than what's [written] there. But I think that kind of opens the door because nobody else. . . . (Session 33)

Five minutes later, "Yes, I think it is going to work. I found another one. It's really beautiful" (Session 33).

Session 33 appeared to complete the work on phrasing and dynamics. The only other comments on these topics were the resolve, expressed repeatedly (Sessions 33, 39, and 41), "To go very, very light[ly]." In Session 41, as she concluded that the piece was learned, Gabriela noted: "I still have to try to lighten up the touch to the maximum, but I have to make sure that the piano responds."

Tempo. There were few comments about changes of tempo. As noted earlier, the Baroque tradition allows relatively little freedom to vary tempo within a piece. In Session 31, however, Gabriela decided to change the tempo of the whole piece and "play it even faster." She mentions this frequently in subsequent sessions, and later in an interview:

Ever since I was a kid I have been a terrible speed freak. I think if I did not have the piano it would be terrible because I would get it out of my system somehow. I think it is the thrill of it. I actually relate it to race car drivers. I can just tell it's the same kind of feeling.

I have to recognize that [feeling] in me as a performer because it is dangerous. As a kid, I was always playing everything faster than I was supposed to. My piano teacher always said she would need Valium before a concert of mine because I would show up on stage smiling, looking perfectly fine. Then I would sit down and she would just hang on to the seat. . . . Of course it was the adrenaline. . . . So it was an imbalance that I had trouble with. But I do like speed. Neuhaus [the Russian teacher and pianist] said that pianists who at some point in their lives do not have the desire to beat the life out of the piano are never going to amount to anything.

With the Bach [Presto], the people who say you shouldn't play these pieces fast are terribly wrong. To me it is ridiculous to claim that speed was not the Baroque way. The violinists were playing fast. Listen to Vivaldi. It's wild, and it's fine, and everyone says, "Go ahead." But when pianists play in that tempo, people say, "No, no. The harpsichord didn't go that fast," that it was a limitation of the instrument, the composer was not feeling that kind of speed. But, as a matter of fact, the harpsichord is a much lighter instrument, so you can play most things faster on the harpsichord than on the piano. And, in the case of the Bach, I also felt that people played it slower because of some technical restrictions, because they couldn't play it faster. I wanted to try to actually play it as fast as it felt it should go. And it is presto, and it's in cut time. So you know you have every indication from the old Bach that you could do it [that way]. It's like a green light.

So it was a very clearly calculated risk. I knew exactly what I was doing. I was actually constantly battling my instinct to go faster just for the sake of it, for the pleasure of it. I usually try to find an excuse for it. The excuse can be choosing the right music or, like in this case, I think it's real. There's something that comes out that does not come out at any other speed. This really wild chitter-chatter. A different music, like a hidden polyphony, that if you play a bit slower you don't hear. It doesn't gel.

And I think it is devilishly hard to play this way. Now, the fun part is, that once you can play it that way, you can go down [in tempo] a little bit. . . . You want to make sure you can play it faster than you will in performance, so that you have that little cushion there. That's good to know, [when you want] to play it that fast.

In Session 31, the pianist first checked her playing for stability: "I'm going to run it with the metronome . . . See what happens. [See] if I'm shifting the tempo a lot." After playing through the entire piece, she concluded,

That was miserable playing, but at least there's no tempo problem. Much less than I expected. I usually can tell, if I'm not feeling comfortable with the metronome, that there's some technical, [or] some rhythm problem. But it doesn't seem like I'm getting off [tempo] so much. It's [just] more concentration [that is needed], as usual.

She then played the piece through at a faster tempo that met with her approval.

Okay, that's pretty exciting. I'm going to check this tempo and write it down because it's fairly fast. . . . I would say that is an excellent tempo, and it's metronome [marking] 132 [beats per minute], which is up there. As you see, I'm having enormous problems with the fugue. I'll have to get on it.

She postponed that task, however. After working on some remaining points of interpretation, she tried the new tempo again, "Mainly to just try to let it adjust by itself. See how much I can do without too much practice. But try to change technically what I need to change to go to warp speed." Later Gabriela explained that she was seeing how far she could go while still continuing to attend to the same performance cues she had been using at the slower tempo: "Every time you raise the general tempo you have to get rid of more performance cues because there is a limit to how many active cues the brain can handle." She had hoped that she might be able to manage the new tempo without eliminating performance cues, but this proved impossible. Particularly in Section D, major thinning and reorganization was needed:

> It would be real exciting without that fugue. I have a couple of places where I have serious left hand problems. You notice it in [bar] 97 and . . . about [bar] 132. I'll have to actually sit down and practice real hard, slow practice. I need more patience (Session 31).

The hard, slow practice began the next day.

At the beginning of Session 32, Gabriela gave herself one last chance, playing the piece through twice at the new tempo (132 beats per minute) to see whether slow practice might not be needed after all. She concluded,

> Okay, well . . . I have to sit down with this piece of metronome, this terrible bit of equipment and work on the fugue. Actually, the whole page that contains the fugue, because I still can't get through that [at the new tempo]. I'll open my music, and I'm going to set the metronome to a slower, very slow speed actually. I'll move it up slot by slot, very patiently. So I have to remember my goal is 132. I usually count back from that about 20 [notches on the metronome]. It's going to be very, very slow, but it usually works.

Gabriela worked with the metronome throughout Session 32 and again in Sessions 37, 38, and 41, gradually becoming more comfortable with the new tempo. In Session 33, she noted, "I still feel like it's a struggle in this tempo, and I need to work more to make the tempo comfortable. It's very hard and sticky here." In Session 35, she was "Still cracking up here and there, but its getting better." In Session 36, "Well, as you see, the mistakes are starting to fade out a little bit. . . . It's coming along." By Session 41, she was able to report, "Now, this is [the] tempo that I . . . set about three weeks ago [132], and [then] it seemed like top notch, maximum. [Now] it is quite comfortable." Even so, use of the metronome "Is probably going to be pretty standard routine for a while."

In Session 42, she began to use the metronome in a new way, not increasing the tempo gradually, but playing with it set at her targeted tempo. Gabriela explained, "The metronome seems to have helped, because it seems to me that it is much more stable." The metronome was used again in this way in Sessions 43, 44, 45, and 49. Gabriela explained, "The metronome is necessary because it helps me reach a steadiness that is vital for this. And sometimes unsteadiness is due to real technical problems. So, . . . we need to even those out."

The question of the optimum tempo for performance remained open. In Session 31, Gabriela had decided that a tempo of 132 was "pretty exciting."

But she also wanted to play expressively, with all of the interpretive decisions she had made at the slower tempo. Indeed, she continued to make interpretive decisions in Sessions 31 and 33 even after deciding on the new tempo. There was a conflict here. Playing faster gave the excitement that she wanted, but made it harder to bring out some of the nuances of interpretation. In Session 35, she observed,

> I may still take the tempo down a little for the recording. I don't know yet. I just don't want it to sound super frantic. I have to somehow make it sound easy. If I manage that, the tempo is going to work. If I don't, I'll have to slow down. [Meanwhile], practicing fast is not going to hurt at all. Every time I slow down just a little bit it seems like it is so much easier.

In Session 37, she pushed the tempo up to 148 before commenting,

> I was experimenting. This is brilliant. An insane tempo. I just wanted to see if it has anything to offer. It was too fast. I may play it slower. I just don't like it very very fast, so I may slow it down. Let's see.

She settled on a tempo of 138.

In Session 41, the exercise was repeated as she pushed the tempo up to 148 again: "I might try to see one notch up, just to see what happens, maybe two. [I will] just try to play much lighter. It's an experiment." She reached the same conclusion: "It's too much. It's ugly." After playing the piece through again a little slower, she concluded, "That's fast, that's 138 and it's just about maximum, I think, for that piece. It just can't take more [or] it sounds frantic."

A tempo of 138 became the new standard for the remaining practice sessions. Yet, as she had forecast in Session 35, she did take the tempo back down (to 132) for the recording. Gabriela was not prepared to sacrifice either the nuances of her interpretation or the excitement of the faster tempo. With hard work, she managed both—the nuanced interpretation and the "warp speed".

Performance Issues

The fast tempo and formal complexity of the *Presto* demand a high level of attention. Retrieval cues must be brought to mind at a great rate, and retrieval from long-term memory has to be rapid and automatic. With bars going by at the rate of more than one per second, there is little time to think about what comes next. Because this is largely a memory issue, most of Gabriela's comments about performance appear in chapter 9, which deals with this topic. Here we simply outline the issues and indicate the points in the learning process where they became salient.

Attention. Gabriela first commented on the need for concentration in Session 5.

> Now for me to actually [play it at a] tremendous speed level, I think one of the biggest problems for performance is going to be that, literally for seven pages, . . . probably about five minutes, there's absolutely no place to relax . . . it is pure concentration.

Comments about the need for attention appeared again in Session 24 as Gabriela described the things she needed to think about as she performed. Attention became a central issue again in Sessions 31 to 44 as Gabriela pushed the tempo up, increasing the rate at which attention had to be switched from one memory retrieval cue to the next.

Memory and Use of the Score. Memory was a subject of comment throughout the learning process. We have already noted comments indicating that ease of memorization played a role in the selection of fingerings and comments about the difficulty of remembering unfamiliar patterns. The first comments about playing from memory appeared in Session 8, when Gabriela mentioned that she had just played the piece through without looking at the score. In Session 12, she mentioned that she was going to play without the score to demonstrate that she did have the piece memorized. Comments about memory appear again in Session 17, as Gabriela described how she was getting ready to play without the score by looking at some pages and not others. Memory continued to be mentioned from time to time throughout the rest of the learning process during which the piece was generally played from memory.

Formal Structure. The formal structure is the organization of the piece into sections and subsections based on thematic similarity. As noted in chapter 6, the complex formal structure of the *Presto*, with its multiply embedded repetitions of the A and B themes, is a major source of difficulty. The multiple repetitions of the same theme, each time a little different, made it essential to identify the differences, which we call *switches*, and to keep track of which switch was coming up next.

This formal organization was the subject of comment in the practice by sections stage (Sessions 1–6) when it was used to divide up the piece for practice. The formal structure also appeared prominently in Session 24 as the pianist reviewed her understanding of the piece and talked about her interpretation.

Gabriela made her first comment about the thematic structure at the end of Session 2, when she flipped through the remaining pages of the score looking for the various returns of the A and B themes she had been practicing.

> The last page is pretty much a repeat of the first, at least some of it is. . . . Tiny changes sometimes are the worst. . . . Oh, this is not going to be hard. Again we have a pattern and it's not hard. [PLAYS], [I] recognize the problem. So, a lot of the third page is going to be fairly easy. . . . The last two pages are very much repeated material, . . . transposed in different keys.

As she worked out the structure, Gabriela marked critical places on the score, "The reason I circled the D is because that's where the two . . . , the theme splits up." In Session 4, she again noted the similarity between the section she was working on and an earlier one: "I'm confusing [it] with a similar place. . . . "

As this last comment indicates, similar passages are a potential source of interference. In the first session, Gabriela had commented on the difficulty of distinguishing the A theme at the beginning and end of the piece: "The left hand is a problem too, because it changed the pattern after [PLAYS]. Instead of going to the top G, it goes to the left bottom G." At the end of Session 5, she reviewed the places that still needed to be "ironed out", many of them switches.

> There are glitches like [PLAYS]. Absolutely identical. . . . There's some difference there, let's see [PLAYS]. The first group is different for sure because in the first version it is [PLAYS]. It's a different key [PLAYS] . . . and then there are a couple more differences at the end of this passage. And at the entrance [PLAYS]. See [PLAYS]. And here, circling down [PLAYS]. And then there's one more difference at the end.

In session 12, Gabriela noted another switch. "I am confusing this bar with the one that is [an] almost identical start for left hand. . . . "

At the beginning of session 12, the pianist responded to a request from Roger to describe how she divided the piece up for practice: "As you asked, I am going to tell you the main sections where I have stopped. . . . The big sections that . . . I've basically learned one at a time, or less." Gabriela then listed stopping places at the ends of Bars 24, 64, 92, 122, 149, and 174, dividing the piece into seven sections. Representing the sections of the formal structure by capital letters, stopping places with slashes and page breaks with asterisks, the piece was divided:

A, A1/ B, B1/* A2, C/ A3, D/* A4,B2,A5/ A6,C1,B3a1,B3a2/* B3d1,A,A1.

Five of the stopping places were at divisions between major sections of the formal structure. The sixth was at a subsection boundary (between B3a2 and B3d1) that coincided with a page break. This was the only page break that did not fall on a major section boundary, and Gabriela was less definite about it as a stopping point. "Somewhere around, huh, [bar] 175. Most times I've tried to patch that."

The comment suggests that this was not an ideal stopping place and she was trying to "patch on" the final subsection of the B3d1 subsection to the rest of the B3 section from memory without turning the page. In fact, in the section by section stage, the last page never did get practiced separately. It was simply added on to run throughs from other sections to the end. Thus, the organization of the piece for practice, at this point, was determined primarily by the formal structure, but was also constrained by the physical layout of the music on the page.

A little later in Session 12, Gabriela further explained the role of the formal structure in organizing her practice:

> Those starting-points, ... they are arbitrary. They are based on musical endings and semi-endings. But, eventually I do break away from them [in my practice]. Especially, [in order] not to have cuts in my memory. . . . And also when there are very difficult passages. As you see, I do take [difficult passages] apart and practice them separately. Sometimes [I]] take out . . . sections [as small as] one bar or less and build around them. I still have [passages which are] my nemesis, more than one, which [will] probably need constant maintenance. . . . They are always going to be tough.

At the end of the session, Gabriela promised, "Those starting points that I told you about, I will mark them on . . . the Xerox . . . that I am sending you." After the session was over, she marked the sections of the formal structure onto a copy of the score, identifying the 17 sections and 37 subsections mentioned in our description of the *Presto's* formal structure in the last chapter. There was some later revision of the numbering system for the sections and subsections, but it is clear that by this point the pianist was aware of the hierarchical nature of the structure into repeating sections and subsections and that this had determined the division of the piece for practice.

Another occasion on which the formal structure figured prominently in the comments was at the end of Session 24 just before the first performance when Gabriela went through the piece: "I'll try to spend a couple of minutes telling you what I am working on." The description makes it clear that Gabriela's understanding of the piece was organized in terms of the thematic structure. Although most of what she had to say concerned interpretation, the location of these features is dictated by the formal structure.

> I just save a little bit of a crescendo for the return of the [B] theme in bar 45. . . . The next section [at bar 53] I do reverse dynamics again and that actually prepares this ending, this return of the [B] theme [in bar 59].

A little later, "It's a big jump [at bar 93], but I want to emphasis it because it's a theme. . . . Again the return of the theme [at bar 123] is robust."

Metacognitive Issues

We suggested in chapter 5 that attention to metacognitive issues is probably one of the hallmarks of expert practice (Hallam, 1995a, 1995b; 1997a, 1997b). Gabriela's awareness of her own learning processes is evident in many of the comments already described—from her preference for fingerings that are easy to remember to concerns about maintaining concentration. Attention to metacognitive issues is also reflected in the continual monitoring and evaluation of the effectiveness of her practice, concern with the progress of the learning process, and plans and strategies for practicing.

Evaluation. One characteristic that undoubtedly characterizes effective practice is diligent monitoring of the performance quality. Gabriela's constant monitoring of her playing is evident in the evaluative tone of many of her comments on other topics (e.g., "That was memorized, as horrible as it sounds"). In addition to the evaluation of specific dimensions, many comments were evaluative without mentioning specific aspects of the music. These miscellaneous evaluative comments were more numerous than any other single category of comment, accounting for 38% of the total. Many were critical.

> Well, I am not sure if . . . that is going to work. (Session 1)

> I'm making an enormous [number] of mistakes. (Session 5)

Oh, it's still not good. It's really far from what I'd like it to be. It's just so difficult. (Session 7)

Well, that was just about as lousy as it can get. (Session 9)

That's bad, that's bad, that's bad. (Session 9)

What is going wrong. That's terrible. (Session 13)

I just hate the way that sounds. I don't know what to do with it. (Session 33)

Sometimes Gabriela even apologized: "That was so bad. I'm sorry. That was really bad" (Session 16). These negative evaluations were balanced by a smaller but substantial number of positive comments.

It's fun. (Session 4)

It's better. (Session 9)

That's about a million times better than two days ago. (Session 20)

I cleaned up the right hand and I'm very happy with that. (Session 30)

It's quite comfortable. (Session 40)

Whether positive or negative, evaluations were generally delivered dispassionately with an air of detachment: "I'll have to check everything. I think I am slipping occasionally and fluctuating [in tempo]" (Session 30). Negative evaluations were often softened by acceptance that the problem was unavoidable: "I made a couple of really bad mistakes, but it's going to go like this for a while" (Session 20). Often negative comments were balanced by positive ones: "That needs work too. It's coming along" (Session 10) or "It'd be real exciting without that fugue. I have a couple of places where I have serious left hand problems" (Session 31). The dispassionate character of these appraisals may well be a characteristic of effective practice not previously identified.

Affect. From time to time, however, dispassionate evaluation gave way to stronger feelings. Some were positive: "It's kind of fun" (Session 20), or "I'm all fired up" (Session 40). Others were more mixed: "This, it makes my head spin. . . . Every time you get through something like this clean, you feel so euphoric . . . and then you fail at something . . ." (Session 20). Others were extremely negative: "It feels like walking through a mine field. . . . Still I don't feel comfortable even on the first page" (Session 2), or

"I don't like it. It's irritating, maddening. I hate it" (Session 42). Gabriela's strongest negative feelings were reserved, however, for the mechanics of recording her practice, in particular the balky microphone. "We are experiencing technical difficulties, Roger, yet again. I cannot stand it. I'm just so furious. I could just kill somebody" (Session 24).

Yet we all managed to survive.

Plans and Strategies. Gabriela sometimes gave brief outlines of her plans, usually at the beginning of a session, sometimes at the end. These comments give the impression that she generally had a clear idea of what she wanted to accomplish:

> When I sit down again, I have to clean up this . . . and then it all needs to be put into motor memory, and probably I'll be able to learn the third page. (end of Session 2)

> So, I think in another hour I can pretty much have this up to be playable. I still have tons of work, but [PLAYS], let's just call it a rough draft. (end of Session 5)

> What I am going to do today is just touch it up. . . . Run through it a couple of times. Polish it up and make sure that I play it a few times slowly as well. (start of Session 24)

> I have . . . a couple of places that need refreshing—the fugue, rondo, 140 and on. I'll probably play it from the beginning and stop everywhere I need practice. (Session 28)

> I'm going to mostly focus on the fugue and then run through a couple of times [at] medium tempo and that's about it. (Session 35)

> I'm going to play this with the metronome three times. (Session 41)

> I'm just going to run through . . . fixing little things, just basically once or twice through everything. (Session 42)

Similar comments in the middles of sessions described goals for parts of practice sessions:

> I'm going to try to play it from beginning to end a couple of times. Then I might even try to play it from memory. (Session 8)

> Okay, I'm going back to the first page or two to get them really good. (Session 9)

Sometimes plans included the description of detailed strategies. In Session 4, Gabriela described how she was going to segment a passage:

"So, I'm going to . . . chunk it in half-bars, and I am going to . . . add [each] group to the previous one and always start and stop on the first note of a certain group. (After doing this for a while.) [Now] I'm going to try to add the groups backwards, so that this ending, which is really the hardest, is going to [get played the most]."

In Session 8, she used the same strategy again, but with larger chunks. "I'm going to try to add a measure and just stop on the first note of each measure. I think I'm going to use measures as chunks." In Session 6, interference between two different versions of the B theme needed attention: "I have to rework [this] pretty carefully. . . . It's never been solid, but now [as] I put the two versions together. . . . I just have to work on it. It's going to take another half an hour" (Session 6).

Other strategies involved the size of unit to think about during practice:

I can't think at this speed [at anything] smaller than a half-bar, maybe a whole bar. . . . If my brain starts to split that half bar apart, it really troubles me and I have to give these commands [to] my hands for half-bar chunks, otherwise I get tangled up like crazy. (Session 4)

Other strategies included use of the metronome and slow practice, which were both used frequently during polishing for the first performance (Sessions 18–24) and for the final performance (Sessions 31–44).

Gabriela had a large number of different practice strategies available to her, and she used them as the situation demanded. We noted in chapter 6 the enormous amount of time devoted to thinking during practice. Much of this time was probably spent selecting practice strategies on a moment-to-moment basis as she played. This kind of flexible use of practice strategies is probably one characteristic of expert practice. Certainly, Hallam (1995a, 1995b) found it in descriptions of practice given by professional musicians. Here we see the same thing in actual practice.

The Learning Process. Gabriela also evaluated her progress on a larger time scale and reflected on the factors that made the *Presto* hard to learn. The comments indicate a rich understanding of the wide range of factors involved. For example, in Session 8, she commented on the effects of page turns on motor memory:

That is something else that is a pain in the neck. Turning pages takes your hands off and that does a lot of damage to muscle memory. So, doing page turns [is] difficult. They are usually memory traps where people really have trouble. . . .

One of the issues that most concerned Gabriela during the initial section-by-section stage was her inability to find the time to practice regularly (see chap. 6). She knew it was making the learning process more difficult.

[It's] a couple of days later and I'm getting back to the Bach. So, it's going to be quite a disaster. Not much left from what I've done a couple of days ago. I have to go very slowly and probably a lot of the work is going to be wasted. [Plays.] Not as bad as I thought. [Plays.] There is absolutely no consolation about losing so many days except when you come back after a few days of not playing something, you do have a fresh idea about whether the decisions you have made are right or wrong. (Session 2)

I just get to practice this in bits and pieces and this makes it much more painful. (Session 5)

I'm afraid this is going to be a disaster [PLAYS]. Sorry about that. It's been about four or five days since. . . . I haven't touched this. (Session 7)

You remember the time I told you that every time you leave the piece for any amount of time, especially in such an early stage, it drops down several levels, and it is something I dread and hate [because] it is so frustrating and embarrassing because you are doing the same things over. (Session 9)

Gabriela also demonstrated her awareness of her own learning processes in her identification of problem passages. We have already seen comments about many of these passages from the initial section-by-section stage. By Session 9, they were acknowledged with a weary familiarity.

The same old places as usual. The rest of this has always been okay, but shaky. (Session 9)

All the old places, just as we suspected. I still have to continue with a big work out. . . . (Session 10)

Energy and Fatigue. Another way in which Gabriela reveals an awareness of her own learning processes was in monitoring her energy level. Most of the comments were about fatigue. "I'm going to go through the last few pages, then I am going to stop because I am very tired" (Session 2). In

Session 4, after almost an hour of practice, "Aagh, I'm getting very tired." She continued to practice for a while, carefully weighing how much was left to do.

> The last two pages are alright, but the next two are sheer hell. . . . So actually, oh gosh, I'm not even half way thorough. Anyway, if I eliminate the last two pages, I have two more to go, and they're . . . going to be the hardest.

It was too much, and 15 minutes later she stopped. "Maybe I'll stop now and take a break and come back and do it."

On two other occasions, Gabriela mentioned being tired shortly before ending the session. "I definitely feel like I am running out of steam" (Session 30), and "I guess I am pretty tired" (Session 32). On only one occasion did Gabriela mention *not* being tired: "It's 2:30 in the afternoon, a very energetic time of day."

These comments about energy level show that Gabriela was concerned about the effectiveness of her practice. She was monitoring her energy level and stopping when she could no longer practice effectively. A concern about the effectiveness of practice may be one of the keys to developing high levels of skill. Certainly, Gabriela's concern about fatigue is reminiscent of an observation by Ericsson, Krampe, & Tesch-Römer (1993) that the more accomplished young performers in their study took more naps.

INCOMPLETENESS OF THE COMMENTS

Gabriela's comments during practice provide a fascinating and essential window into the learning process by identifying problems she was working on and decisions she was making. However, they give an incomplete picture. The comments are about problems that seemed important at the time. For example, there are a lot of comments about memory because that was our main interest. Other problems may not have been mentioned because they seemed too mundane or obvious, because they were hard to put into words, or because to do so might have seemed vain. Even if Gabriela had tried to give a complete description of her actions, it would be impossible. There is too much going on. It is not possible to mention each decision, let alone the reason for it. Besides, Gabriela was not trying to give a complete description. Long stretches went by, sometimes entire sessions, with no comment at all. The comments were only intended to provide signposts to the things that she thought were most important. The rest of the story is told by what actually went on at the keyboard, which we turn to in the next chapter.

Psychologists tend to be skeptical of first-person accounts—people's descriptions of their own behavior and thought processes. People tend to focus on the novel and exceptional and ignore the mundane and commonplace. Also, many mental operations are not open to introspection (Nisbett & Wilson, 1977). This is certainly true for the mental processes responsible for the rapid, overlearned actions involved in piano performance. Although reports about the goals of ongoing problem solving and actions are generally reliable (Ericsson & Simon, 1980), it would add greatly to the objectivity of our description if we could give an independent, third-person description of what Gabriela was working on in the various practice sessions. An outside perspective would allow us to determine how accurate a picture the comments provide and might help fill in some of the gaps.

This is why we taped Gabriela's practice. The tapes provide an independent, third-person record of what went on during practice to complement Gabriela's first-person account. We use the practice record to verify, elaborate, qualify, and amend Gabriela's description of what she was doing. To do so, it is necessary to link the practice that went on in each session and Gabriela's goals for that practice. That is the topic of the next chapter.

ENDNOTE

1. The transcript was divided into short passages so that, as far as possible, each passage concerned a single topic. When a passage dealt with more than one topic, the number of topics covered was noted. Segments were then classified independently by two judges, one unconnected with the project. The agreement rate was 86.8% (Kappa = .78).

The grouping of sessions into sets is slightly different than that used for the practice data in chapters 6 and 8. Frequencies are not given for Sessions 14 to 16 because there were few audible comments in these sessions, nor are they given for Sessions 25 to 26 because there were no comments in these sessions. Comments for Session 24 are reported separately from those for Sessions 20 to 23. At the end of Session 24, Gabriela went through the score giving a lengthy and detailed description of how she performed the piece. Because most of the comments in this session were part of this description, it was tabulated separately from the preceding sessions. (Similar descriptions of performance cues in Sessions 12 and 17 were much shorter and were not tabulated separately.)

EIGHT

Effects of Musical Complexity on Practice

Roger Chaffin and Gabriela Imreh

I n this chapter, we look at what Gabriela actually did in practice in contrast to the previous chapter where we looked at what she said. The practice record provides us with an outsider's view of the learning process—the kind of objective record of behavior that scientific psychology tends to be most comfortable with. This allows us to see whether the issues Gabriela mentioned in her comments while practicing correspond to what she was doing at the keyboard. To the extent that they agree, our confidence in the conclusions we draw are strengthened. There may be disagreements, and these may be informative too. Some practice goals may have seemed too obvious and mundane to mention, others too grandiose, and still others too vague or ineffable.

We look at the relationship between how a passage was practiced and the sort of complexities or problems it contains. By looking at whether some passages were repeated more than others, we can ask what musical features were responsible for the extra practice. If some passages served as starting places more than others, we can ask what features were singled out for this special attention. If practice segments stopped or were interrupted in some places more than others, we can ask why. For example, if bars with technical difficulties were repeated more than bars without them, this tells us that technical difficulties were being practiced. If practice segments start or stop more on bars containing dynamic features, this tells us that dynamics are a focus of attention. Once we have identified the effects of different kinds of musical complexity on practice, we can compare these with Gabriela's comments during the same sessions. If practice is focused on fingering in the same sessions that Gabriela is talking about fingering, then we have a link between her own report of what she was thinking and our observation of what she was doing.

To begin, we needed a bar-by-bar description of the features of the music. This description was provided by Gabriela, who reported each decision she had made about the piece, organized in terms of 10 dimensions. These reports provided the basis for measures of musical complexity on each dimension.

TEN DIMENSIONS OF MUSICAL COMPLEXITY

The aspects that a pianist attends to and makes decisions about while learning can be captured by 10 dimensions. A pianist must attend to three basic dimensions (fingering, technical difficulties, and familiar patterns) to produce the notes and four interpretive dimensions (phrasing, dynamics, tempo, and pedaling) to shape the musical character of the piece. Implementation of most of these decisions becomes automatic with practice. A few, however, still require attention during performance, and these become performance cues—features of the piece that the pianist practices thinking about while performing. The performance cues can be organized into three performance dimensions (basic, interpretive, and expressive). These dimensions are summarized in Table 8.1. The idea of basic, interpretive, and performance dimensions was introduced in the last chapter as part of the framework for describing Gabriela's comments. Here we use the framework in the context for which Gabriela originally developed it, to summarize her decisions while learning the *Presto*. First, however, we need to give a more precise characterization of each dimension.

Basic Dimensions

To play a piece through, a pianist must identify familiar patterns of notes, make decisions about fingering, and decide how to cope with passages containing technical difficulties. Familiar patterns are the scales, arpeggios, chords, harmonic progressions, diatonic triads, and other more complex patterns that the pianist has learned to recognize and produce

TABLE 8.1
Dimensions of a Composition That a Pianist Must Attend to and Make Decisions About While Learning and Performing

Dimension	Description
Basic: require attention to simply to play the notes	Fingerings—decisions about unusual fingerings Technical difficulties—places requiring attention to motor skills (e.g., jumps) Familiar patterns — scales, arpeggios, chords, rhythms, etc.
Interpretative: shape the musical character of the piece	Phrasing—groupings of notes that form musical units Dynamics—variations in loudness or emphasis Tempo—variations in speed Pedaling—use of pedal
Performance: represent features requiring attention during a performance	Basic—familiar patterns, fingering, and technical difficulties Interpretive—phrasing, dynamics, tempo, pedal Expressive—emotion to be conveyed (e.g., surprise)

through long years of practice. These are the conceptual and motor chunks that experienced pianists bring to the task of understanding and memorizing a score (Halpern & Bower, 1982). The beginning pianist starts with scales, arpeggios, and simple examples of each of the major styles of composition. Practice of these basic patterns continues through the student years, while more complex and subtle patterns are learned through exercises and études and through mastery of a varied repertoire. As a result, a pianist is able to recognize a large number of standard patterns and perform them automatically. The presence of familiar patterns makes memorization easier because it is only necessary to learn the deviations that give each passage its individuality. One of the characteristics that makes Bach's music hard to memorize is that he often departs from familiar patterns so that nothing ever goes as expected.

The pianist must also make decisions about fingering. When possible, standard fingerings for familiar patterns are preferable, but the obvious choices must often be modified because of the context (Sloboda et al., 1998).

A standard fingering may put the hand into a configuration that makes it difficult to play the next pattern or may not allow a critical note to be executed with sufficient strength or sensitivity. For example, the first three fingers of each hand are stronger and can be more finely controlled than the fourth and fifth. The pianist can use these differences to enhance performance of particular notes by choosing fingers appropriate to the type of effect she wants to produce. Such choices help give each performer's interpretation of a piece its unique character.

There are two main criteria to be considered in choosing a fingering: how well it suits a particular interpretation and its ease of execution. When the two sets of goals are opposed to one another, a balance must be struck. Once the decision has been made, it must be remembered. Fingerings also serve as memory cues. Thinking about the placement of a particular finger reminds the pianist of the passage she is about to play while ensuring that the hand is in the correct position to execute it.

Technical difficulties require movements that are particularly awkward, fast, or vulnerable to error. For example, in a jump, the pianist moves the hand from one location on the keyboard to another. In a fast piece, such as the *Presto*, it may not be possible to move the eyes to monitor the landing. Instead, the hand's trajectory is judged solely on the basis of kinesthetic information. On other occasions, an interpretive decision, such as a particular phrasing, may create a technical difficulty by requiring a certain emphasis or separation of notes that is difficult to execute with the necessary precision.

Interpretive Dimensions

Attention to four dimensions concerned with interpretation is required to shape a musically sensitive rendition. The pianist must make decisions about phrasing, dynamics, tempo, and use of the pedal. Phrasing involves the identification of notes that belong together to form melodic, harmonic, or rhythmic patterns. Phrasing is a useful tool for thinning out the texture of the fast and complex polyphonic structure of a piece like the *Presto*. Often notes can be grouped into phrases by virtue of some familiar pattern, such as a scale or arpeggio. However, many opportunities for phrasing are less obvious. Finding these implicit structures is an essential part of learning a new piece. Choosing among the possibilities determines the performer's unique and personal interpretation. Discovering a new pattern is a delight. To find one that other performers, perhaps even the composer, have not discovered is to find a treasure all one's own. An example of this kind of discovery appears in Gabriela's comments during Session 31.

The way the music is written, I think it easily could be interpreted as a little error in editing [or] writing. Those syncopes [syncopations] are very, very exciting and I think worth bringing out. And there is one that is in the left hand, not written out as such, in bar 112 . . . , and I think I am going to do it as a syncope. It is much better. And, I don't know, there are two of them. Actually, there is one in 109 too.

Changes in dynamics and tempo help highlight the phrases the per-former has identified and emphasize or moderate the impact of the melodic and harmonic structure. Dynamic features in Bach are fairly simple. Changes in overall loudness are made in steps rather than continu-ously, reflecting the limitations of the harpsichord and clavichord on which dynamic changes are produced by changing manuals. Phrasing dynamics allow a note to stand out or a series of notes to be perceived as belonging to the same phrase by virtue of being played in the same fashion (e.g., louder or shorter). Gradual change in these qualities can also help tie a sequence of notes into a phrase.[1] Abrupt changes in either loudness or tempo can mark the end of one phrase and the beginning of another, and they also build and release tension within and across phrases.

The two pedals of the modern piano provide another tool for pianists to implement their interpretations. The pedals allow the performer to control tone quality and duration of resonance within the piano, altering the color of the notes. Because there was no pedal on early keyboard instruments, pianists tend to use it sparingly when playing Baroque music. Gabriela did use it for the *Presto*, however, to assist with phrasing. Pedaling a series of notes in the same way can unite them into a phrase as does giving notes the same dynamic emphasis. These uses of the pedal are represented by the features of the pedal dimension.

Performance Dimensions

The many decisions a pianist makes about basic and interpretive dimen-sions during practice become automatic as they are built into motor and auditory memory. In performance, a pianist does not have time to think of every feature. Each must be known so well that it occurs without conscious thought, leaving the pianist free to attend to the instrument, hall, and audience. For the performance, the pianist selects a relatively small num-ber of the most critical basic and interpretive features and attends to these. For example, particular fingerings that are critical to setting up a hand position for the following notes, or a phrasing that is still not fully reliable, continue to require attention during performance. These become the performance cues.

Unlike the basic and interpretive dimensions, which are familiar to any musician, the idea of performance cues is new. At least we are not aware of any previous discussion that has dealt with these issues in the same way.[2] The idea emerged during our early discussions of how preparing for performance is a matter of making sure that retrieval cues operate automatically (chaps. 2 and 4). Exploring this idea and learning more about how performance cues function was an important motivation of our research.

Performance dimensions represent those features of the music that help performers play the piece the way they want. Thinking of each performance cue at the right moment brings the necessary information to mind when it is needed—not so far ahead so as to distract attention from the preceding passage, but not too late to guide the forthcoming movements. Practice of performance cues gives the artist control over what happens during the performance of a rapid piece like the *Presto* and also provides the means to correct things if they begin to go wrong. Thinking of a performance cue elicits the corresponding actions and provides access to more detailed information stored in long-term memory. Performance cues are thus retrieval aids. Memorizing a piece is a matter of establishing performance cues that serve as retrieval cues to elicit the music from memory (see chap. 9).

We divide performance cues into three types: basic, interpretive, and expressive. Basic and interpretive performance cues are subsets of the complete sets of basic and interpretive features already described—the ones that still require attention during performance. In addition, expressive performance cues represent the pianist's expressive goals, the emotions to be conveyed to the audience, and the sense of how these are articulated in the relationship between the various sections of the piece. Expressive cues give the piece its overall musical shape, specifying the ebb and flow of feelings that are the artist's most personal, subjective contribution to a performance. They are based on the basic and interpretive features of the music coupled with the performer's knowledge of related works and of the history, taste, and musical tradition of the composer's era.

Performance cues evolve over the course of learning a new piece. By the time she is ready to perform in public, Gabriela aims to be thinking about the piece in terms of expressive cues (e.g., surprise, gaiety, excitement). As she makes her final preparations for a performance, she looks for the central expressive intent behind each passage, distilling this from the mass of more detailed interpretive and structural features. Playing while thinking of these goals establishes links between the expressive intentions and the motor responses that embody them as well as with the more specific basic and interpretive cues that guided playing earlier in practice. By the time polishing is complete, the expressive goals have coalesced and it is possible to mentally rehearse the entire piece in terms of the expressive goals of each passage. This rechunking creates a new level of organization in the retrieval hierarchy, providing the memory cues to be used in performance. As noted in chapter 3, when pianists talk about their performances, their descriptions are often given entirely at the level of expressive cues.

Ideally, the performance of a piece that is thoroughly learned would be guided solely by expressive cues. This would provide the maximum freedom to play expressively and respond to the immediate context. When this happens, the performer experiences the trancelike state Ivo Pogorelich described in chapter 3: "The notes have become you and you have become the notes." Yet each performance is different, and on another occasion a performer may have to work hard to keep things on track. This is when the basic and interpretive performance cues come into play to keep the performance going through perturbations and distractions.

The different dimensions are a tangled hierarchy, representing different levels of organization of the same material. Decisions on one dimension are often linked to decisions on another. Fingering decisions are often made to solve an interpretive or technical problem. Technical problems may be given an interpretative gloss. Instead of thinking of a technical difficulty during performance, it is better to wrap it with the interpretive effect that is produced (e.g., a particular phrasing or emphasis). Interpretive effects can, in turn, be subsumed under the expressive goal they serve. For example, the phrasing may provide an exciting or powerful moment. Thinking of the excitement rather than the phrasing during performance provides a more convincing execution.

So the same musical feature may be encoded in different ways at different points in the learning process. Most of the basic and interpretive features simply become automatic, fading from awareness. A few are retained to become basic and interpretive performance cues by being monitored during later stages of practice. During performance, they hover on the fringes of awareness, which is focused on the expressive cues. Expressive performance cues represent the highest level of organization and incorporate the combined effects of all the other basic and interpretive features.

Measuring Musical Complexity

To report the features of the *Presto* on each of the 10 dimensions, Gabriela identified the decisions she had made or features she had paid attention to during practice by marking them on a copy of the score with an arrow

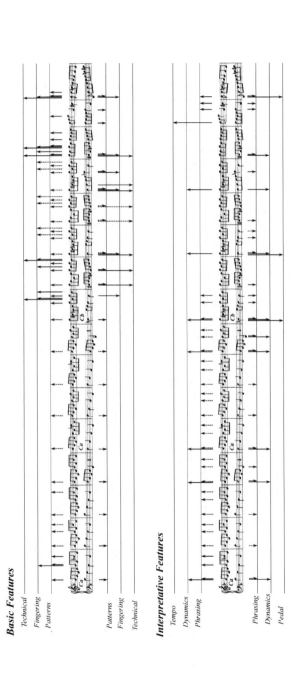

FIG. 8.1 The location of features (indicated by arrows) that the pianist reported attending to during practice of Section C of the *Italian Concerto (Presto)*. Features are shown separately for three basic, four interpretive, and three performance dimensions. From "A comparison of practice and self-report as sources of information about the goals of expert practice," by R. Chaffin and G. Imreh, 2001, *Psychology of Music, 29*, p. 44. Copyright 2001 by the Society for Research in Psychology of Music and Music Education. Adapted with permission.

pointing to the location of each feature. Figure 8.1 shows an example for Section C. Each dimension was represented by a different set of arrows. The complexity of a bar on each dimension was measured by counting the number of features reported for the bar. For example, the first bar of Section C contains four familiar patterns and one fingering, four phrasing, and two dynamic features, one interpretive performance, and one expressive performance cue. In Figure 8.1, the performance cues are labeled, although these labels were not part of the analyses described here.

In chapter 6, when we looked at a graph of the practice of Section C (Fig. 6.2), we saw that Section Cb was practiced more than Section Ca. In Figure 8.1, we see a possible reason for this difference. Section Cb was more complex than Section Ca on the basic dimensions. Section Cb may have required more practice because it contains more fingering decisions, more technical difficulties, and more different patterns than Ca. We are looking for just this kind of correspondence between complexity and amount of practice. To see whether the relationship between the amount of practice and complexity occurred for other passages and in other sessions, we used regression analyses to look at the effects of the 10 dimensions on practice more generally (Chaffin & Imreh, 2001).

Another characteristic of the practice of Section C in the practice record (Fig. 6.2) was the tendency to start practice segments at the beginnings of sections. Gabriela appeared to use the sections of the formal structure to organize her practice. Again, we want to know whether this occurred more generally. To answer this question, the location of the boundaries was included in the analyses along with the serial position of each bar in its section and another important aspect of formal structure—the location of switches. The location of each bar in the formal structure was represented in the analyses by four measures: whether the bar was the first or last in its section (two measures), the serial position of the bar in the section (numbering from the beginning), and the number of switches in the bar.[3] Switches are places where two or more repetitions of the same theme diverge (see chap.6).

How many times did Gabriela use the pedal? How many different familiar patterns did she find in a typical bar of the *Presto*? How many switches can a single bar contain? The answers to these and other similar questions can be found in Table 8.2, which gives descriptive statistics for the 10 dimensions, switches, and number of notes in a bar. The answer to how many times the pedal was used is to be found in the first column (total), which gives the total number of features reported for the entire piece (45 uses of the pedal). The second column (mean per bar) gives the average number of features reported in each bar and shows that, for Gabriela, the typical bar contained 3.59 familiar patterns. The third column

TABLE 8.2
Descriptive Statistics for Complexity on Basic, Interpretive, and Performance Dimensions and for Switches and Number of Notes in the *Italian Concerto* (*Presto*)

	Total for Piece	Mean per Bar	Standard Deviation	Range	Number of Zero Values
Basic					
Fingerings	259	1.71	1.27	5	41
Technical difficulties	204	0.97	1.01	4	69
Familiar patterns	741	3.59	1.41	7	2
Interpretive					
Phrasing	518	2.47	1.76	7	22
Dynamic Changes	270	1.29	0.91	3	53
Tempo Changes	5	0.02	0.15	1	205
Pedal	45	0.21	0.47	2	170
Performance					
Basic	147	0.70	0.66	3	85
Interpretive	139	0.66	0.56	2	80
Expressive	72	0.34	0.49	2	139
Other					
Switches	49	0.23	0.53	3	168
Notes	2794	13.3	2.32	15	0

(standard deviation) shows that there was sufficient variability for purposes of regression analysis for every measure except perhaps for tempo.[4] Additional information about variability is provided by the last two columns (range and number of zero values), which together indicate that the answer to our third question—about switches—is that the maximum number in a single bar was 3.

Did the different dimensions describe different aspects of the music? Table 8.3 suggests so. The table shows the correlation of the 10 measures of complexity with each other and with serial position in a section, number of switches, and number of notes. The relatively low values indicate that each measure provided somewhat different information about the piece. The highest correlations were for basic performance cues with technical difficulties and interpretative performance cues with dynamic features. This is because the basic and interpretative performance cues were subsets of the larger sets of basic and interpretative features. The moderate size of the

TABLE 8.3
Correlation Matrix for Measures of Musical Complexity, Switches, and Number of Notes ($N=210$)

	Patterns	Fingers	Technical	Phrase	Dynamics	Tempo	Pedal	Basic Perf.	Interp Perf.	Express. Perf.	Serial Position	Notes
Patterns												
Fingers	0.30											
Technical	0.36	0.29										
Phrase	0.39	0.21	0.09									
Dynamic	0.14	0.29	0.16	0.24								
Tempo	0.05	0.04	0.00	0.10	0.12							
Pedal	-0.02	0.16	-0.11	0.26	0.15	0.26						
Basic	0.11	0.18	0.46	-0.01	0.35	0.02	0.09					
Interpret.	0.02	0.18	0.04	0.26	0.48	0.04	0.19	0.30				
Express.	0.04	0.07	-0.10	0.24	0.35	0.15	0.33	0.25	0.45			
Serial	-0.09	-0.15	0.11	-0.21	-0.15	-0.03	-0.17	0.06	-0.02	-0.14		
Notes	0.29	0.16	0.23	0.07	0.01	-0.05	-0.22	0.13	-0.01	-0.08	0.17	
Switches	0.10	0.11	0.02	0.21	0.15	0.05	0.09	0.22	0.24	0.34	-0.09	0.15

correlations indicates that the basic and interpretive performance cues were distinct from the complete sets of basic and interpretive features from which they were derived. These correlations also tell us that the technical and dynamic dimensions were bigger sources of performance cues than the other basic and interpretive dimensions.

DOES THE FOCUS OF PRACTICE CHANGE DURING LEARNING?

Our division of dimensions into basic, interpretive, and performance contains an implicit ordering. It suggests that practice might focus on each type of problem in turn: first basic, then interpretive, and finally perform-ance. This general idea of a progression can be stated more precisely as four hypotheses. Practice should focus on:

- the complete set of features for the basic dimensions before the complete set of features for the interpretive dimensions,
- the complete sets of basic and interpretive features before the subsets selected as basic and interpretive performance cues,
- the basic performance cues before the interpretive performance cues, and
- the basic and interpretive performance cues before the expressive perform-ance cues.

We discuss the basis for each of these expectations and consider why they may or may not prove correct. First, the basic dimensions are so named because their features have to be settled on simply to play the notes. So there is good reason to expect that practice will focus on basic dimen-sions first. However, there is also good reason to think that an expert might make decisions about interpretation and expression right at the beginning so that these goals can shape decisions about fingering and technical difficulties. We saw some evidence of this in Gabriela's comments in the section-by-section stage (chap. 7). For example, she mentioned in Session 2 that notes needing more emphasis should be assigned to stronger fingers.

Our second hypothesis concerns the basic and interpretive performance dimensions that are subsets, respectively, of the complete sets of basic and interpretive features. If the selection of performance cues does not occur until the pianist begins to practice the piece as a performance, it would seem that their practice would begin during putting it together or perhaps during the polishing stage. However, because performance cues occur at critical points in the piece, they might be a focus of practice even before their future role in performance has been decided. This kind of sensitivity to the difficulty of different passages might be one of the characteristics of expert practice. If so, it would parallel the kind of intuitive anticipation characteristic of experts in other fields (Gobet & Simon, 1996b).

Third, practice of the basic performance dimension might be expected to precede practice of the interpretive performance dimension for reasons similar to those given earlier for the complete sets of basic and interpretive features. Basic performance cues provide the initial landmarks necessary for playing the piece as a whole, whereas interpretive performance cues come later, adding refinement. Yet, if interpretation develops throughout the learning process, then basic and interpretive performance cues may emerge together.

There are similar considerations for our fourth hypothesis. We have suggested that a small number of basic and interpretive features are established as performance cues in case they are needed, and that their final selection and practice occurs toward the end of the learning process. We also suggested that, in the final preparation for a performance, expression must become the central focus of the artist's attention. The piece must be reworked or rechunked so that the performer can direct full attention to expression, leaving everything else to take care of itself automatically. So it seems that practice of expressive cues should come after the groundwork has been laid through earlier practice of basic and interpretive performance cues. Nevertheless, expression surely cannot be simply ladled on at the end of the learning process. Expressive intentions must guide interpretive choices, as well as decisions about the basic features on which they rest, throughout the process. If so, then we may find effects of expressive cues on practice well before the final polishing stage.

In summary, although Gabriela's grouping into basic and interpretive dimensions and performance cues suggests a temporal ordering from basic to performance, this is by no means a foregone conclusion. Effects of interpretive features and performance cues on the early stages of learning may be characteristic of expert practice.

THE EFFECTS OF MUSICAL COMPLEXITY ON PRACTICE

Regression analyses were used to identify effects of musical complexity and structure on practice. We have tried not to be technical, but readers more interested in conclusions than details can skip this section. In addition, the implications of the practice of performance cues for memorization are discussed in chapter 9 while chapter 10 redescribes the six stages of the learning process taking into account what we have learned here.

The predictor variables for the regression analyses were the 10 measures of complexity and four measures of structure, together with the number of notes in each bar. The dependent measures were the number of starts, stops, and repetitions for each bar. The number of starts is the number of times a practice segment begins on a bar. The number of stops is the number of times a segment ends on that bar. The number of repetitions is the number of times the bar was played.[5] These three measures were counted separately for work and runs.[6]

Interpreting the Effects

The regression analyses identify which dimensions the pianist focused on in each set of practice sessions. A significant effect of a dimension indicates that Gabriela was consistently paying special attention to (or having special trouble with) bars containing that type of feature. The effects were mostly positive, indicating that bars with more of a particular kind of feature were repeated more or involved more starts or stops than other bars. Negative effects indicate that features were repeated less frequently or were the location of fewer starts or stops.

Effects have different meanings for runs and work. Effects on work are generally simpler to interpret. Work on a dimension results in more repetitions, starts, or stops for bars containing those features. The interpretation of runs is more complex. For starts, the situation is similar to work. An effect generally means that the pianist is choosing to start at the feature in question. In contrast, repetitions and stops generally indicate interruptions. Because runs cover a lot of bars, those that are the object of special attention during the run are not necessarily repeated more than other bars. Repetitions and stops generally occur in places where runs are interrupted.

Work and runs differ in the demands they place on memory. Memory is not a problem during work because the passage only has to be retrieved from long-term memory the first time it is played. On subsequent repetitions, the memory representation is already activated. During runs, each succeeding passage has to be retrieved from long-term memory as the run progresses. For this reason, interruptions to runs are often due to memory-retrieval problems. If the upcoming passage is not retrieved from memory quickly enough, the run must stop until retrieval is completed or the information is read from the score. Early on, runs may be interrupted by "finger tangles" when conflicting motor patterns interfere with one another and the pianist is not able to think fast enough to consciously select the correct pattern. This is also a kind of memory-retrieval problem. Runs may also be interrupted by a deliberate decision to go back and repeat something to think about or evaluate it.

Some indication of the nature of the interruption is provided by the measures affected. Effects on stops during runs generally indicate memory-retrieval problems—the run could not continue because Gabriela was not quick enough in thinking what had to be done next. In this case, there may also be effects on repetitions or starts depending on how far the pianist backs up before continuing the run. Effects on repetitions in the absence of an effect on stops may also reflect memory problems, but they are more likely to be due to deliberate evaluation.

Overview

How did the effects of complexity and musical structure change across the course of learning? Table 8.4 shows the dimensions of complexity and musical structure that affected runs and work in each of the 11 session sets. Only statistically reliable effects ($p < .05$) are listed, and they are indicated by an abbreviation of the measure affected: repeats (r), starts (s), and stops (p).[7]

Because of the large number of effects, we begin with a quick overview. Practice in the section by section stage (Sessions 1–6) was distinguished by effects of all three basic dimensions. The gray stage (Sessions 7–16) of developing automaticity was distinguished by effects of performance cues, technical difficulties, and interpretive features. Performance cues continued to affect practice in the putting it together stage (Session 17), when the piece was memorized and effects of technical difficulties were absent for the first time. Polishing for the first performance (Sessions 20–24) produced the widest array of effects: building up confidence for trouble spots with practice of basic features, continued practice of phrasing and other interpretive features, and practice of interpretive and expressive performance cues. Re-polishing in Period 3 was distinguished initially by the effect of expressive cues (Sessions 28–30). Then the decision to increase the tempo (Sessions 31–44) required reworking of fingering, technical difficulties, and interpretive performance cues.

The report card is mixed for our hypotheses about the order in which effects of basic, interpretive, and performance dimensions would appear. Examination of Table 8.4 suggests that effects of basic dimensions were present right from the start, whereas most effects for interpretive dimensions did not appear until later. In contrast, the effects of the performance

TABLE 8.4
Significant Effects of the Dimensions of Musical Complexity on Repetitions (r), Starts (s), and Stops (p) per Bar for Runs and Work

	Learning Period 1							
	Sessions							
Dimensions of Musical Complexity	*1–6*		*7–8*		*9–10*		*11–12*	
	Runs	*Work*	*Runs*	*Work*	*Runs*	*Work*	*Runs*	*Work*
Basic								
Fingering	r	r	r,p	.	.	.	.	r
Technical	p	r,p	.	r,s	.	r,s,p	.	r,s,p
Patterns	.	r,p	.	.	.	.	.	.
Interpretive								
Phrasing	.	-r	.	.	.	.	.	.
Dynamics	r	.	.	.	-r	.	.	.
Pedal	.	.	.	.	-r,p	.	.	.
Tempo	.	.	.	.	.	.	.	.
Performance								
Basic	-r	.	r,s	r,s,p	r	.	r,p	.
Interpretive	.	.	p	p	r,p	s	r	.
Expressive	.	.	s	.	s	.	.	.
Musical Structure								
Begin	s	s,p	.	.	.	.	s	s
End	.	.	.	.	.	.	.	.
Serial pos'n	r	.	-r	r	r	r	.	.
Switch	r,s,p	r,s,p	-r	-r	-r	-r	.	.
Num Notes	.	-r,-s	.	s	.	.	.	.
R^2 repeat	0.14	0.18	0.29	0.37	0.30	0.25	0.24	0.23
R^2 starts	0.25	0.25	0.17	0.23	0.16	0.14	0.17	0.17
R^2 stops	0.23	0.19	0.20	0.20	0.13	0.10	0.20	0.05

TABLE 8.4 *(continued)*

Dimensions of Musical Complexity	Learning Period 2							
	Sessions							
	13		14–16		17		20–24	
	Runs	Work	Runs	Work	Runs	Work	Runs	Work
Basic								
Fingering	r,s	.	.	.	.	.	r,p	r,p
Technical	.	r	.	r,s	.	.	-r	-r,-p
Patterns	.	.	.	.	-s	.	.	r,p
Interpretive								
Phrasing	-p	r	.	.	.	.	r	r
Dynamics	-r	-r,-p	.	.	.	-r	-r	.
Pedal	.	.	.	.	.	.	.	-r
Tempo	.	.	p	.	.	.	.	.
Performance								
Basic	.	.	r	r	r	r	.	.
Interpretive	.	r,s	r	p	.	r	r,p	.
Expressive	.	.	.	.	.	.	-p	.
Musical Structure								
Begin	s	.	.	s	.	.	s	s
End	.	.	p	.	p	.	p	p
Serial pos'n	r	r	-r	.	.	.	r	.
Switch	p	-r	.	s	.	.	.	-p
Num Notes	.	-r	p	.	.	.	.	.
R^2 repeat	0.25	0.44	0.21	0.24	0.08	0.19	0.17	0.26
R^2 starts	0.15	0.10	0.14	0.21	0.15	0.09	0.13	0.09
R^2 stops	0.11	0.07	0.13	0.07	0.07	0.05	0.16	0.19

dimensions were not limited to the later learning periods, but affected practice from the beginning of the gray stage.

Basic Dimensions

Fingering. Work on fingerings began in Sessions 1 to 6, with bars containing more nonstandard fingerings being repeated more. The goal of this repetition was to try out fingerings and then integrate the chosen

TABLE 8.4 (continued)

Dimensions of Musical Complexity	Learning Period 3					
	Sessions					
	26–27		28-30		31-44	
	Runs	Work	Runs	Work	Runs	Work
Basic						
Fingering	.	r	.	.	r,p	.
Technical	s	.	.	.	.	r,p
Patterns	.	.	.	.	.	.
Interpretive						
Phrasing	.	r	-r	-r,-s	r	.
Dynamics	-r	-r	.	.	-r	.
Pedal	.	-p	.	.	.	-r
Tempo	s,p	.	.	.	.	.
Performance						
Basic	r	.	-r	.	.	.
Interpretive	r	r,p	.	.	r	r,s
Expressive	.	.	r	.	.	.
Musical Structure						
Begin	s	.	.	p	s	s
End	.	.	.	.	.	.
Serial pos'n	r	r	.	-r	r	r
Switch	-r	.	s,p	r,s,p	p	.
Num Notes	.	-r,-p	.	.	.	-r,-p
R^2 repeat	0.33	0.39	0.11	0.11	0.26	0.20
R^2 starts	0.22	0.14	0.09	0.09	0.13	0.14
R^2 stops	0.10	0.09	0.10	0.09	0.15	0.12

fingering into a smooth motor sequence. While the motor integration developed, runs were interrupted by "finger tangles" as conflicting motor impulses disrupted the smooth flow of movements. This was responsible for the effect of fingering on runs, which were interrupted by fingerings having to be repeated. The solution was repetition in short work segments.

However, fingering continued to interrupt runs in Session 7 to 8 as Gabriela began to play longer runs from memory. Now in addition to fingerings needing repetition, runs were actually stopping right on the troublesome fingering. These effects were probably due to lack of automaticity when nonstandard fingerings were played without the opportunity to think ahead. When a wrong fingering was used, the run stopped and the passage was repeated with the correct fingering. There was no work at this point, however. Gabriela knew that automaticity takes time to develop and that "It's going to take weeks until it settles."

Fingerings continued to be a problem and in Sessions 11 to 12, when she was "just run[ning] through it . . . and fix[ing] whatever goes wrong," they were one of the things that needed fixing. Fingerings were a problem again in Session 13 when memory for the piece was rusty after the long interval of not playing. In this session, however, Gabriela was relying on the score to avoid mistakes. She had written many of her fingering decisions into the score and refreshed memory for them by using fingerings as starting points for runs. Fingerings also needed refreshing at the beginning of Period 3 (Session 26–27). This time, however, Gabriela was playing mostly from memory, and motor memory was reawakened by repeating the fingering resulting in an effect on work rather than on runs.

There was also renewed attention to fingering during the polishing for the first performance (Sessions 20–24), when fingering affected both work and runs. This is curious because, at this point, there had been no effects of fingering since Session 13. Why would fingering suddenly start interrupting runs and needing work again just before the first public performance of the piece? This may be evidence for the rechunking in preparation for performance that Gabriela described. She said that she was practicing performance cues—reworking every detail of the piece to link them to the interpretive and expressive performance cues that she wanted to think about as she performed. Was this responsible for the renewed work on fingering? We think so. We know that Gabriela was using slow practice for the first time to check her conceptual memory and improve articulation. Playing slowly reduces the ability to find the correct fingering automatically, giving conceptual memory the chance to come up with it before the fingers make their choice. Engaging in slow practice at this point certainly provided an opportunity to link the fingerings to new, higher level retrieval cues. The repetition of bars containing fingering decisions during these sessions is evidence that this was happening.

Fingerings also required attention during the final polishing in Sessions 31 to 44. As in Sessions 7 to 8, fingerings were interrupting runs, but Gabriela did not respond by working on them. There we suggested that the problem was interference from motor memory for the usual fingerings. But why should these cause problems in Sessions 31 to 44 when the nonstandard fingering has been successfully used for months? The answer is the increase in tempo. Playing faster involved changing the movement patterns, and the nonstandard fingering were not fully automatic in the new contexts. The solution was to practice playing long runs with the metronome, correcting fingering errors as they occurred, and steadily increasing the tempo until the fingerings became as automatic at the new tempo as they had been at the old.

Technical Difficulties. There was work on technical difficulties in every session set from the beginning to Sessions 14 to 16 (Table 8.4). Technical difficulties were repeated in short work segments. Except for Sessions 1 to 6 and 13, these work segments generally started at the technical difficulty. These are places where an unusually complex or difficult series of movements requires attention. The multiple repetition involved in work establishes a motor memory for the movements that eventually makes attention unnecessary. While this is happening, starting at the difficulty maximizes the attention that can be devoted to it. By Session 17, this work was completed and technical difficulties were no longer a problem.

While this work on technical difficulties was going on, runs were unaffected except at the beginning in Sessions 1 to 6. This contrasts with the effects of fingering on runs during the same period. The absence of corresponding effects for technical difficulties can be attributed to two things. First, technical difficulties are more distinctive and easier to remember than fingerings. Second, failure to remember a technical difficulty before it appears may slow things down or make the execution messier, without actually stopping the run. This would be a signal that more work was needed. So technical difficulties affected work, but not runs. However, whenever a wrong fingering was used, it was immediately corrected, so fingering did affect runs.

After technical difficulties had been worked on consistently from Session 1 to Session 16, in Sessions 20 to 24 the pendulum swung the other way and they were ignored. Technical difficulties were worked on less than other bars. The explanation lies in the injury to Gabriela's hand. By avoiding technical difficulties she minimized stress to the injured hand. Apparently she felt secure enough that she was willing to prepare for the first performance under this restriction.

Technical difficulties did, however, need some more work in Sessions 31 to 44 when the new tempo made it necessary to streamline movements. The altered motor patterns had to be reestablished through repetition just as they had been at the beginning.

Patterns. The number of different patterns of notes, or chunks, in a bar affected the initial work in Sessions 1 to 6. Each familiar pattern has a motor sequence associated with it. In bars containing more familiar patterns, there are more discrete, preestablished motor sequences to be integrated, and these bars required more repetition. Unlike the effects of fingering and technical difficulties, the integration of separate motor patterns was completed in Sessions 1 to 6, and there was no effect on the number of different patterns in subsequent sessions until Sessions 20 to 24. The reappearance of the effect during the polishing for the first performance is similar to the reappearance of fingering effects at the same time. Both appear to result from the process of rechunking, in which the basic motor patterns of the piece were linked directly with higher level expressive performance cues.

Interpretive Dimensions

Interpretive dimensions generally affected practice differently than basic dimensions. Effects were often negative rather than positive. Bars with more interpretive features tended to be repeated less and occasioned fewer starts and stops than other bars. Why might this be? There are two main possibilities. One is that bars containing interpretive features tend to occur in passages that are less complex harmonically or rhythmically and so require less practice. The reason the pianist needed to make interpretive decisions about these passages was that there is less going on musically than in more complex passages, providing both the need and opportunity to add interest and complexity through the use of interpretive devices. Needing less repetition, these bars would also be the location of fewer starts and stops.

Alternatively, interpretive features may be the location of fewer starts, stops, and repetitions because they require *practice in context*. Interpretive features often involve relationships between adjacent bars. For example, the polyphony involved in the creation or accentuation of a voice or theme against the background of other voices often extends over several bars. Other interpretive features, such as changes in dynamics or tempo, involve contrasts between longer passages, each consisting of several bars. Features of this sort must be played as part of their larger context. To practice them, the pianist must avoid starting or stopping at the bar in which the feature begins. This would result in negative effects for starts and stops. With this preamble, we can now turn to the effects of the interpretive dimensions.

Phrasing. Much of the phrasing used in the *Presto* consisted of grouping eighth notes into sets of four, emphasizing the first of each group, so that the emphasized notes form a melody or figure against the background of the others. Gabriela's comments in Sessions 1 to 6 indicate that she considered this kind of phrasing in making basic decisions about fingering and technical difficulties. Her comments were largely concerned with the difficulties this created. For example, in Session 5, "Right here, it's purely a technical problem. I am having trouble because I am trying to phrase similar notes different[ly]. . . . " This attention to phrasing is reflected in the regression analyses by the negative effect of phrasing on repetitions in Sessions 1 to 6. Bars with more phrasing decisions were repeated less frequently during work—an effect that may indicate practice in context or that work on phrasing was postponed by avoiding places that needed it until later.

There was no effect of phrasing for the rest of Period 1, not even in Sessions 9 to 10, when interpretation had become a major topic of comment (chap. 7). For example, "I have to work in one accent that I haven't got, and it's still a shifty place." Although Gabriela was making decisions about phrasing, this comment suggests that she was still working at the level of the individual notes making up each phrase, which may explain why effects of entire phrases on practice had not yet appeared. In the following remark from Session 10, she appears to accept the fact that phrasing might not always be fully implemented. "The notes were there but it was uncomfortable. It didn't feel right and, of course, I missed that phrasing I was working on."

Work on phrasing did, however, begin in Session 13. Bars containing more phrases were repeated more during work, and runs stopped on these same bars less frequently than on other bars. The positive effect on work is straightforward enough. It indicates hard work—many repetitions of the bar in question. The negative effect on stops for runs probably indicates practice in context of phrasing during runs. To practice or evaluate the phrasing of a particular bar, the bar was played as part of the longer context, and so it was important that the run not stop on the critical bar. The negative effect of phrasing for runs tells us that Gabriela was using runs to practice phrasing in the context of the surrounding sections. It is interesting that this pattern of practice appeared in the first session of Period 2. One of the reasons for taking a break from a new piece is to be able to hear it with a fresh ear. When she did this, what apparently struck Gabriela was the need for work on phrasing.

The other time during the second learning period that Gabriela focused on phrasing was in Sessions 20 to 24, when bars containing more phrasing decisions received more repetitions in both run and work segments. In these sessions, Gabriela was refining the interpretation in preparation for the first public performance. "I am trying to . . . bring out the left hand, just every other note, forcing it out a little bit. . . . I [still] can't decide whether I am going to do the echo in bar 99" (Session 24). The effects of phrasing reflect this concern. Repetitions during work were the result of trying out a new phrasing, whereas repetitions during runs may reflect the initial evaluation that led to the work or continued dissatisfaction with its results.

The work on phrasing was completed in the first half of Period 3. In Sessions 26 to 27, bars with phrasing features were again repeated more than other bars during work. In Sessions 28 to 30, the character of the work changed to practice in context, with more complex phrases being repeated less frequently and work segments starting on them less often than other bars. This new pattern of practice undoubtedly reflects decisions to bring out a few themes mentioned in the comments about these sessions.

Dynamics. Dynamics also affected practice in the section by section stage. Runs tended to be interrupted by the repetition of bars containing dynamic features. As mentioned earlier, the dynamic features in the *Presto* often served to bring out a particular theme. The effect on runs early in the learning process means that Gabriela was attending to this aspect of interpretation from the start. However, she was not sufficiently prepared to execute these dynamic affects ahead of time, but had to back up and replay the relevant bar. This particular effect did not appear again, suggesting that the interruptions caused by the dynamic features at this early stage may have been different from their effects when they later became a more central focus of practice.

Later effects of dynamics were all negative, and there were a lot of them. Bars with dynamic features were repeated less often than other bars during runs and work. This was the most consistent effect observed, occurring in either runs or work, or both, in more session sets than any other dimension (Sessions 9–10, 13, 17, 20–24, 26–27, and 31–44). As mentioned earlier, these effects may reflect practice in context, or passages containing more dynamic features may have needed less practice because they were harmonically simpler than other passages.

Pedal. Bars involving use of the pedal were repeated less often during runs in Sessions 9–10 and during work in Sessions 20–24 and 31–44. Work was also affected by pedaling in Sessions 26 to 27, when there were fewer stops at these locations. These are all sessions in which Gabriela's comments indicate that she was focusing on interpretation. Apparently she avoided interrupting runs on bars where she used the pedal so that she could practice bringing out the theme.[8]

Tempo. We do not discuss the effects of tempo because the small number of tempo features makes it likely that the particular effects are accidents of their location in the piece.

Performance Dimensions

When she first described her use of performance cues, Gabriela reported selecting them to guide her performance during the final polishing of a new piece. It was with some surprise, therefore, that I [Roger] first saw the results in Table 8.4. Practice was apparently affected by performance cues from the outset. When I went to Gabriela for an explanation, she was delighted. First, her novel idea that there are such things as performance cues had received empirical support—they really did influence practice. Even better, their early effect seemed to indicate that early on she had started thinking in terms of the musical effects of her decisions. She was very gratified. She now said that she did indeed make note of likely performance cues early on, but had not liked to say that she could pick them out so early for fear of seeming to boast. She was aware of how bad practice sounds initially—there is little real music to be heard. She knew that most of her attention was focused on basic issues. She did not expect that the arcane technique of regression analysis would pluck from her practice evidence of the innermost creative intentions that guided her work.

> The [basic and interpretive performance] cues are there from the beginning, I would say about 75% of the ones that will be performance cues. I know which ones are essential and I groom them from the beginning. But, in the beginning, there is no way to know for sure. You have to do it as a process and as the piece evolves it sort of narrows down to a few really key places [which are finally selected as the performance cues].

We return to the effects of performance cues in chapter 9, where we examine their role as memory-retrieval cues. Here we focus on the question of timing: When did practice of the different performance dimensions begin and end?

Basic Performance Dimension. Many of the basic performance cues were apparently identified at the beginning of practice in Sessions 1 to 6. These were the fingerings, technical difficulties, and patterns that she would still need to attend to during performance 10 months later. The negative effect of basic performance cues on runs indicates that bars containing these features were played less frequently than other bars. Either they were being practiced in context or work on them was being postponed. The latter explanation seems more likely because work began in the following sessions (7–8). Performance cues were played repeatedly in work segments that started with them. The need for this work is apparent in the identical effects for runs that were interrupted at these same points. Gabriela was beginning to play from memory, managing to play through the whole piece "mostly from memory" for the first time in Session 8. The fact that she was having trouble with basic performance cues during runs suggests that they were beginning to function as memory-retrieval cues.

Further evidence that basic performance cues were acting as retrieval cues comes from their continued effects in period 2, when they interrupted runs as memorization of the piece was completed in Sessions 14–16 and 17. The work needed to make the basic performance cues fluent was also completed at the same time. There was no further work on them after Session 17, although the basic performance cues did need some refreshing at the beginning of Period 3, when they again interrupted runs (Sessions 26–27). In Sessions 28 to 30, the direction of the effect reversed, and for the first time these cues were repeated less than other bars. The effect may represent practice in context, although why this should be necessary only at this one point in the learning process is unclear. In the final session set, there were no effects on runs or work.

Interpretive Performance Dimension. The interpretive performance cues first began to affect practice in Sessions 7 to 8. These were the phrasings, dynamics, tempo changes, and pedallings that Gabriela would need to attend to during performance months later. At this point, they were apparently beginning to take on their role in guiding performance and were singled out for work in Sessions 9 to 10 when they served as starting points for work as well as interrupting runs by getting repeated. This apparently provided the musical shape the piece had been lacking because it was at the end of Session 9 Gabriela noted, "It's getting there. It's so [much] fun to see some music finally coming out of it."

Attention to interpretive performance cues continued throughout the rest of the learning process. They interrupted runs in Sessions 7 to 8, 9 to 10, 11 to 12 and were worked on from Sessions 7–8 until Session 17. Despite this work, interpretive performance cues continued to interrupt runs and required repetition during polishing for the first performance in Sessions 20 to 24 and through much of Period 3. In short, work on interpretive performance cues began soon after work on basic performance cues and continued to the end of the learning process long after work on basic cues had been completed.[9]

Expressive Performance Dimension. Initial decisions about expressive goals were made early in the first learning period. Their effects appeared in Sessions 7 to 8, when Gabriela first began playing the piece as a whole after learning it in sections. Expressive cues served as starting places for runs in these sessions and continued to do so in Sessions 9 to 10. Using expressive cues as starting points would have established them as memory-retrieval cues, associating the expressive intention with the passages that followed.

Expressive cues did not affect practice again until the polishing for the first performance (Sessions 20–24), when Gabriela avoided interrupting runs on expressive cues (a negative effect on stops). The effect seems to represent practice in context and may be yet another reflection of the rechunking needed to focus attention during performance on expressive cues.

Effects of the expressive performance cues reappeared again in Sessions 28 to 30 as Gabriela made "more musical decisions" involving "stereo effects," "trying to thin it out," and getting "a very nice rich tone." Repetition of expressive cues during runs allowed her to evaluate and rehearse her expressive intentions.

Formal Structure

In the graphs for Section C (Figs. 6.2 and 6.3), practice appeared to be organized by the boundaries of the formal structure, with work segments tending to start at the beginnings of sections. The regression analyses show that section boundaries were used as starting places at many points during the learning process. The importance of the formal structure in organizing practice was also evident in numerous effects of switches and serial position in a section. These effects are discussed in chapter 9, where we explore the use of the formal structure as a retrieval organization.

HOW DID PRACTICE CHANGE ACROSS THE LEARNING PROCESS?

The outsider's view of the goals of practice described in this chapter largely agrees with the insider's view reflected in Gabriela's comments (chap. 7). Both practice and comments show that Gabriela initially attended more to basic than to interpretive dimensions, and that this balance reversed as learning progressed. Both views also agree that she attended to performance issues throughout the learning process. The two perspectives support each other, providing converging evidence that Gabriela's reports of the musical and performance features of the piece were accurate and that the regression analyses were able to identify their effects on practice (Chaffin & Imreh, 2001).

Our success in identifying practice goals by looking at the frequency of starts, stops, and repetitions of different kinds of features was by no means a forgone conclusion. The regression analyses involve several levels of abstraction, beginning with Gabriela sitting down with the score 2 months after the recording session to recall decisions she had made during practice. There is no necessary relationship between these retrospective reports of features and the details of what she did in practice sessions that, in some cases, had taken place almost a year earlier. Each of the large number of significant effects in the regression analyses represents a correspondence between her retrospective reports and what happened in practice. These effects provide an impressive demonstration of the accuracy of her memory and the validity of the features she reported.

The goals of practice did change over the course of the learning process, and this was apparent in the changing effects of the different dimensions on practice. First, basic dimensions were practiced before most of the interpretive dimensions. Second, for basic features, practice of performance cues followed practice of the complete sets of basic features, whereas for interpretive features this order was reversed—practice of interpretive performance cues preceded practice of the complete sets of interpretive features. Third, work on the basic performance dimension began before work on the interpretive performance dimension and was completed sooner. Fourth, practice of the basic and interpretive performance dimensions preceded practice of the expressive dimension. These conclusions depend on distinguishing between the initial decision making about a dimension and its systematic practice. For example, expressive cues appear to have been identified and memorized at the same time ɜ the other performance cues, but did not become a focus of practice until much later. We now summarize the evidence for our four hypotheses, focusing on the first appearance of systematic practice for each dimension.

First, basic dimensions were practiced before most of the interpretive dimensions. The motor and perceptual skills required by basic features of the piece (fingering, technical difficulties, and integrating familiar patterns) were developed in Sessions 1 to 6. Work on these three basic dimensions was the main focus of the initial practice sessions. There was also evidence of attention to phrasing and dynamics in Sessions 1 to 6. We discuss the effects of dynamics later, but this early effect of phrasing was negative and probably indicates that the need for work on phrasing was recognized but postponed. Work on phrasing did not begin in earnest until Session 13. Attention turned to the other interpretive dimensions earlier in Sessions 9 to 10, when dynamics and pedal received practice in context. Attention to dynamics and pedaling at this time may have laid the groundwork for the later work on phrasing in Session 13, because dynamic emphasis and pedaling were used primarily in the service of separating phrases from the polyphonic background.

Although practice on most of the interpretive dimensions occurred later than for basic dimensions, many interpretive decisions were made earlier during the initial work on basic dimensions in Sessions 1 to 6. Interpretation was taken into account in the choice of fingerings and solutions to technical difficulties. This is indicated both by effects of phrasing and dynamics for these sessions and by comments about interpretation in Sessions 1 to 6 (chap. 7).

The one dimension that was an exception to the pattern of later practice of interpretive features was dynamics. Dynamic features were repeated during runs in Sessions 1 to 6. Runs were interrupted to insert the dynamic emphasis on a series of notes needed to create the phrases practiced later. We already noted the practice in context of these same dynamic features in Sessions 9 to 10 and the work on the resulting phrasing in Session 13. The practice of dynamic features in Sessions 1 to 6 appears to have been the first step in this process of using dynamic emphasis to create phrases and is thus an exception to the general conclusion that practice of basic dimensions began before practice of interpretive dimensions.

The second hypothesis—that work on performance dimensions would begin after the initial work on the corresponding basic and interpretive dimensions had been completed—held only for basic dimensions. Work on the basic performance dimension began in Sessions 7 to 8 after the initial work on the corresponding basic dimensions had been largely completed in Sessions 1 to 6. (The negative effect of basic performance cues in Sessions 1 to 6 appears to indicate that the need for work was recognized and postponed.) The sequence for the interpretive dimensions was the opposite. Work on interpretive performance cues began in Sessions 7 to 8— before the initial practice in context during runs of dynamics and pedal features in Sessions 9 to 10. It seems that the interpretive performance cues were established first because they provided the big picture—the interpretive framework within which the more detailed interpretive effects were developed. The setting up of this framework in Sessions 7 to 8 was followed by practice in context of the more detailed interpretive decisions about dynamics and pedaling. At this point, if a particular interpretive detail, such as the emphasis of a particular note, could not be managed, playing simply continued. As Gabriela put it,

> I think interpretation starts from the big picture, where you are going. It has to do with the overall architecture of the piece, comparing climaxes and low points. Comparing the repeats of the A theme, making sure that they are not exactly the same as each other. These concern the big structure of the piece.

It was only later that work on the more specific interpretive features began, starting in Session 13 with dynamics and phrasing and continuing with tempo in Sessions 14 to 16, with work on pedaling not taking place until the repolishing stage in Sessions 26 to 27. The practice of the more specific interpretive dimensions thus appears to have come after practice of the corresponding interpretive performance dimensions.

Third, work on the basic performance dimension began at the same time as work on the interpretive performance dimension but was completed earlier. Work on basic performance cues began in Sessions 7 to 8, when Gabriela began to play through the whole piece, at least partly from memory, achieving a rough draft, "A level of performance that is relatively, I'd say 'sufficient'. It's pretty much in tempo. The sound is not very good, but . . . I am trying to play everything out quite rough. . . . " (Session 8) The work on basic performance cues in this session suggests that these critical milestones of the piece were an essential part of her rough draft. Basic performance cues were needed in Sessions 7 to 8 because they served as retrieval cues to elicit the necessary memories. Still lacking, however, was the interpretation that would turn it all into music.

The effect of the interpretive performance cues on both runs and work in the same session set suggests that these were providing the interpretive landmarks needed to make the performance musical. At the end of Session 9 Gabriela remarked with satisfaction, "It's getting there. It's so [much] fun to see some music finally coming out of it, because until now it's just been pulling teeth and torture." The interpretive performance cues had provided the overall interpretive shape that was needed.

> Musically I could do more [in the gray stage than earlier] because I had the whole picture. I wasn't just looking at one little segment at a time. And I had the freedom to have the emotional flow without being interrupted all the time by difficulties.

The work on interpretive performance cues had brought musical coherence to the emerging performance.

Work on the interpretive performance cues began at the same time as work on the basic performance cues, but it continued longer. The last session in which the basic performance cues were worked on was Session 17. In contrast, work on the interpretive performance cues continued through Sessions 26 to 27 and 31 to 44. Thus, work on interpretive performance cues began at the same time as work on basic performance cues and continued until the end of the learning process.

The evidence for the fourth hypothesis—that practice of the basic and interpretive performance dimensions precedes practice of the expressive dimension—was more equivocal. Expressive cues were established early on, but did not become a focus of practice until later. On balance, the hypothesis was more wrong than right, although the story is more complex than the hypothesis allows. Contrary to the hypothesis, the first effects of the expressive performance cues occurred at the same time as those of the basic and interpretive performance dimensions and immediately before the first work on interpretive performance cues. Expressive cues served as starting points for runs in Sessions 7 to 8 and 9 to 10. This would have provided the overall framework for the "emotional flow" of the piece at the beginning of the gray stage, establishing Gabriela's expressive goals as retrieval cues. This was at the same time as the first work on the basic and interpretive performance cues in Sessions 7 to 8. These effects suggest, therefore, that the expressive framework for the piece was established at the same time that the basic performance cues were identified and was a precursor to the identification of the interpretive performance cues. Interpretation did indeed start "from the big picture."

However, practice of expressive cues at this early stage of the learning process was limited to starting runs at them. Basic and interpretive performance cues, in contrast, were subjected to a much more intensive type of practice, being played repeatedly as part of short practice segments. This kind of practice is not of course appropriate for expressive cues, which were never worked on in this way. However, expressive cues were the object of a different kind of practice during the polishing stage. In Sessions 20 to 24, they were avoided as stopping places during runs (practice in context), and in Sessions 28 to 30, they were repeated during runs. These effects reflect the evaluation and polishing of expressive effects that is evident in Gabriela's comments as she prepared for the first performance (Sessions 20–24) and put the finishing touches on her interpretation (Sessions 28–30). If the focus on expression evident in these sessions is regarded as equivalent to the work on basic and interpretive performance cues in Sessions 7 to 8 and 9 to 10, then we could say that practice of expressive cues did indeed begin much later than practice of the basic and interpretive performance cues.

SUMMARY

The regression analyses suggest there was a progression in practice in both directions—up and down the hierarchy of basic, interpretive, and performance cues. For basic features the progression was up the hierarchy, whereas for interpretive features it was down. On the one hand, basic dimensions were practiced before most of the interpretive dimensions, and practice of the complete set of basic features preceded practice of the subset of basic performance cues. On the other hand, for interpretive features, the progression was in the other direction. The big picture provided by the expressive cues was established first, followed by the interpretive performance cues, followed by work on the particular interpretive dimensions.

The final wrinkle to this complicated tale is that, although the development of interpretation began with the expressive cues, systematic practice of these cues did not occur until the final polishing for performance. Expression provided the initial framework for the many hours of work spent in developing the interpretation. At the end of this long process, expression again provided the framework for conceptualizing the piece as it was performed. In the next chapter, we propose that the retrieval hierarchy was reorganized during the polishing stage so that memory could be directly accessed through the expressive cues.

ENDNOTES

1. It is somewhat arbitrary whether phrasings created in this way are regarded as decisions about dynamics or phrasing. We chose to treat them as dynamic features.

2. The idea that what a musician attends to during a performance is critical to its success is the central message of Barry Green and Timothy Gallwey's (1986), *The Inner Game of Music*.

3. Position as the first bar in a section or subsection was represented by a dummy variable, in which the first bar was coded as "1" and all other bars as "0." Position as the last bar was represented by a separate dummy variable, with the last bar coded as "1" and all others as "0." Serial position was coded by numbering each bar consecutively from the beginning of the section (or subsection). Thus, the first bar was always "1" and the value for the last bar depended on the number of bars in the section.

4. Tempo was included anyway for the sake of completeness.

5. A bar was counted as having been repeated if more than a single beat (more than half the bar) was played.

6. All predictor variables were entered simultaneously. Preliminary analyses were performed with 15 predictor variables, 10 measures of musical complexity, 4 representing position in the formal structure, and number of notes. The results led to a small reduction in the number of predictors. Repetitions were affected by serial position in a section, but not by location at the beginning and end of a section, whereas the reverse was true for starts and stops. As a result, slightly different sets of predictor variables were used for repetitions than for starts and stops. Serial position in a section was used for the analysis of repeats and location at the beginning and end of a section was used for the analysis of starts and stops. Thus there were 14 predictor variables for starts and stops and 13 for repetitions.

Another difference between the analyses of repetitions compared to stops and starts was that the first and last bars were eliminated from analyses of starts and stops. This avoided distorting effects with the large number of practice segments that started and ended, respectively, on these two bars.

We tried two different units of analysis for the *Presto*, bars, and subsections. (Beats is another possible unit that we did not try.) Bars appear to be the unit best suited to the examination of work and interruptions of runs. Work is typically organized in segments of a few bars, and many interruptions to runs also have their effects in the space of a bar or two. Sections are probably a more suitable level of analysis for runs because the selection of what to play in a run is probably made at the level of sections. Here we limit our description to analyses of bars because there were enough of them to give the power needed to identify reliable effects.

7. More complete reports of these analyses giving regression coefficients can be found in Chaffin and Imreh (2001, in press). There were 902 possible effects: 286 for repetitions (13 predictor variables x 11 session sets x 2 [runs/work]) and 308 each for starts and stops (14 predictor variables x 11 session sets x 2 [runs/work]). With so many effects being tested, some of the significant effects are undoubtedly due to chance. If the analyses were being used to test hypotheses, this would require use of a more conservative criterion for significance to minimize the risk of incorrectly identifying effects. Our use of regression analysis is, however, descriptive. The question asked is whether, during the learning of a particular piece, the pianist consistently used some kinds of features as starting or stopping places or consistently repeated some kinds of features. From this perspective, the significance level of an effect provides a measure of its robustness and reliability for the particular set of practice sessions analyzed and can be used to identify which dimensions the pianist attended to most consistently. Because our goal is to provide a complete description of the learning of the *Presto*, we have used a liberal ($p < .05$) level of significance to ensure that we did not omit interesting effects. However, the overall character of our description does not change when a more conservative criterion is used (Chaffin & Imreh, 2001)

8. The possibility that passages involving use of the pedal were easier to learn is an unlikely explanation because most of these effects occurred at the end of Period 2 and in Period 3, when the piece was already well learned.

9. Note that the effects of the basic and interpretive performance dimensions were independent of the effects of the complete sets of basic and interpretive features. The fact that the performance cues affected practice independently of the complete sets of features indicates that they were, as Gabriela reported, serving different functions. The effects of the interpretive performance dimension were not only independent of, but also in the opposite direction to the effects of the complete sets of interpretive features. This also suggests that the role of the interpretive performance cues was different in kind from that of the larger sets of interpretive features.

NINE

Memory and Performance

Roger Chaffin and Gabriela Imreh

P erformers deal with mistakes—their own and other people's—all the time. Usually the recovery is graceful. The potential catastrophe is averted, and only the performer feels the rush of adrenaline that comes from teetering on the verge of disaster. Gabriela remembers watching the conductor turn several pages by mistake at a critical point in Beethoven's *Emperor Concerto* and search desperately to find his place again while she played on, waiting for the crash. On that occasion, disaster was averted. The conductor found his place and the performance went on, but memory of the feeling remains.

Mistakes do happen, even to experienced performers, and when they do artists have to cope as best they can. Two of us (Roger and Mary) were present at a wonderful recital given by the soprano Kathleen Battle at the University of Connecticut in 1999. It earned her six standing ovations, but she had a memory lapse. At the beginning of one piece, about four bars in, she stopped, leaned over to confer with her accompanist, made a self-deprecating gesture to the audience, and started over. The incident lasted just a few seconds and by the end of the evening most members of the audience probably did not even remember it. A more glaring memory lapse occurred during the performance of a Mozart concerto in New York that Gabriela attended. The renowned pianist, Alicia de Larrocha, stopped, got up, left the stage, returned, and started again at the beginning. This time she got through the troublesome passage successfully and gave a beautiful performance. Gabriela's worst memory lapse was in a recital as a student. She came off the stage elated by what she thought to be a perfect performance of a Bach *Partita*, only to see the horrified expression on her teacher's face. She had left out an entire section.

The performer has to continually guard against the possibility of a catastrophe of this sort. Memory is both the source of the problem and its solution. To prevent performance failures, a concert artist needs to have a conceptual representation of the music clearly in mind at all times during performance. To recover, you have to know where you are in the music— which section, which bar, where the switches are, and what is coming next. You use that knowledge to restart the motor program. The novice can start only at the beginning; the expert can start anywhere, using retrieval cues strategically placed throughout the piece. When something goes wrong, the performer jumps to a suitable retrieval cue and the show goes on. In this chapter, we see how one pianist sets up those retrieval cues and trains them until they operate fast and reliably enough to get her out of any impeding disaster.

Our account of this preparation for performance accords surprisingly well with the theory of expert memory developed by Anders Ericsson and his colleagues, although that theory is based on the study of very different kinds of expert memory—largely memory for chess boards and random strings of digits (Chase & Ericsson, 1982; Chase & Simon, 1973; Ericsson & Kintsch, 1995; Ericcson & Oliver, 1988, 1989). We described this research in chapter 4 and review the main points only briefly here. Experts are able to memorize with an efficiency that seems beyond the norm (Chase & Simon, 1973). This feat has been explained in terms of three principles of skilled memory: meaningful encoding of novel material, use of a well-learned retrieval structure, and rapid retrieval from long-term memory (Chaffin & Imreh, 1997, in press; Ericsson & Kintsch, 1995).

According to the first principle, experts' knowledge of their domain of expertise allows them to encode new information in terms of ready-made chunks—knowledge structures already stored in memory (Bousfield, 1953; Mandler & Pearlstone, 1966; Tulving, 1962). For a musician, these include chords, scales, arpeggios, phrases, and harmonic progressions whose practice forms an important part of every pianist's training. These chunks and the ability to play them automatically are built up during the long years of training required to develop high levels of expertise (Ericsson & Charness, 1994; Ericsson, Krampe, & Tesch-Römer, 1993). Their presence in long-term memory allows the expert to immediately recognize novel situations as variations of more familiar ones (Anderson, 1983; Ericsson &

Kintsch, 1995), think in larger chunks than the novice (Halpern & Bower, 1982), identify and remember large amounts of information rapidly (Chase & Simon, 1973), and make snap decisions about complex situations (Gobet & Simon, 1996b).

According to the second principle, expert memory requires a hierarchically organized retrieval scheme to provide cues to be associated with new information (Ericsson & Oliver, 1989). These cues can be used to retrieve the newly learned information when it is needed. For a pianist, the formal structure of a piece provides a ready-made hierarchical organization (Chaffin & Imreh, 1997, in press; Snyder, 2000; Williamon & Valentine, 2002). Figure 9.1 shows a hypothetical retrieval scheme for the *Italian Concerto* showing its hierarchical organization into movements, sections, subsections, and bars. The expressive cues make up the next level of the hierarchy below the subsection and typically include several bars that share the same expressive goal. The figure shows the hierarchy unpacked to this level, as if the pianist is currently thinking about the expressive cues in the first Ca section. Interpretive and basic performance cues are shown at the next level, representing specific features of the music within each bar. Still lower levels in the hierarchy represent more detailed knowledge of basic and interpretive features and, at the bottom level, the individual notes.

According to the third principle of expert memory, retrieval of conceptual knowledge from long-term memory is normally a slow process. Prolonged practice in the use of a retrieval scheme dramatically increases the speed with which the expert can access stored information (Ericsson & Kintsch, 1995). This allows the expert to rely on conceptual memory in situations where most people would need to rely on external aids, such as the score. Unlike other kinds of expert memorists that have been studied, however, performers do not have to rely on conceptual memory.[1] Instead, they could depend on motor and auditory memory. Some pianists probably do play this way early in their careers, but it is just a matter of time before the limitations of this strategy become apparent. When something goes wrong during a performance, as it inevitably does, the pianist must know where he or she is in the music and be prepared to restart the motor program to get the performance back on track. This requires conceptual memory. The hierarchical representation of the piece in working memory allows the pianist to select a suitable point for reentry and to activate the appropriate retrieval cue.

Because retrieval from conceptual long-term memory is so much slower than from motor memory, one of the main tasks in learning a fast piece like the *Presto* is to bring retrieval from conceptual memory up to the pace of the performance (i.e., to match retrieval from motor long-term memory).

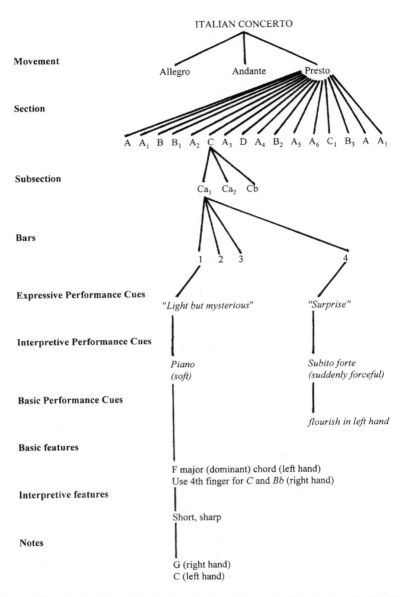

FIG. 9.1 Hypothetical hierarchical retrieval scheme "unpacked" for Section C of the *Presto*. Main themes (sections) are represented by capital letters. Section C is "unpacked" into subsections (Ca₁, Ca₂, and Cb). Subsection Ca₁ is further "unpacked" into its performance cues. The first performance cue in Ca₁ is further linked to the basic and interpretive features from which it is derived. At the bottom is the note to which these features refer.

The main task of achieving this integration begins in the gray stage. It is the lack of integration that makes this stage so frustrating. Practice of basic and interpretive performance cues, which begins at this time, is the key to the problem. Performance cues are a conceptual representation of the music that is linked to the corresponding motor response, so that thinking of the cue directly elicits the performance. Retrieval of these cues from conceptual long-term memory requires practice, however, and it is in the extended practice of these cues that the third principle of expert memory applies to Gabriela's learning of the *Presto*.

Chapters 6 to 8 have provided a wealth of information about how the *Presto* was learned. In this chapter, we explore how well Gabriela's strategies for memorization fit the three principles of expert memory. We begin with the comments (chap. 7) and regression analyses (chap. 8). What we are looking for is evidence that the pianist used knowledge structures already stored in memory as building blocks (Principle 1), used the formal structure to encode the music in practice and retrieve it in performance (Principle 2), and engaged in extended practice in the use of this retrieval scheme (Principle 3).

An additional window into the memorization process is provided by a memory test administered more than 2 years after the performance. Gabriela wrote out the first page of the score from memory. Recall is typically affected by serial order, with items at the beginning of an ordered chunk being recalled better than later items (Broadbent, Cooper, & Broadbent, 1978; Murdock, 1960; Roediger & Crowder, 1976). If music is organized in memory by sections, then beginnings of sections should be recalled better than later portions.

We also look closely at the first few times the pianist played from memory. This did not happen all at once. Gabriela's initial efforts were full of hesitations and pauses while she searched her memory for how to continue. These moments are particularly revealing because they indicate that a retrieval cue was not functioning up to speed. If the formal structure provides the retrieval scheme needed to play from memory, then hesitations should occur at the critical points in this structure—at beginnings of sections and switches. If performance cues also serve to retrieve features from long-term memory, then we may expect hesitations at these points as well.

PRINCIPLE 1: MEANINGFUL ENCODING OF NOVEL MATERIAL

In the initial stages of learning, it is the expert's ability to recognize familiar patterns (e.g., scales, arpeggios, diatonic triads, broken chords, etc.) that sets him or her apart from the less skilled. These familiar patterns are already stored in memory together with the motor programs required to execute them. They provide the building blocks or chunks that a musician relies on to play and remember a new piece, greatly reducing the time and effort required to learn it.

One thing that makes Bach's music more difficult than most is that even though he was a true innovator and made a tremendous contribution to the development of writing for keyboard instruments, he was still near the forefront of what we know today as modern keyboard technique. It was later composer/performers like Beethoven, Liszt, and Chopin who developed a way of writing for the piano that we call "pianistic". From that perspective, Bach's music seems unpredictable. A familiar pattern begins and then immediately changes into a different pattern, equally familiar perhaps, but unexpected in that context. The difficulties that this created were evident in Gabriela's comments during the initial practice sessions and in her practice—she devoted more practice to passages containing more patterns. A bar with more patterns takes more practice because it is unpredictable. Gabriela complained of the lack of familiar patterns, but what is lacking are familiar patterns that continue for more than just a few notes. The problem is really that there are too many patterns, so that none of them goes anywhere. Combining all those little chunks into a unified conceptual and motor sequence takes a lot more time than if the initial patterns were larger.

Familiar patterns have familiar fingerings (Sloboda et al., 1998). When the patterns keep changing, nonstandard fingerings are needed. These are at least as much of a burden on memory as the rapidly changing patterns that make them necessary.

Comments

The dearth of predictable patterns was a frequent topic of comment, as Gabriela worked through the piece section by section, setting fingerings, solving technical difficulties, and making decisions about phrasing and articulation. She noted the problem immediately: "I have my hands full here. Mostly the trouble with this movement is ... places where the patterns are erratic and unpredictable, and sometimes very uncomfortable" (Session 1). Although she made use of familiar patterns wherever possible, in "every bar [there] is something that has almost nothing to do with the idea before." In Session 1, Gabriela thought that this made the *Presto* "The hardest I've ever tried to memorize." After she had learned the first movement in a couple of days, she came back to the *Presto* and compared it unfavorably.

If you really look at the first movement though, almost everything is a pattern. . . . That's something the hand understands. Now babbling around like in the third movement is just very hard because it doesn't make sense. [For example], that's half of a scale . . ., that's part of a trill, and this is [a] rotation, and that is [an] absolutely horrible tangled up mess. So, out of four bars there's nothing to rely on.

One way to create an organized pattern where none appears to exist is to impose one through the selection of fingerings. Gabriela began to do this in Session 1.

Here I change the fingerings to be perfectly symmetrical, because I know that the first finger on each beginning of a group is going to give me stability, and also [help me] memorize it.

Of course, creating patterns in this way added its own burden to memory because the fingerings had to be remembered. In Session 2, Gabriela explained,

The reason I need so many [fingerings] written [into the score] is because the music is much more unpredictable. . . . Within one phrase you have five different things . . . [with] no connection. There's . . . absolutely nothing that can be used in the next bar that you've had in the bar before. So in this case, the hand has a much harder [time] picking up the patterns and storing [them] into muscle memory and, so, good fingerings [are essential]. You can't afford to confuse the hand by giving it mixed messages. You have to be consistent.

Consistency of fingering was not, however, always possible:

It would be ideal to keep the same fingering as much as possible, [but] the hand gets too close, so eventually on the top it must be changed. This is too close. (Session 2)

Effects on practice

In recording the features of the piece that she had paid attention to in practice (see chap. 8), Gabriela reported an average of 3.5 different familiar patterns of notes in each bar and 1.7 nonstandard fingerings. At performance tempo, she would have to cope with an average of four different patterns each second as well as two nonstandard fingerings. In order to cope, these have to become automatic and that takes practice. The practice occurred at the outset, in the section by section stage (Sessions 1–6), when the regression analyses showed that it was bars containing more different patterns and more nonstandard fingerings that received the most work (Table 8.4). It was in these same sessions that the complaints about the lack of patterns occurred.

The identification of familiar patterns was accomplished in the initial section by section stage of practice, and patterns did not affect practice in the ensuing gray stage. This was not so with fingerings, which continued to disrupt runs in Sessions 7 to 8. Nonstandard fingering have to be prepared ahead of time. The pianist has to remember, "Here, I am going to use the fifth finger on the G, not the fourth." If the mental command is not sent soon enough, the wrong finger is used and playing stops while the pianist goes back to take another go at it. It is this continual effort to control the rapidly moving fingers with the much slower conceptual thought processes that makes gray stage practice so frustrating.

Eventually nonstandard fingerings become automatic, triggered by attending to a performance cue. So why did nonstandard fingerings (and not basic performance cues) start disrupting runs again in Sessions 31 to 44, after the increase in the tempo? The tempo increase required a reorganization of motor patterns that apparently disrupted the automaticity of nonstandard fingerings, although these had been functioning fine since Sessions 7 to 8. The solution was twofold. First, whenever a wrong fingering was used, the run was immediately stopped so that traces of the mistake could be erased by playing the passage again correctly. Second, slow practice allowed time for thought before the key was pressed.

Fingering also needed rehearsing at two other points in the learning process: at the start of Periods 2 and 3 after the piece had not been played for 2 or 3 months. In Session 13, this was done by starting runs at fingering features. In Sessions 26 to 27, fingering features were repeated during work. The difference in the type of practice on these two occasions may be because in Session 13 the pianist was still reading fingering from the score, whereas in Sessions 26 to 27 she was relying more on memory, so that if a fingering was hard to retrieve she immediately repeated it several times to make it more available.

The first principle of expert memory is at work here. In the initial section by section stage, Gabriela looked for patterns of notes to use as the building blocks for her performance. Finding familiar patterns greatly reduced the amount of new material that had to be learned and made it possible to play the piece through from memory, however imperfectly, by Session 8. Evidence of Gabriela's search for familiar patterns comes from her lamentations about the unpredictability of the music and her use of fingering to impose organization. Evidence of the use of familiar patterns as building blocks comes from the extra work needed to put together bars that contained more of them. Fingering too, provided evidence of the importance of familiar patterns. In choosing a nonstandard fingering, the pianist is deciding to use a conceptual representation in working memory to override an already established motor pattern. In the disruptive effects of nonstandard fingerings, we can see in mirror image the beneficial effects of the familiar motor patterns that made most fingering relatively unproblematic and effortless.

PRINCIPLE 2: USE OF A HIERARCHICAL RETRIEVAL SCHEME

Many of the pianists in chapter 3 talked, in one way or another, about the importance of formal structure. Even those, like Rudolf Serkin, who described their memorization as automatic or unconscious acknowledged the importance of studying the architecture or harmonic structure of a piece. It is a standard recommendation to students to divide   piece into sections for practice on the basis of its formal structure (Hughes, 1915; Lehrer, 1988; Matthay, 1926; Sandor, 1981; Shockley, 1986). Structure is so important because it is the key to memorization as well as interpretation.

Memorization is largely a matter of finding the necessary information in long-term memory when it is needed (Bousfield, 1953; Mandler & Pearlstone, 1966; Tulving, 1962). In chapter 4, we saw that a student (SF) was able to recall strings of up to 80 digits by chunking them as familiar running times and dates. Recall became largely a matter of remembering the order of a series of familiar chunks—did the 2-mile time come before the 1-mile time? To keep things in the right order, SF used a standard retrieval scheme that helped him recall the information he needed in the right order (e.g., four 4-digit then three 3-digit times). The formal structure of a piece of music provides the musician with the same kind of mental tool—a ready-made hierarchical organization to use as a retrieval scheme.

The retrieval scheme for the *Presto* in Figure 9.1 draws attention to one important characteristic of this kind of hierarchical organization: Nodes at each level include all the information linked to them at lower levels. This reflects the obvious point that we can conceptualize a piece at different levels of detail. We can think of the *Presto* as a whole or of its themes. We can focus on one theme, a subsection, an expressive phrase, a bar, and so on down to the individual notes. In the figure, the hierarchy is shown the way Gabriela reported thinking about the piece during a performance, with the expressive performance cues at the center of her attention in working memory. Once in working memory, the expressive cues act as retrieval cues, eliciting the associated motor sequences and summoning later nodes in the retrieval hierarchy from long-term memory. The retrieval hierarchy can also be used to recall the more detailed information from lower in the hierarchy if need be.

One aspect of the formal structure not represented in Figure 9.1 is switches. Switches are places where one repetition of a theme diverges from a similar version of the same theme elsewhere in the piece. Playing one version puts the performance at one point in the piece, playing the other version puts it at another location. The switch is the point at which the choice is made, where what is played determines which track is taken. To make the right choice, the performer must know the location of the switches with respect to the current location of the performance. Conceptual memory is needed because auditory and motor memory cannot always make the switch automatically. When a performer does make the wrong switch, conceptual memory is needed again to make a graceful recovery. With luck and good preparation, an experienced performer is able to jump back onto the right track and the audience is none the wiser.

We know that Gabriela was thinking about the formal structure as she practiced because she commented on it as she worked and also because it affected the organization of her practice. In the section-by-section stage, each practice session focused on a different set of sections. The regression analyses tell us that, then and later, practice within sessions was further organized by sections, with practice segments tending to start and stop at section boundaries and switches. Starting at these critical points in the formal structure establishes them as retrieval cues. Thinking of a particular location in the piece and then playing it links the thought to the action.

Initially, of course, the music is read from the score. Yet after the first time through, memory begins to form, and looking at the score increasingly serves more as a retrieval cue than as an opportunity to really read the notes. The notes no longer have to be read because they are already in memory in both motor and conceptual forms. The score simply reminds the performer of what he or she already knows. But this reminding, or cuing, function is critical. Without it, the performer cannot get through the piece. Only when the cuing function has been internalized and the score can be dispensed with is the piece said to be memorized. When this happens, each retrieval cue is summoned into working memory from conceptual long-term memory slightly ahead of the motor program so that it is fully activated at the center of attention as the associated motor sequence is executed. Memorization is a matter of making sure that these cues automatically arrive in working memory when they are needed. We turn now to the evidence for this account in Gabriela's comments, practice, and recall of the score after more than 2 years.

Comments

Comments about the formal structure were particularly frequent at four points during the learning process: at the beginning (Sessions 1–6), in Gabriela's overviews at the ends of Periods 1 and 2 (Sessions 12 and 24), and while putting the piece together (Session 17). In the practice by sections stage (Sessions 1–6), Gabriela was mapping her general understanding of the Italian rondo form onto its instantiation in the *Presto*. We can see this happening early in Session 1 as she worked her way through from the beginning. When she reached Section B, she announced, "This is going to be my first stop, as a goal for today." In Session 2, Gabriela took up Section B and, after working her way through it for 20 minutes, she came to the reappearance of Theme A and noted, "Uh, [I] probably hit another repeat of the main theme [A2]." By Session 4, she was beginning to think about putting the different sections together: "At the seams [between sections] I should probably practice more. . . . "

Similarities between sections are an aid to memory, but they are also a potential source of confusion. Gabriela dealt with this problem by noting similarities and differences between repetitions of the same theme. Sometimes she played the two sections side by side: "I have to rework pretty carefully this section. It's never been solid, but now I have to put the two versions [of the same theme] together . . ." (Session 6).

This sorting out of confusions between sections is a matter of identifying switches, the places where two different versions of a theme differ. "And here it's basically the same theme but . . . the bottom G steps down, and, um, it's a very subtle change" (Session 4). The first mention of the term *switch* came in Session 5.

> . . . And, of course, many subtle [differences between sections] are going to surface . . . [which are] just going to mean that I will really have to concentrate on this switch every time I play either one of them.

But it was not until Session 12 that she explained the basis for this metaphor.

> Mostly being able to switch to a different section is like being a train engineer, where you have to switch tracks; and that's basically what I have to do. Otherwise you end up in all kinds of places.

When Gabriela began the task of putting the piece together (Session 17), she began with the switches for the A theme.

It's bar . . . 9 and 10, around there, and number two [bars 194–5]. The difference is really minor, but it has to be drilled in [PLAYS]. Here [PLAYS], all the difference is in the left hand. . . . Okay, [let's] see if we can come in from an earlier place [PLAYS].

Then, "I'll try [both passages] again, [PLAYS]." "Uh, I made a mistake. I really want to play the first one and that's the irregular one."
After 10 minutes, she moved onto the B theme.

And actually there's another conflict here, on bar . . . 25. [PLAYS] That's one, and the other [bar 167] is in the same key, but both turns are different. The left hand turns down in the middle and the ending is different. . . . I should probably practice. . . .

She then put the two themes together. "I think I am going to work on these larger sections. There are definitely a lot of conflicts going on between the first two pages and then the last page and a half. . . . " Five minutes later, referring to the A theme, "Oh, it still is driving me crazy. There's another one that's different here. I have no idea how it goes. I'm all confused." But the confusion was soon dispelled, and after another 5 minutes' work she was ready to begin practicing without the score: "I'll try to play the first page. Let's see, how can I do this? I'll play the first . . . two [pages] by memory . . . and keep the last page for memory again."
After playing the piece through without the score five times in succession, Gabriela described the retrieval scheme she was using:

Eventually, at this level [of practice], you start to have a sort of a map of the piece in your mind. And you start to sort of focus on certain places in it. I'll try to tell you [what they are]. There are a couple of key places, like bar 8. . . . I was really concentrating on the left hand to make the [correct] switch. Bar 23, the left hand again. Bar 32, right hand mostly. . . . I have to concentrate on the switching in 74 [Aba]. . . The next switch is 145. The next one is 150, the . . . third finger in left hand. . . . "

And so on to the end of the piece.
By the next time Gabriela described how she was thinking about the piece during performance (at the end of Session 24), only a few particularly troublesome switches and section boundaries were mentioned.

I still have to think a bit at bar 32 [the boundary between sections A1 and B] just to make sure that it goes on the right track and I don't take off . . . I still have a few places where I really do have to think hard and concentrate on the turns [switches]. . . . In 154 I have to remember not to play a regular theme. . . . I still have to remember 187 [start of the final Aa section], and then the switches . . . between 190 and 191 [between the Ab sections], and then jumping down in left hand in 194. And, anyway, by then I'm pretty much through the worst.

The memorization that went on in Session 17 had involved sorting out the details of the formal structure, getting a clear idea of the switches, and getting this organization into memory. It then served as the retrieval scheme. Summoning a particular section or switch from long-term into working memory activated the corresponding motor sequences. Playing the *Presto* from memory was now largely a matter of thinking of each section and switch in turn and letting motor memory do its job automatically.

Effects on practice

Although comments about the formal structure were limited to times when the pianist was thinking about the piece as a whole, the regression analyses show that the use of this structure to organize practice was much more widespread (Table 8.4). The use of section boundaries and switches as starting points for practice established them as retrieval cues, while the effect of the serial position of a bar in its section suggested that the organization of practice by sections was reflected in memory.

Beginnings and Ends of Sections. Section boundaries served as starting and stopping points in preference to other locations (Table 8.4). Starting at a particular location forms a link in memory between thinking of the location and starting to play. So the use of section boundaries as starting places would have established them as retrieval cues. This occurred at the beginning of each learning period (Sessions 1–6, 13, 26–27) and again at the end (Sessions 11–12, 20–24, 31–44). At these times, the pianist was thinking of the piece as a whole, and its structure was more salient than at other times.

At the beginning, in the section by section stage, attention to structure was needed as the location of the different themes was identified. At the beginning of Periods 2 and 3, attention focused on sections once more to refresh the memory for their locations. At the end of each learning period, Gabriela was getting ready to perform which again requires that the entire structure of the piece be clearly in mind. At the end of Period 1, Gabriela wanted to show that she had the music memorized and played through it for the first time without the score. She was also preparing to play from memory at the end of Period 2 for her first public performance and at the end of Period 3 for the recording session. Preparation to perform from memory probably also accounts for the stops at section boundaries in Sessions 14–16 and 17. At this time, Gabriela was getting ready to put the piece together and play from memory.

Attention to structure at the ends of Periods 2 and 3 also served another purpose. An important part of preparing for performance is polishing the interpretation. This involves thinking about the structure of the piece in relation to its character (e.g., how the continually returning themes of the *Presto* reinforce its sense of headlong momentum). The artist must create a balance among different sections to bring out similarities and contrasts among related themes. The ebb and flow of tension and emotion has to be modulated at each level of the hierarchy so that the piece has an overall coherence, the rise and fall of tension within each phrase contributing to the rise and fall within the section and the sections to the flow of the whole piece. This balancing and tuning of each unit in relation to its neighbors extends beyond the individual piece to the larger work and to the entire program of which it is a part. The artist is shaping the way an audience's experience unfolds across the performance, and it is attention to structure that makes this possible. Attention to structure serves the double purpose of preparing both the interpretation and the retrieval structure. Indeed, the two are not readily separable.

Serial Position in Section. Further evidence that practice was organized by the formal structure comes from the effects of serial position, which show that the formal structure was affecting practice even when practice segments did not start at section boundaries (Table 8.4).[2] Moreover, not just practice was organized by the formal structure, but memory as well. The effects of serial position appear to be due to the ubiquitous effect of serial order on memory—items earlier in a sequence are easier to remember probably because they receive more attention (Fischler, Rundus, & Atkinson, 1970; Rundus, 1971). Positive effects on repetitions indicate that bars later in a section were repeated more than earlier bars, negative effects that earlier bars were repeated more. Both appear to be due to the greater difficulty of remembering later bars.

Positive effects appeared whenever repetition was needed to establish or refresh memory: throughout most of Period 1 (Sessions 1–6, 7–8, 9–10), at the beginnings of Periods 2 and 3 when memory had faded during the break (Sessions 13 and 26–27), and after the increase in tempo required memories to be strengthened (Sessions 31–44). On these occasions, memory was weaker for bars later in a section, and they were given more rehearsal. Negative effects appeared when Gabriela was trying to play from memory but was having trouble with gaps in her memory: when beginning to play longer segments from memory (Sessions 7–8, 14–16).[3] On these occasions, when memory failed, the pianist backed up to a place where her memory was more secure and tried again to get through it. Because gaps tended to occur later in a section, earlier bars were repeated more.[4]

Switches. The interference caused by the subtle differences among sections at switches required intense repetition to establish distinct motor patterns. In Sessions 1–6, switches received more repetitions, starts, and stops than other bars for both runs and work, the only instance of effects on all six measures at the same time (Table 8.4).[5] It is interesting that, despite the attention she gave them, Gabriela had little to say about switches at this stage. Apart from the three comments reported earlier, her intense practice of switches went unremarked. It seems that there were other, more important things to think about. Getting the motor patterns for the switches to work was a fairly routine matter; once they were working, she ignored them. This is indicated by the negative effects of switches in Sessions 7–8, 9–10, and 13, which suggest that she was avoiding them whenever possible, even though in Session 13 they were disrupting runs. Switches were just not a priority at this point, and Gabriela put off thinking about them until she was ready for memorization.

Preparation for this began in Sessions 14–16 when work on switches began again. The purpose was evident in the following session, when Gabriela finally set out to memorize the piece in Session 17. Although the attention given to switches did not show up in the regression analyses, her comments show that Gabriela spent the first half hour carefully going through the piece comparing the different switches. "Let's see, [switch] number 1 is [PLAYS]. Number 2 [PLAYS]. Number 1 is right. Now number 2 [PLAYS] I'm going to use a different fingering from the original." She was putting the *Presto* together, getting ready to play without the score, and she had to know exactly which path to take at each switch.

Switches continued to affect practice in Sessions 20–24, when work segments tended not to stop on switches. Because it seems unlikely that Gabriela would still be avoiding switches during the final polishing for the first performance, it is likely that this represents practice in context— playing through switches without stopping to ensure that the appropriate track was taken. Gabriela explained that at this stage, "Switches don't take a lot of repetition. They are more a matter of concentration and attention. It is a matter of building up endurance."

Building concentration and endurance for switches continued during the third learning period with intensive practice of switches during both runs and work in Sessions 28–30. Despite the additional practice, switches still gave trouble when the tempo increased in Sessions 31–44. This is when concentration and attention really became an issue. We have seen Gabriela's complaints about it: "I'm still cracking up. . . . If you miss any beat, you're gone" (Session 35).

The switches were the main problem. They were still interrupting runs in these final sessions (Table 8.4). Prolonged practice was needed and it had the desired effect. By Session 36, Gabriela reported that, "The mistakes are starting to fade out a little bit." By the end of Session 41, the task was almost complete and she concluded, "There isn't that much more that I can do."

Recall After Two Years

Additional evidence that Gabriela's memory of the *Presto* was organized into chunks based on the formal structure comes from a memory test administered more than 2 years later. During practice, Gabriela generally tried to set things up so that when she played from memory she was successful. For example, in Session 17, she reviewed the switches before beginning to practice without the score. This was a good strategy for her as a learner. As a psychologist, on the other hand, Roger usually likes to look at situations where there is sure to be plenty of forgetting to reveal the effects of mental organization.

So one day, 27 months after the recording session, I [Roger] paid Gabriela an unexpected visit and made a strange request. Would she try to play the *Presto* without looking at the score first? Gabriela was not pleased. She had not played it since the recording session, and she knew she would make mistakes that would interfere with relearning the piece when she wanted to perform it again. Instead, she offered to write it out. Starting at the beginning, she worked for about 15 minutes, until the task became too tedious. When she stopped, she had completed the first page of the score, 32 bars, containing six subsections of the piece. At this point, Gabriela was prepared to play and took her manuscript to the piano. While playing through it, she added more notes and made some corrections. When she was done, she had correctly recalled 65% of the notes (Chaffin & Imreh, 1997, in press). This is pretty good by everyday standards (Neisser, 1982), although fairly normal for an expert (Gobet & Simon, 1996a). More important for our purpose, it provided enough errors to reveal the effect of her mental organization of the piece.

As already noted, memory is generally better for beginnings of lists. Serial position effects thus indicate the nature of the chunks into which memory is organized (Mandler & Pearlstone, 1966; Tulving, 1962). If the *Presto* was organized in Gabriela's memory in terms of its formal structure, memory should be better for bars at the beginning of a section and decline bar by bar across the section. This is what we found. The top row of Table 9.1 shows the mean probability of correct recall, including the changes made at the piano, as a function of serial position from the section boundary. Recall of the first bar of each section was almost perfect (97%), with memory for each successive bar decreasing step by step down to a mere 28% for final bars of the two longest sections.[6]

This kind of serial position effect is the signature of a memory organization in which access is via the first bar of the section, with each successive bar providing the cue for next one. Failure to recall one bar means that all the bars after it are lost until the start of the next chunk provides a new starting point. The effect of serial position in a section provides compelling evidence that Gabriela's memory for the *Presto* was chunked by sections, as predicted by our second principle of expert memory (Ericsson & Kintsch, 1995).

What about the effect of the other retrieval cues? Shouldn't the performance cues embedded in each section provide access to memory and provide starting points for recall at intermediate points in a section? To find out, regression analyses similar to those reported in chapter 8 for practice were performed on the recall data (see Table 9.2). Because we have recall data for only 35 bars, the number of predictor variables was limited to those most likely to affect memory retrieval: three measures of location in the formal structure and three performance dimensions. The measures of musical structure show the effect of serial position already seen in Table 9.1.[7]

The effects for the three performance dimensions are a surprise. Yes, basic and expressive performance cues affected recall, but in opposite directions. Recall of bars containing expressive performance cues was better than other bars, whereas the recall of bars containing basic performance cues was worse. The positive effect of expressive cues is what we expected. A well-rehearsed retrieval cue provides access to the conceptual memory for the piece at this point, producing better recall. In contrast, the negative effect of basic performance cues is a surprise. It suggests that attention to basic performance came at the expense of other features, which were consequently recalled less well (Fischler et al., 1970; Rundus, 1971).

Why would basic and expressive performance cues affect recall in such totally different ways? If the advantage of the section beginnings is due to the availability of more attentional resources at those points, then the disadvantage at basic performance cues may be the result of less attentional resources being available at these points. This seems likely when we consider the different roles played by the two types of cue. (The results for interpretive performance cues suggest that they fall somewhere in between, which is also plausible.) Ideally, a pianist would like to dispense

TABLE 9.1
Mean Probability of Correct Recall and (N) as a Function of Serial Position From Section Boundaries and From Expressive, Basic, and Interpretive Performance Cues

	Serial Position				
	1	2	3	4	5–8
Section Boundaries	.97	.90	.87	.69	.28
	(6)	(6)	(6)	(6)	(1–2)
Performance Cues					
Expressive	.85	.85	.74	.43	.00
	(11)	(10)	(5)	(3)	(3)
Basic	.68	.77	.78	.77	.46
	(11)	(7)	(6)	(5)	(3)
Interpretive	.75	.78	.61	.00	.
	(19)	(8)	(4)	(1)	(0)

with basic performance cues altogether during performance, relying totally on the automaticity of motor memory to implement these features. Basic performance cues are only used to ensure accurate execution of a critical movement, such as the placement of a particular finger or the trajectory of a hand. In these cases, the pianist learns to monitor the motor response with the result that other features receive less attention. The pianist concentrates on the basic cue and so cannot pay attention to the rest, resulting in poorer recall. The basic performance cue reminds the pianist where to place a finger or how to move an arm, but not what the rest of the notes are.

Attention to expressive cues in contrast does not come at the expense of other features. Rather, expressive cues include the other features. Expressive cues encapsulate or chunk an expressive phrase in much the same way that a section encapsulates or chunks all of the more detailed information in the section. This idea of encapsulation or inclusion is represented in the diagram of levels of the retrieval hierarchy in Figure 9.1. Thinking of a node at one level activates the next level down, providing access if more detail is needed. It is this access to lower levels of the retrieval hierarchy that accounts for the better recall of bars containing expressive cues. Expressive cues provide access to the details of expressive phrases in the same way that the beginning of a section provides access to the details of the first bar and to those that follow, which make a prediction!

TABLE 9.2
Regression Coefficients and R^2 for the Effects of Musical Structure and Performance Cues on Probability of Recall

Variable	Regression Coefficient
Musical Structure	
Serial position	-.15***
Begin section	-.03
End section	.47***
Performance Cues	
Basic	-.28**
Interpretive	-.01
Expressive	.24**
R^2	.76***

$* = p < .05.$ $** = p < .01.$ $*** = p < .001.$

If expressive cues and section boundaries work in the same way, then expressive cues should show the same serial position effect as section boundaries. The relevant data are shown in the second row of Table 9.1, which shows the mean probability of recall as a function of serial order numbered successively from each bar containing an expressive performance cue. As predicted, there was a serial position effect, with the bar containing the cue and the one immediately following it being recalled best and succeeding bars being recalled successively less well.

What about basic and interpretive performance cues? Do they produce the same kind of serial order effect? Table 9.1 shows the same analysis for these other performance cues. There was no effect. (The apparent trend for interpretive performance cues was not statistically reliable.) Again, we see that basic performance cues did not operate in the same way as expressive cues, and that interpretive performance cues were somewhere in between.

In summary, the use of section boundaries and switches as starting places ensured that these locations became retrieval cues, establishing the hierarchical organization of the formal structure as a retrieval structure just as Ericsson and Kintsch's (1995) account of expert memory predicts. Expressive cues appear to represent the next level in this retrieval hierarchy, marking the start of expressive phrases that further subdivide subsections. This is exactly what Gabriela claimed when she reported rechunking memory cues during the final polishing for performance. Expressive cues came to form a new level in the retrieval hierarchy that could elicit the motor responses that make up the performance, the basic and interpretive performance cues, and the more detailed knowledge of the piece represented by the complete sets of basic and interpretive features. We turn now to the third principle of expert memory, which maintains that using such a retrieval structure requires the kind of extended practice that Gabriela's 33 hours of practice of the *Presto* provided.

PRINCIPLE 3: PRACTICE AT RETRIEVAL

Retrieval from long-term memory is a slow process. Finding an idea in long-term memory generally takes several seconds, and can take much longer. This is a problem for a fast piece like the *Presto* in which notes fly by at a rate of 15 a second. Speeding up the retrieval process to the point where it can keep pace with the music requires extended practice. This was the main reason that the *Presto* took so long to learn and why it took 14 sessions to increase the tempo in Sessions 31–44:

> It was a matter of learning exactly what I needed to be thinking of as I played, and at exactly what point, so that as I approached a switching point I would automatically think about where I was, and which way the switch would go.

At the tempo Gabriela eventually played the *Presto*, sections were going by at the rate of one every 5 seconds, expressive cues one every 2 seconds, basic and interpretive performance cues every half second. During performance, Gabriela relied primarily on expressive cues. The basic and interpretive performance cues were going by too quickly. They were only there in case some perturbation threatened the stability of the performance.

> [Basic and interpretive performance cues] are the ones that I maintain as active [during performance]. So when I practice, I try to really keep them [in mind]. They are that important. Those are the ones that, even to the very end, I have to . . . monitor closely. But in a performance, hopefully, I will need to use maybe five or ten percent, because I think the performance is better if you don't use any of them.

The extra security provided by basic and interpretive performance cues is essential because of the pressures of a public performance:

> When it actually comes to that adrenaline rushing in and you really having to land . . . it's like an ice skater. They can do triple and quadruple jumps all the

time . . . in practice. But in the performance. . . . Somehow the performance takes something else, and that's what the final [performance] cues are about. And so what I am trying to do, . . . is to create a security blanket, where my percentage [of success] goes up.

While the performer attends mainly to the expressive cues, she must be prepared to focus on particular basic or interpretive performance cues when necessary. These are the "security blanket". Ensuring that they were activated required extended practice: 33 hours and 57 sessions in all.

We have seen that practice of the retrieval structure (section boundaries and switches) continued until the end. If we are right that what was being practiced was memory retrieval, then we should find evidence that practice was affected by the features that Gabriela identified as performance cues and that these effects continued to the end of the learning process.

Comments

Performance Cues. The first clear reference to performance cues came at the end of Session 17.[8] Gabriela had just learned to play without the score. In describing her "map of the piece", she listed features of the music that needed attention as she played from memory. We already mentioned some of the switches; the other landmarks in the map were all basic performance cues:

I have a thing in bar 52 where I have to remember to go all the way to the G, but I can get through it. . . . I have to concentrate on the fingering in bar 67. . . . I have the scale in the left hand at [bar] 124, the two fours in a row. . . . The fingering in 186.

Like the larger set of basic features, basic performance cues are stored in motor and auditory memory as well as being represented in conceptual memory. Unlike the other basic features, however, the basic performance cues still need attention during performance. This takes practice. Retrieval from conceptual and motor memory have to mesh so that the conceptual cue is retrieved slightly before the motor responses. Earlier, in the gray stage, this had been problematic. In Session 17 it was becoming smoother. Where previously the conceptual memory had lagged behind, it now became faster and more automatic so that the conceptual memory for the feature was arriving in working memory first—in time to serve as a retrieval cue for the motor response rather than the other way around.

The next time Gabriela talked about performance cues was at the end of Session 24, when she went through the piece giving a much more detailed description of what she was paying attention to in her practice immediately before the first performance. In other words, she was describing her current set of performance cues. She had little to say about either basic performance cues or switches. Her thinking about the piece had moved to a new level, and the focus had shifted to interpretive performance cues. Basic performance cues were now wrapped in an interpretive gloss so that, instead of talking about a specific fingering or technical difficulty, she would describe the interpretive effect that it produced.

> I try to put the accents in. It's very hard. Most times I'm lucky, but in 93 I sometimes miss that D below the staff. It's a big jump and it goes awfully fast. But I want to emphasize it because it's a theme.

Phrasing is the most frequent topic mentioned: "And again the . . . double counterpoint that I've been working on ever since in bar 45. And then it changes in bar 49—the hands switch roles." Other interpretive performance cues involve tempo and dynamics: "I'm doing a little bit of ritard, just smaller than the other one in bar 75." A few expressive performance cues were also mentioned: "I'm playing this whole next section [Bc] quite transparent and light [from] 38 on . . . I am trying to bring [the theme] out in a more lyrical way in bar 52 and maybe not quite so short."

However, this was about it for expression. In the four pages of transcribed comments that make up this report, there was nothing else that could be identified as talking about expression. This is curious. Gabriela was about to perform the piece for the first time the next day. Was she about to give a performance that lacked expression? No, expression had been built in at every level from the fingerings to the calibration of one section against another. Expression was in there, but Gabriela was not yet at the point where she could focus on it as she played. Attention was still on the more detailed interpretive performance cues through which her expressive goals were accomplished. This is why she was not yet ready to perform without the score. The process of adding the final level of expressive cues to the retrieval hierarchy was still in progress and continued into the third learning period.

Unfortunately, Session 24 was the last time Gabriela went through the piece giving a systematic description during practice. She did, however, write out the expressive cues for Section C midway through the third learning period between Sessions 31 and 32. This is the report shown in Figure 8.1, in which Gabriela first described features of the piece on the 10 dimensions. The expressive cues were, "Light but mysterious . . . Surprise . . . Hold back . . . Surprise . . . Start building crescendo . . . No holding back

... Prepare for return of the A theme." The detailed enumeration of expressive cues at this point suggests that the process of distilling them out of the larger set of interpretive performance and structural cues was more or less complete. This is consistent with our earlier observation that the development of phrasing appeared to be largely completed in Session 33 and that subsequent sessions were devoted to increasing the tempo. The expressive cues were in place by this time, and the goal was to make them function effectively at the faster tempo.

Although there were no comments directly about performance cues during Sessions 31 to 44, there were many comments about the difficulties created by the new tempo. Attending to performance cues at just the right moment required intense concentration, and there were frequent complaints when it was not sufficient.

Concentration. Gabriela noted the need for concentration early on: "It is pure concentration.... As soon as my concentration goes ... I'm making an enormous amount of mistakes" (Session 5). Comments like this run through the practice sessions like a refrain: "I ran out of steam on the last few pages and you can tell my concentration dropped dramatically" (Session 17).

The fact that Gabriela talked about concentration more after she started playing from memory in Session 17 (chap. 7) gives us a clue as to why it is so important. Concentration is needed so that the right performance cue is brought to the center of attention in working memory at the right moment. This is clear when Gabriela describes her "map of the piece":

> [In bar 8] I have to really concentrate on the left hand to make the right switch.... [In bar] 52, I have to concentrate on the fingering.... I have to concentrate on the switching in 74. The next place I really have planned to concentrate was, an old friend, 118.... And if I can get through all those, one by one, without making mistakes I'd probably.... " (Session 17)

In the next systematic description of "What I am working on" at the end of Session 24, the refrain about concentration is more muted but still there. Now instead of switches, it is basic and interpretive performance cues that need more attention:

> I keep the fugue [section D], from 104 on, quite light, and just try to concentrate on really just getting through it. There are so many jumps, I try to be accurate. Right now they are taking most of my attention, like [bar] 108. The left hand jump [in bar] 110.... They're quite difficult. In 119 the whole

attention now goes to those fairly large accents I put on the whole notes in right hand. I bring them out with accents. . . .

Gabriela goes on to explain how attention to a feature strengthens the link between the conceptual representation and the hands as the music flies along:

> I still have to concentrate on 150, on the fingering in left hand. I tend to put the fourth finger somewhere. It's the regular A minor fingering, and I forget that [it] is. I mean, I don't forget, but sometimes it goes by so fast that I forget. So usually if that happens, I finally manage to just remember that there's an A with fifth finger in 151. And if I don't get that, I'm in trouble. But most times, if I'd skip through the scale and I miss the fingering, I still try to land on A with fifth finger (Session 24).

Concentration is necessary to *remember*. The motor program will carry on regardless. But if she does not attend to the performance cue at the right moment, the motor response may not be executed with the desired fingering. This comment also explains nicely how performance cues can help in recovering from this kind of slip. If she misses the fingering in Bar 150, she will improvise, skipping through the scale, relying on auditory and motor memory, until she comes to the next performance cue. Hitting the A with the fifth finger in Bar 151 will put her back on track.

The decision to increase the tempo in Session 31 strained attentional resources to the limit: "I'm still cracking up here and there, but it's getting better. The intensity of concentration that's required is amazing. If you miss any beat, you're gone" (Session 35).

Concentration like this is exhausting. The solution was to increase the automaticity and speed of retrieval through repetition. By Session 36, "It's coming along. I think it will need technical maintenance a lot, because it takes enormous endurance to play so many notes, so clearly, so fast."

There was also another way to achieve the faster tempo—using fewer retrieval cues.

> To increase speed it is necessary to unclutter both your thinking and your manual work. It is like building a castle out of cards. You build a complex and fragile structure, putting in plenty of reinforcements to make sure it is stable. Then you start taking cards out, one at a time, until you are left with just enough to support the whole edifice. So, when you first learn a piece, you put in lots of movements and mental cues to make sure you do it right. Then, when you speed up, it is a matter of taking some of them out. You leave out

some of the cues and lighten up, or leave out some of the motions. The secret is to guide the listener to what to listen to. As it gets faster, the listener can hear less detail. So you have to guide them with good clues as to what is important.

Effects on Practice

The effects of the three types of performance cues were among the most consistent and numerous effects in the regression analyses (Table 8.4). Starting and stopping at performance features and repeating them during work and runs established these locations as retrieval cues. Thinking of them while playing kept the performance on track, ensured that particular features were implemented, and provided a safety net if things began to go wrong.

Basic and Interpretive Performance Dimensions. The first positive effects of basic performance cues appeared in Sessions 7 to 8 at the beginning of the gray stage (see Table 8.4). The initial decision making about basic dimensions was finished, and Gabriela was beginning to pay attention to larger musical goals, playing through the whole piece, relying on memory when possible. This was when she announced that she had been playing "largely from memory" (Session 8) and that she was able "to see some music finally coming out" (Session 9). The emerging musicality, playing from memory, and attention to performance cues are all part of the same process. As she began to give musical shape to longer runs, Gabriela would stop and restart at basic and interpretive performance cues to collect her thoughts for what she was trying to accomplish musically. These places were already beginning to function as retrieval cues—points where the performer refocused her attention on the next musical goal.

Work to strengthen the automaticity of these critical spots began immediately for the basic performance features (Sessions 7–8) and soon after for the interpretive performance cues in Sessions 9 to 10. This work came to an end temporarily with the end of Period 1. In Sessions 11 to 12, Gabriela was "just running through" the piece. Work on the interpretive performance cues began again in Session 13 and work on the basic performance cues resumed a little later in Sessions 14 to 16. Once the performance cues were in place, it was time to start playing entirely from memory. This happened in Session 17. Work on both types of cues continued during this session, but it was basic rather than interpretive performance cues that interrupted runs, suggesting that Gabriela was relying more on the basic cues at this point. We have already seen that

Gabriela's description of her mental map at the end of this session points to the same conclusion.

By Sessions 20 to 24, this had changed, and it was interpretive perform-ance cues that interrupted runs. Basic cues no longer had any effect. As the first performance approached, interpretive cues were becoming more central. Again, the effects on practice are consistent with the description of performance cues at the end of Session 24, which focused on interpretive rather than basic performance cues.

Memory for both basic and interpretive performance cues needed refreshing after the 3-month break between Periods 2 and 3, and runs were once again interrupted at both kinds of cues (Sessions 26–27). For basic performance cues, practice during runs in Sessions 26 to 27 and 27 to 28 completed the learning process.[9] In contrast, the interpretive performance cues still needed work and were still interrupting runs in Sessions 31 to 44. Interpretive decisions about phrasing were still being made as late as Session 33.

Expressive Performance Dimension. Gabriela had decided on her main expressive goals by the beginning of the gray stage, and in Sessions 7 to 8 and 9 to 10 she used expressive cues as starting points for runs (Table 8.4). This established these expressive goals as memory cues, setting in place the main musical outline for the piece. It was at this point that Gabriela announced that it was beginning to sound like music, and she prepared to bring the first learning period to a close, concluding that the piece was 60% learned. Meanwhile the focus turned to filling in the details to realize the expressive framework she had established.

As the first performance approached, it was time to distill a final set of expressive cues to access both the motor responses and the more detailed conceptual knowledge of the piece. There is evidence in the practice record that this was happening in Sessions 20 to 24 (Table 8.4). In these sessions, expressive cues affected practice again for the first time since Sessions 9 to 10. They were avoided as stopping places during runs, thus providing them with practice in context. At the same time, nearly all the other dimensions also affected practice—the only time that this happened. In particular, fingering and patterns were reworked in a way that had not been seen since the beginning (Sessions 1–6). These effects suggest that the retrieval hierarchy was being reorganized to link all of the features of these other dimensions directly to expressive cues.[10]

Another way in which Sessions 18–24 were distinctive was in the prolonged use of slow practice. By reducing the effectiveness of motor memory, slow practice provided an opportunity to rehearse the performance cues. By making sure that the performance cues were clearly in mind as the notes were played, their links to each other and to the motor performance were strengthened.

Although the practice record is consistent with the idea that expressive cues were becoming the top level of a reorganized retrieval hierarchy, Gabriela's account of these sessions, described in the previous section, suggests that her focus was still more on interpretation than expression. To develop this point further, here is Gabriela's description from an interview of how she would normally think about expressive cues right before a performance:

> Something else happens before a performance. . . . With very little warm up and practice you [need to] be emotionally in tune. You have to sort of rev yourself up. You say, "Okay, I want to be like this," and you have to have that reaction really fast. If you watch me warm up before a concert you would think I was a total lunatic because I play three notes or one bar, and then I go on to something else, because I am going from one end of the piece to the other. Basically what I am doing is just trying to catch the moment to make me look forward. . . . You try to make sure that they [the feelings] come fast and they'll be there. . . . Through practice and work you get dulled down and before a . . . performance you try not to let that happen. So you try to put a twinkle on these things. . . . You try to inspire yourself. It keeps things alive.

There is more to the rechunking process than simply thinking of a new set of cues. It is a matter of linking the motor activity and all of the interpretive and basic performance cues with the emotions they are intended to express. The emotion—that is, the idea of the emotion—has to be center stage in working memory during the performance. To prepare for this, the idea of the emotion and its articulation through the structure of the music must become the primary way of thinking about the piece during practice. Gabriela's description of her practice goals at the end of Session 24 does not suggest that she was yet thinking of the piece this way. This, and her unwillingness to perform without the score the following day, suggest that the final level of the retrieval hierarchy, the expressive cues, was not yet firmly in place at the time of the first performance.

The expressive cues needed more development, and they continued to be a focus of practice as polishing continued in Sessions 28 to 30 (Table 8.4). Now bars containing expressive cues were played more often than other bars during runs. This is the only time that expressive cues were repeated, and it indicates that Gabriela was thinking about them, interrupting runs to go back and try them again. However, this practice appeared to complete the development of the expressive cues because Gabriela was able to report expressive cues for Section C at the end of Session 31, and their effects on practice did not continue in Sessions 31 to 44.

In Session 32, there was a shift in the goals of practice. The target was still expressive—to give the piece "more excitement", and make it "more dramatic". The route was new—an increase in the tempo. The expressive cues were apparently not an obstacle because, unlike switches and interpretive performance cues, they did not interrupt runs. Expressive cues were apparently functioning well, and they do not appear in the practice record or comments for these sessions. The evidence that Gabriela was using expressive cues at all in this final stage of the learning process comes from her recall of the piece 2 years later, when it was the expressive cues, along with the boundaries of the formal structure, that provided the primary way of retrieving her knowledge of the music from memory.

In summary, the effects of performance cues on memory are consistent with the third principle. Speed of retrieval from long-term memory was indeed the major difficulty in learning the *Presto*, and this was exacerbated by the increase in tempo after Session 31. The problem was not primarily a matter of executing movements rapidly enough. The difficulty was in the mind.

> A lot of my later practice of the Italian Concerto was practicing throwing those switches. My fingers were playing the notes just fine. The practice I needed was in my head. I had to learn to keep track of where I was. It was a matter of learning exactly what I needed to be thinking of as I played, and at exactly what point, so that as I approached a switching point I would automatically think about where I was, and which way the switch would go.

HESITATION DURING MEMORY RUNS

For the most part, playing from memory and from the score are so interwoven in Gabriela's practice that they cannot be separated. Memorization occurred gradually. She generally practiced with the score open in front of her and, with time, came to rely on it less and less. This is reflected in her comments about memory, which occurred at every stage of the learning process. But, just because the process was gradual does not mean that it was effortless. On the contrary, on the first two occasion—when we can be sure Gabriela was playing from memory because she said so at the time—the effort required was readily apparent. She stumbled through the piece, hesitating repeatedly as she struggled to recall the next passage. These renditions are painful to hear, but they provide a unique window onto the process of retrieval. Each hesitation represents a memory cue that operated too slowly, each stop or repetition a cue that failed to activate the necessary long-term memory trace on the first attempt.

The Effort of Remembering

Session 8. The first run through the entire piece largely from memory occurred about 40 minutes into Session 8, the long practice session in which Gabriela set out to "really accomplish something" and get the *Presto* "wrapped up". Although the score was still open on the piano, she announced, "That was memorized, horrible as it sounds. At least I know what I am doing. I still have a couple of fairly deep gaps in memory."

The effort involved was extraordinary. The run began smoothly enough at a steady tempo of 116. The trouble began in Section C. The tempo slowed and, for the remainder of the piece, fluctuated from moment to moment, punctuated by pauses, sometimes speeding up, back to the original tempo, and sometimes crawling along at half the pace. Watching the video, the viewer is struck by the pianist's dogged persistence. You wish she would just look up at the music a few inches in front of her, but she does not. Instead she battles on, slow and halting, dredging up the music from memory. In the end, she did have to look at the score in a couple of places, but these capitulations were hard fought. The overwhelming impression is one of unyielding effort. For Gabriela, the experience was one of exhilaration.

> It feels so liberating, to be able to put the music away and to play the first time from memory. It is thrilling! There is such a huge contradiction between how horrible the music sounds and how I feel. It bothers me so little because I know I can fix all that. I know what it will sound like.

We can get a rough idea of the time spent in struggling with recall by comparing the observed performance duration of the entire run through from memory (5 mins 1 s), with the expected duration that would have resulted if the initial, target tempo of 116 beats per minute had been maintained (3 mins 37 s).[11] The additional playing time was 1 min 24 s— 39% more than the expected duration (see Table 9.3).

How much of this additional time was spent struggling to retrieve the music from memory rather than to mechanical difficulties or intentional, expressive variation in tempo? There were four other runs through the entire piece in the same session. For these runs, Gabriela did not report playing from memory, so for comparison purposes we assume that memory retrieval difficulties did not add to their performance duration.[12]

TABLE 9.3
Duration of Memory Runs and Target Tempo With Estimates of Additional Playing Time Due to Difficulties When First Playing From Memory

	Memory Run				Performance
Variable	8.1	12.1	12.2	17.1–17.4	CD
Observed duration	5:01	5:53	4:13	4:07	3:04
Target tempo (beats/min)	116	118	118	116	138
Expected duration (420 beats/tempo)	3:37	3:34	3:34	3:37	3:03
Additional playing time (observed-expected)	1:24	2:19	0:39	0:30	0:01
% additional playing time ([additional/expected]*100)	38.7	64.9	18.2	13.8	0.0

The four comparison runs lasted an average of 12% longer than dictated by their target tempi. This means that in the memory run, at least 27% (39%–12%) of the extra playing time is attributable to retrieval difficulty.

Reader, think of the last time you struggled to recall something from memory. Stop for a moment and think of a particular occasion. Remember how much effort it took. Did you spend the best part of a minute trying to remember? Most of us do not. We give up a lot sooner or never make the effort at all. (For example, did you follow these directions to think of a particular example? Probably not, which makes the point.) Recall is hard work. We do not engage in it lightly, just to satisfy a whim of an author for example. It may be this willingness to do the hard work of recollection that distinguishes people who can memorize from the rest of us who simply proclaim the task too difficult.

Session 12. The second time Gabriela played from memory was at the end of Session 12. It was the end of the first learning period and time to set the *Presto* aside for several months. Gabriela wanted to show that she had it memorized even if retrieval was still a struggle.

There is one thing I have not done yet for you [Roger] and that is to completely put the music away and try to play it by memory. One of the reasons is that. . . . I know it is going to sound so much worse than what I can do with the music [score]. . . . It is going to be a lot of stumbling and babbling and stuff. So I didn't want to inflict that on you.

She closed the score and began to play (run 12.1). It was true, there was a lot of "stumbling and babbling". The first trouble came in the initial statement of the A theme. Gabriela spent 2½ minutes on Bars 9 and 10, playing them over and over, trying to get them right. She tried starting from the beginning again five times. In the end, she had to admit defeat and opened the score to look. She started at the beginning again; this time she sailed through the roadblock without a problem. After this, things went better, although there were still hesitations and fluctuations in tempo. At one point she did have to flip open the score for a quick look, but she did not come to a complete stop again.

Again, we can estimate the time spent in retrieval (Table 9.3). The performance duration was 5 minutes, 53 seconds, not including the initial 2½ minutes spent on the first 10 bars. This was 2 minutes, 19 seconds or 65% longer than the expected duration. How much of this extra time was due to retrieval problems? There was one complete run through in Session 12 with the score open, which we can use as a comparison. This run took 12% longer to perform than expected on the basis of its target tempo. So hesitations due to retrieval increased the performance duration of the memory run by at least 53% (65%–12%) over the expected duration. This is double the estimate for Session 8. Gabriela was working even harder. She had to because she had put away the score. Recall that in Session 8 Gabriela had the score in front of her and glanced at it at least twice.

Another factor contributing to her difficulties in both Sessions 8 and 12 was that Gabriela was performing in front of the camera. As she put it later, "The pressure was on. It was not like playing for myself. It was a challenge." In Session 12, when she ran through the piece from memory for the second time (run 12.2), Gabriela reported that she "relaxed a bit", and we can see the effect. This time she did not need to consult the score, and there were fewer hesitations. The performance duration was 4.13 minutes—a substantial 1.40 minutes faster than the previous attempt and only 39 seconds or 18% over expected performance duration (Table 9.3). This is a striking improvement in fluency. Either the effort put into the first memory run had paid off, or she had indeed "relaxed".

Session 17. Gabriela next played without the score in Session 17. After a review of the switches and a preliminary run through looking at some pages of the score, Gabriela was ready to try it from memory. She closed the score and played through the piece four times (runs 17.1–17.4), fairly fluently compared with the memory runs in Sessions 8 and 12. The average observed duration for the four memory runs was 4.07, which was 30 seconds or 14% more than the expected duration (Table 9.3). Was the additional 14% due to retrieval problems or was it perhaps due to expressive slowing at the ends of sections? To answer this question, the final performance recorded for the CD was used as a comparison. The observed duration of 3.04 is almost exactly the same as the expected duration of 3.03, the difference of less than .05% being well within the margin of error for the measurement of target tempo.

In a comment at the end of Session 17, previously quoted in chapter 5, Gabriela compared her memory for the piece to the last time she had played from memory in Session 12:

> The last time I played from memory, if you remember . . . I was relying very much on motor memory . . . I had very few reference places, that I knew exactly what I was doing. I had a lot, but compared to now it was much less. So, now I think, even though I make a few mistakes, I know what the mistake was, and how to fix it.

These "reference places" are the retrieval or performance cues, where the pianist can take stock of where she is, locating what her hands are currently playing in a conceptual representation. Knowing where she is allows her to access the performance cues for the current section. If she takes a wrong turn at a switch or if something sounds wrong, she can retrieve the relevant performance cue from long-term memory and correct the problem immediately without having to consult the score. She knows where she has been, where she is now, and where she is going next. She knows "how to fix it".

Bar Duration as a Measure of Hesitation

Which features of the music were responsible for the hesitations and slow downs in these initial memory runs? If we are right, then they should be the retrieval cues: the section boundaries, switches, and performance cues. To see if this was so, Helma de Vries measured the duration of each bar in the memory runs in Sessions 8 and 12 and for the CD performance as part of an undergraduate research project (Chaffin et al., 1999). (Bar duration could not be accurately measured for Session 17 because of the poor quality of the recorded sound signal).[13] We measured the first complete playing of each bar. This provided a clean measure of the time required to play each bar once, but it had the drawback of omitting cases in which Gabriela stopped in midbar. This resulted in omitting or underestimating some of the most substantial hesitations (e.g., the 2½ minutes spent trying to recall Bars 9 and 10 in run 12.1). As we shall see, this way of measuring duration still left more than enough hesitations to demonstrate retrieval problems.

Bar durations decreased and became less variable across the three memory runs and were most uniform in the CD performance (Table 9.4). These reductions suggest that much of the variability was due to lack of fluency. What exactly was the source of the problem?

Effects of Memory and Expression on Memory Runs

If we are right about the features of the *Presto* that served as retrieval cues, hesitations should tend to occur at boundaries between sections (as the pianist thinks of how the next section begins), at switches (as she tries to remember which switch to make), and at performance cues (as she remembers a critical decision, perhaps a phrasing or fingering). This would provide further evidence that boundaries, switches, and performance cues were serving as retrieval cues. Regression analyses were performed with bar duration as the dependent variable and the same predictor variables as in the regression analyses of starts, stops, and repetitions.[14] Just as the earlier analyses identified the types of features at which practice segments started and stopped, the bar duration analyses identified the types of features at which hesitations occurred.

Changes in bar duration might be due to mechanical problems, deliberate expressive variation in tempo, or retrieval difficulties. Mechanical problems would result in longer bar durations for basic dimensions. Expressive variation would produce effects, either positive or negative, at interpretive or expressive cues and at the ends of sections. Effects in the CD performance can be assumed to reflect acceptable, expressive variations in tempo, so when the same effect occurs in practice, we assume that it was intentional. Other effects in practice are more likely due to problems— some inability to maintain the target tempo—and the mostly likely source of these problems is memory retrieval.

The three memory runs (8.1, 12.1, and 12.2) and the CD performance were each analyzed. In addition, adjusted bar durations were calculated for each memory run by subtracting the bar duration for the CD performance. This should remove most of the expressive variation in bar duration from the practice runs so that effects are most likely due to problems of some kind—either mechanical or memory retrieval. Comparing the adjusted and unadjusted practice data with the CD performance data allows us to separate effects that are most likely due to intended expressive variation from those more likely due to a lack of fluency.

TABLE 9.4
Mean Bar Durations (in secs), Standard Deviation, and
Coefficient of Variation (Standard Deviation/Mean)
for Practice and Performance From Memory

	Memory Run			Performance
Variable	8.1	12.1	12.2	CD
Mean$_{bar\ duration}$	1.86	1.34	1.19	.86
$SD_{bar\ duration}$	1.31	.76	.37	.13
$(SD/\overline{X})_{bar\ duration}$	.70	.57	.31	.15

Effects Due to Memory. We expect retrieval problems to be reflected in effects of performance cues and structure. The performance cues produced the most consistent effects on bar durations and all appear to indicate hesitation due to a lack of fluency. Performance cues slowed playing in all three memory runs and in the adjusted data, but not in the CD performance suggesting that the effects were due to hesitations and were not intentional. Bar duration was longer for bars containing basic performance cues in all three memory runs, at interpretive performance cues in runs 8.1 and 12.1, and at expressive performance cues in run 12.2. (The effect of expressive cues did not appear in the adjusted data, casting some doubt on its reliability). The pattern of the other effects, however, is consistent with the idea that the performance cues functioned as retrieval cues and that the hesitations were due to difficulty with memory retrieval. The hesitations provided more retrieval time, an opportunity to remember what was supposed to happen.

The effects of structure, in contrast, cannot be unambiguously attributed to retrieval difficulties but may have been deliberate, expressive variations in tempo. The effect of serial positions on runs 12.1 and 12.2 looks at first sight like another serial position effect. Bars earlier in a section were played faster, those later in a section more slowly, suggesting that later bars were harder to recall. However, the absence of this effect in the adjusted bar durations indicates that the memory run was not reliably different from the CD performance in this respect. The effects in the memory run may, therefore, have been deliberate, expressive effects. Expression is certainly the most straightforward explanation for the effect of ends of sections in run 12.1. Bar durations were longer for the last bar of a section than for other bars. Slowing at the ends of sections is a standard

TABLE 9.5
Significant Effects of Musical Structure and Performance Features on Log Bar Duration for Practice and Performance While Playing From Memory: *Italian Concerto* (*Presto*)

	Practice			Performance	Adjusted Practice (Practice-Performance)		
Session	8	12.1	12.2	CD	8	12.1	12.2
Variable							
Musical Structure							
Begin section	.	.	.	-0.06	.	.	.
End section	.	.15	.	.	.	.	.
Serial pos'n	.	.02	.01	.	.	.	.
Switch	-.16	.	.	.	-.10	.	.
Performance Cues							
Basic	.27	.09	.11	.	.16	.	.05
Interpretive	.14	.10	.	.	.10	.07	.
Expressive	.	.	.07	.	.	.	.
Basic Dimensions							
Fingering	.	.	.	.	.	.	.
Technical	.	.	.	.	.	.	.
Patterns	.	.	.	.	.	.	.
Interpretive Dimensions							
Phrasing	.	.	-.02	.	.	.	.
Dynamics	-.13	.	.	.	-.08	.	.
Pedal	.	.	.	.05	.	.	.
Tempo	.	.	.	.14	.	.	.
Number of Notes	.04	.	.	-.01	.03	.	.01
R^2	.27	.19	.27	.25	.25	.15	.19

expressive device (Clarke, 1995; Repp, 1992). Since the effect also occurred in the CD performance and was not present in the adjusted data, it is quite possible that the slowing at the ends of sections in run 12.1 was expressive rather than intended to provide more time for the retrieval of the next section.

Bar durations in run 8.1 were also affected by switches. Unlike the other effects of structure, this one was present in both the original and adjusted data but not in the CD performance, indicating that it was not intentional but reflected some kind of problem. We expected problems with fluency at switches, but the effect is in the wrong direction for this interpretation. Switches were faster than other bars, not slower. The effect suggests that switches had some role in playing from memory but what is unclear. Perhaps Gabriela knew that she would have trouble at switches and so glanced at the score before she reached them. Or the extra attention paid to switches in earlier sessions may have made them more fluent.[15]

Effects of Expression. There was one other effect of structure, and it appears to be a deliberate, interpretive variation in tempo. In the CD performance the beginnings of sections were played faster than other passages—a negative effect. Going faster at the beginning of a section underlines the change in thematic material (Clark, 1988). We have seen that Gabriela used tempo to provide excitement and tension in this fast-paced piece. Increasing the tempo at the beginnings of sections added to the feeling, already created by the repetitive return of the same theme, of whirling on a roundabout at full tilt.

Several other effects also appear to be expressive. Bar duration in the CD performance was longer for bars containing tempo changes and use of the pedal. The effect of tempo clearly reflects deliberate, temporary decreases in tempo. The increase in bar duration associated with pedaling may have been designed to draw attention to phrasings created by the use of the pedal.

Dynamics also affected bar duation in run 8.1, but the effects were in the opposite direction than those in the CD performance. Bars containing dynamic features were played more quickly than other bars. A similar effect for bars containing the beginnings of phrases occurred in run 12.2. Since the direction of the effects seems to rule out mechanical or retrieval difficulties, it seems most likely that these are also expressive effects. Why was the effect of dynamics in the opposite direction in the CD perform-ance? Perhaps because of the very different tempi involved. In Sessions 8 and 12, Gabriela was playing at a substantially slower tempo than in the final performance. At the slower tempo, interpretive features could be underlined by increasing the tempo, while at the faster tempo a similar effect had to be produced by slowing down.[16] If this explanation is correct, it reflects considerable flexibility in the realization of expressive goals.

The effect of number of notes on the CD performance also appears to be an expressive effect. Bars containing more notes were played faster than the other bars in the CD performance. Increasing the number of notes in a bar is a way for the composer to create dramatic tension and increasing the tempo at the same time is a way for the performer to accentuate that tension.

Effects Due to Mechanical Difficulties. There were no effects for basic dimensions. This is important because it indicates that hesitations were not due to mechanical problems with fingering and technical difficulties. Mechanical problems with "finger-tangles" are, however, the likely explanation for the effect of number of notes in run 8.1. Bars containing more notes were played slower. The effect is probably due to a lack of fluency. Bars with more notes may have been more difficult technically or more difficult to remember.

Summary

The effects of performance cues and section boundaries on bar duration provide our most direct evidence that these were acting as retrieval cues. It was here that hesitations occurred when the piece was first played from memory. Such hesitations were not caused by technical difficulties, nonstandard fingerings, complex patterns, or any of the interpretive dimensions. They occurred at cues that Gabriela reported attending to during performance. This strongly suggests that the delays were due to retrieval problems.

CONCLUSIONS

Gabriela's learning of the *Presto* is described surprisingly well by the three principles of expert memory, although these principles were derived from domains of expertise in which memory is primarily conceptual and skilled movement is not required. In piano performance, in contrast, motor skill is clearly central. What we have learned here is that conceptual or declarative memory is important for concert pianists, just as it is for other types of expert memorists.

The operation of the first principle of expert memory—that new information is encoded in terms of previously established chunks—was evident in the initial section-by-section stage, as Gabriela looked for patterns of notes to use as the building blocks of her evolving performance. The ability to see these patterns greatly reduced the amount of new material that had to be learned. This made it possible for her to play the piece from memory in Session 8 after only 7 hours of practice. Evidence for the importance of familiar patterns is found in Gabriela's lamentations about the unpredictability of the music, in the greater amount of work devoted to bars containing more patterns, and in the use of fingering to organize notes into chunks.

The second principle of expert memory maintains that a retrieval scheme must be used to allow controlled access to information stored in long-term memory. For Gabriela, the retrieval scheme was provided by the formal structure of the *Presto*. Knowledge of the musical structure is necessary for reliable performance, particularly for the *Presto*, because its complex rondo form requires the performer to be continually mindful of which repetition of each theme is currently being played. Gabriela's attention to the formal structure is evident in her comments as she identified boundaries and switches and from her use of section boundaries to organize practice. Starting at boundaries ensured that the music was initially encoded into memory in sections whose beginnings served as retrieval cues. The effects of this retrieval practice were evident 2 years later when Gabriela was able to recall the early bars in each section much better than later bars. The effect of serial position on recall indicated that the music was organized in memory by sections, which were further subdivided into expressive phrases. The first bar provided access to each chunk, with each bar within a chunk cuing the next.

According to the third principle of expert memory, extended practice is necessary for a retrieval scheme to work fast enough to be useful. Extended practice is evident in the 33 hours taken to prepare the *Presto* for its recorded performance and particularly in the 14 hours of practice that occurred after the first public performance. Much of this time was devoted to practicing memory retrieval, as shown by Gabriela's frequent comments about the need for concentration and the numerous effects of performance cues, section boundaries, and switches. When a cue did not operate quickly enough, runs were interrupted at the cue, boundary, or switch that had caused the trouble. These effects occurred throughout the learning process, including in the final session set when the increase in tempo placed especially heavy demands on rapid memory retrieval.

One characteristic of expert piano performance not addressed by the principles of expert memory is the rechunking that occurred during the final polishing stage. Gabriela reported that in the last stage of readying a piece for performance she practices attending to expressive cues so that she will be able to think about the piece primarily in terms of the emotions she wants to convey. At the same time, she reworks all the details, creating a new level of expressive cues through which to access the retrieval hierarchy.

The behavioral evidence for this account was suggestive, if not conclusive. In preparing for the first public performance, Gabriela paid renewed attention to expressive cues and basic features, in fact, to almost every dimension—something that did not occur at any other point in the learning process. At the same time, she engaged in slow practice for the first time, ensuring that her conceptual memory (and thus the retrieval cues) would be in working memory as she played. Her unwillingness to perform without the score at the end of Period 2, however, suggests that the expressive cues were not yet securely established, and this is supported by the fact that her description of the piece at this time focused on more specific interpretive effects. The continued development of expressive cues is indicated by their effect on practice in Sessions 28 to 30, which appeared to complete the rechunking process. When Gabriela described the performance cues for Section C between Sessions 31 and 32, expressive cues were clearly labeled. The most direct evidence that this attention to expressive cues had established them in the upper levels of the retrieval hierarchy came when the piece was recalled 2 years later. There were serial order effects for both section boundaries and expressive cues, indicating that memory of these two levels of the retrieval hierarchy provided the primary access to memory for the piece.

On the one hand, our conclusion that conceptual memory is crucial in piano performance is not surprising. Piano pedagogues have long emphasized the importance of formal analysis in learning a new piece (Hughes, 1915; Lehrer, 1988; Matthay, 1926; Sandor, 1981; Shockley, 1986). In interview studies, professional musicians describe the importance of cognitive analysis to their memorization (Aiello, 1999; Hallam, 1995a; Williamon, 1999). Many of the concert pianists discussed in chapter 3 talk about the importance of practice techniques that rely on conceptual memory—mental practice away from the piano, slow practice, and analytic memory, to use Claudio Arrau's term.

On the other hand, the role of conceptual memory has not been well understood by pianists. This is apparent in these same interviews. There is a lack of a common terminology for talking about conceptual memory. The artists talked variously about form analysis, harmonic structure, analytic memory and structural memory. Yet these accounts were often combined, confusingly, with disclaimers, as in Bella Davidovich's account of how this information is available "instinctively . . . so there's no conscious thought." We hope that by pulling together these comments about conceptual memory in chapter 3 we have made their commonalities more apparent than in their original contexts, where they were interspersed with talk of other forms of memory. Alhough they describe it differently, most of the artists acknowledge that conceptual memory is important.

The importance of conceptual memory is further obscured by the greater salience of other forms of memory. The fact that motor memory is largely implicit (procedural) adds an air of mystery to the whole topic—Jörge Demus's unconscious approach, Alicia deLarrocha's natural memory that memorizes by itself, and Rudolf Serkin's unconscious memorizing. The other kind of memory that appears in one interview after another is visual memory, often referred to as photographic. Artur Rubinstein sees his photographic memory as an inherited gift, whereas Lili Kraus sees hers as a liability. Even artists who do not rely on visual memory, such as Alfred Brendel and Misha Dichter, describe their memorization in terms of its absence. When the salience of other forms of memory is combined with the lack of a common terminology for talking about conceptual memory, it is no wonder that the significance of the latter has been unclear.

We believe that conceptual memory is important for any concert pianist, and that if the artists in these interviews had been asked about it directly they would have acknowledged this. In four recent studies in which the interviewers were familiar with contemporary memory concepts, the professional musicians who were interviewed reported in every case that they used conceptual memory (Aiello, 1999, 2000a; Hallam, 1995a; Williamon, 1999). For example, Aiello (2000a) asked four concert pianists to describe the musical elements they would use to memorize two Preludes—one by Bach, the other by Chopin. The pianists all marked features such as repeated melodies, harmonic changes, chord progressions, arpeggiated chords, dynamic changes, and the climax—approximately 10 features for each piece.

In contrast, students appear to be less clear about the importance of conceptual memory. When asked whether their segmentation of the music helped them in memorizing, only 6 of Williamon's (1999) 21 student pianists reported that it had, although the practice records showed that they all used some structure to organize their practice. There was greater awareness of conceptual memory among the Juilliard students studied by Aiello (2000b). Yet even among these highly accomplished young pianists, two out of six appeared to memorize without any explicit awareness of their conceptual memory for the music. They were able to mark only a single feature for each of the scores they examined and reported that they memorized by rote. The reports of the other four students were more like those of the professionals.

Conceptual memory is an invaluable tool for reliable performance, but its use appears to develop rather late for most students. We hope the analysis of memorization in this chapter helps change this situation so that in the future more students will be understand how conceptual memory can help in their preparation for performance.

ENDNOTES

1. We use *conceptual memory* in place of the more widely used *declarative memory* (Anderson, 1983) because we have found that the former term makes the idea more accessible to nonpsychologists.

2. Effects of serial position were on repetitions only, not on starts and stops, and serial position was not included as a predictor variable in the analyses of starts and stops.

3. This effect did not occur at the beginning of Periods 2 and 3 (Session 13 and 26–27) because then Gabriela relied more heavily on the score.

4. In Sessions 28 to 30, the negative effect of serial position otherwise associated with runs occurred for work. Unlike previous sessions, work at this point in the learning process was generally by sections, running from beginning to end of a section. When the new phrasing being practiced did not work well, the pianist backed up and tried it again, resulting in more repetition of bars earlier in the section.

5. Gabriela initially distinguished three types of switches: (a) The same material is repeated in nonadjacent bars, (b) the same musical material is repeated in nonadjacent bars but in a different key, and (c) similar material is repeated in adjacent bars. The first type of switch was the most common in the *Presto,* and preliminary regression analyses show that its effects were larger than those of the other two kinds of switches or any combination. Consequently, only the first type of switch was included.

6. One-way analyses of variances (ANOVAs) showed that differences in the top two rows of Table 9.1 were significant ($p < .001$), whereas those for the bottom two rows were not (Chaffin & Imreh, in press).

7. The negative effect of serial position indicates that bars earlier in a section were recalled better than later bars. The effect for beginnings of sections was not significant because it was subsumed under the more global effect of serial position. The positive effect for ends of sections is not apparent in Table 9.1 because sections ended in a variety of serial positions. Also, the effect in the regression analyses indicates only that last bars were recalled better than their serial position would predict, not that they were well recalled in absolute terms. When the analysis was redone without serial position as a predictor, the effect for beginnings of sections was significant, whereas ends of sections was not.

8. The term *performance cue* did not appear in these comments because this term was not introduced until after the development of the description of decisions about Section C in terms of 10 dimensions that occurred between Sessions 31 and 32.

9. When a negative effect of basic performance cues on repetitions during runs occurred in Sessions 1 to 6, we suggested that Gabriela was avoiding these features until she was ready to work on them. A similar explanation for the negative effect in Sessions 28 to 30 seems implausible so late in the learning process.

Another possible explanation for the effects of the basic performance cues is that they needed attention during performance—not because they were retrieval cues, but simply because they were difficult. The interruptions to runs throughout most of the learning process could simply be a reflection of their technical difficulty. This possibility cannot be entirely ruled out, but it does not explain why the pattern of effects for basic performance cues is so different than that for technical difficulties and fingering. If the basic performance cues were simply the most difficult of these basic features, they might be expected to show the same effects, but they did not.

If the problem with the basic performance cues was just that they were difficult to play, then we would expect to see work on them early on until the difficulties were overcome. This was the approach to technical difficulties, which were worked on continuously until they were mastered in Sessions 14 to 16. Basic performance cues, however, were not worked on in this way. At the beginning, in Sessions 1 to 6, when all three of the basic dimensions were worked on, basic performance cues were actively ignored. Practice was postponed as if the importance of these locations had been recognized and was being strategically ignored. Work on the basic performance cues did not begin until Sessions 7 to 8 and was then renewed in Sessions 14–16 and 17. These are the sessions that placed the largest demands on memory—in Sessions 7 to 8 because the entire piece was practiced for the first time and in Session 17 because the piece was played without the score.

Another possible objection to the interpretation of performance cues as retrieval cues is that Gabriela generally played with the score open. It might be argued that retrieval problems should not be disruptive when the score is available to fill in gaps in memory. However, Gabriela often played from memory even though the score was open.

10. It is, of course, impossible to say for sure that the effect of expression on stops in Sessions 20 to 24 was a result of this rechunking process, but the effect certainly reflects renewed attention to expressive cues just before the performance.

Consider the following alternative explanation for the effects of the expressive cues. Perhaps in starting at expressive cues Gabriela was using them as a convenient way to divide the piece into practice segments. Rather than setting them up as retrieval cues, she was simply using them as starting and stopping places. This is not an attractive alternative. First, it does not explain not stopping at expressive cues in Session 20 to 24. Second, whatever the intention, starting in a particular place does establish it as a retrieval cue. Third, the appearance of effects of expressive cues in the sessions devoted to polishing the interpretation strongly suggests that they were related to this goal.

11. The target tempi in Table 9.3 were adjusted upward by one metronome marking from the original measurements to take account of a consistent error in the metronome used to measure target tempo. When this metronome was calibrated against a stop watch, measured tempi were slower than true tempi by 3.4%. A similar error of measurement is indicated independently by the mean bar duration reported in Table 9.4, which indicates an average tempo of 139.5 for the CD performance. The target tempo measure on the metronome for this performance was 132—a difference of 5.7%. The target tempo for the CD performance is therefore reported in Table 9.3 as 138, which is the next metronome marking above 132. Similar corrections were not made to the tempi reported in chapter 6 for the reasons given in footnote 12 to that chapter.

12. This is almost certainly incorrect, but it provides a conservative baseline. To the extent that retrieval difficulties also added to the playing time of the four comparison runs, the true contribution of retrieval difficulties to the memory run are underestimated.

13. Bar durations were measured from the start of each bar to the start of the following bar using a commercially available sound-editing program to measure the temporal location of sound waves on the audio track of the videotape. Judgment of where each bar started was made using both auditory and visual representations of the signal.

14. Log bar durations were used to normalize the data.

15. Another possibility is that playing was disrupted more severely at switches than at other locations so that playing stopped in midbar so that the switch could be repeated. Because we measured the first complete playing of a bar, this could have resulted in switches being played more fluently. Examination of the practice records indicates that of the 17 places in Run 8.1 where a bar was repeated, 4 occurred at switches and 2 in bars immediately before a switch. By comparison, four repetitions occurred at the ends of sections and four at the beginnings. In Run 12.1, six of nine repetitions occurred at switches. Repetition may have played a role in the shorter duration of bars containing switches.

16. The effect was not simply a mirror of the increase in tempo during performance because it occurred in the unadjusted as well as the adjusted data.

TEN

Stages of Practice Revisited

Roger Chaffin and Gabriela Imreh

$\mathbf{W}$e began our description of the learning of the *Presto* in chapter 6 by identifying six stages of the process. We are now ready to fill out that earlier description by adding what we have learned since from both the insider's and the outsider's perspectives. In chapter 6, we saw from an outsider's perspective how the length of runs and the proportion of practice devoted to runs increased from stage to stage, while the length of work segments and the effortfulness of practice remained the same. In chapter 7, we looked at things through Gabriela's eyes as she practiced and saw that she was initially more concerned with basic issues, but that as these were resolved her focus shifted to interpretation.

In chapters 8 and 9, the insider and outsider perspectives were merged through the use of regression analysis, and we saw a similar pattern of development. In the early practice sessions, Gabriela's activity at the keyboard focused more on basic dimensions, whereas interpretive dimensions had more effect later in the learning process. This was because the main work on the interpretive dimensions came only after the overall musical shape of the piece had been established. In chapter 9, regression analysis of the practice record was supplemented by parallel analyses of free recall and hesitations to understand how the *Presto* was represented in memory. We saw how the formal structure of the piece provided an organizational framework for practice and for Gabriela's memory representation. Here we provide a brief recapitulation of how the *Presto* was learned and memorized.

STAGE 1: SCOUTING IT OUT (SESSION 1)

The first stage of learning consisted of a single run through the whole piece at the beginning of the first session. During this initial scouting, Gabriela identified the main structure of the *Presto* so that she would be able to come back and work on it section by section.

STAGE 2: SECTION BY SECTION (SESSIONS 1–6)

In Sessions 1–6, Gabriela worked her way through the *Presto* a few sections at a time. The division into sections was based on the formal structure. Beginnings of sections and subsections served as starting points for both runs and work segments. Already the switches that distinguished different repetitions of the same theme were identified, interrupting runs and receiving special attention during work.

The main task of this stage was establishing motor memory. Familiar patterns of notes had to be merged to form new, larger patterns; in the process, decisions about fingering and technical difficulties had to be made and practiced. The new motor patterns were then tested in longer runs. These were often interrupted by fingering and technical difficulties that had not yet become sufficiently automatic, requiring the pianist to go back and replay them before going on.

Although work focused on basic dimensions, decisions about interpretation were made at the same time. Gabriela mentioned interpretive goals in explaining why she preferred a particular fingering and laid the groundwork for the later development of phrasing by adding dynamic emphases that would bring out harmonic lines and polyphonic voices. Further work on interpretation and the development of an integrated performance was, however, postponed until later. The places that would require the most complex phrasing decisions—those with the most phrasing features—were avoided during work. Also, the most critical basic features, the basic performance cues, were avoided during runs. These negative effects indicate that Gabriela was aware of the issues presented by these passages, but was not yet ready to address them. Thus, the attention to basic dimensions was the result of a strategic decision.

STAGE 3: THE GRAY STAGE (SESSIONS 7–16)

The goal of the gray stage is to make the execution of earlier decisions fully automatic. This is a transitional phase in which some things are automatic, whereas others still require attention and control. Moving back and forward between automatic and controlled performance is difficult and frustrating. The developing motor automatisms are much faster than the conceptual control processes needed to govern them. Gabriela put it succinctly in a comment from Session 12 quoted more fully earlier:" . . . The more I try to control it, the more I . . . interfere with things that are well set up."

Work on technical difficulties was a distinctive characteristic of the gray stage. Its purpose was to make the execution of difficult passages automatic, and the achievement of this goal in Sessions 14 to 16 marked the end of the gray stage. Fingerings also had to become automatic, and remembering fingerings during runs was another source of trouble at the beginning of the gray stage (Sessions 7–8) and again after the piece had not been played for 5 weeks (Session 13). For fingerings, however, unlike technical difficulties, the solution was not more work, but runs, to provide practice at memory retrieval.

Another task of this stage was to link the short segments learned in the section by section stage into longer passages. The length of runs increased steadily during the gray stage from 16 bars in Sessions 7 to 8 to 29 bars in Sessions 14 to 16. Linking sections puts new demands on memory. What happens in the new section you are just entering? The knowledge is stored in long-term memory; the problem is to find it before it is too late to be useful. Memory was generally better for the beginnings of sections with the result that, as Gabriela began playing from memory (Sessions 8–9 and 9–10), interruptions to runs tended to occur toward the ends of sections.

Memorizing began during the gray stage, and the first run through the entire piece "largely from memory" occurred in Session 8. Interruptions and hesitations during this first memory run identified the location of retrieval cues: section boundaries, performance cues, and switches, although the evidence for switches was ambiguous. Section boundaries and switches had been used as starting places for practice segments since the beginning and were already established as retrieval cues. In contrast, practice of basic and interpretive performance cues only began in the gray stage. Work on the basic and interpretive performance cues established them as retrieval cues, while the interruptions to runs at these points demonstrated that retrieval was often not fast enough to keep pace with the activity of the hands.

As the ability to play the piece as a whole developed, the emergence of an overall musical architecture was marked by the use of expressive cues as starting points for runs in Sessions 7 to 8 and 9 to 10. By the end of Session 9, Gabriela reported that she could finally "see some music . . . coming out of it." This was accompanied by a new focus on interpretation. In Sessions 9 to 10, dynamics and pedal affected runs in ways that suggested that these features were being practiced in context, and interpretation became the dominant topic of comment.

At the end of the first learning period, in Session 12, Gabriela clearly was still enmeshed in gray stage problems of automaticity and cognitive control. We already quoted the clear statement of gray stage concerns made at this time: "It still gives me palpitations to play through it, because . . . I feel like I really have to concentrate and control." At the same time, however, she was beginning to think about putting the piece together—the next stage in the learning process. This was evident in the two performances from memory at the end of Session 12, after which Gabriela noted, "Probably now the seams [between sections] are quite obvious. . . . I have to now check each transition [from the A theme] because every time it is something different."

The concern with transitions between sections anticipates the next stage of putting it together. However, moving onto this the next stage was postponed by the end of the first learning period. In taking a 2-month break, Gabriela made it necessary to relearn much of what had already been done. At the beginning of Period 2 (Session 13), three effects indicate that relearning was needed. First, runs tended to start on fingerings, indicating that these features, which had been functioning automatically, once again needed attention. Second, switches, which had not been a problem in Sessions 11 to 12, were now interrupting runs again. Third, basic and interpretive performance cues no longer interrupted runs as they had in Sessions 7 to 12 because Gabriela was once again relying heavily on the score to avoid making mistakes.

Otherwise, the 2-month break had surprisingly few detectable effects. Session 13 looks remarkably like Sessions 9 to 10 and 11 to 12. The length of runs was similar to Sessions 11 to 12, an average length of 25 bars, indicating that the integration of the piece that had been accomplished by the end of Period 1 had not been lost. The same focus on interpretation continued to develop, with practice in context of phrasing and dynamics during runs, work on interpretive performance cues, and the first appearance of work on phrasing and dynamics.

Attention returned to memorization in Sessions 14 to 16 with a new intensity as practice focused on features that serve as memory-retrieval cues: the basic and interpretive performance cues and the boundaries and switches of the formal structure. This was the first time that work on all these dimensions involved in playing from memory occurred in the same set of practice sessions. It pointed the way to the memorization that was to occur in Session 17. Gabriela was getting ready to play without the score.

STAGE 4: PUTTING IT TOGETHER (SESSION 17)

In Session 17, Gabriela learned to play the *Presto* from memory. As befits a session in which the main goal was to play straight through the music, the average length of runs, 79 bars, was longer than in any other set of sessions. The only effects that reflect the concern with memory were those of the performance cues that had also marked the previous stage. Basic and interpretive performance cues were both worked on, and the basic performance cues continued to interrupt runs.

By the end of the session, Gabriela had played through the entire piece fluently from memory five times. Much more practice at playing from memory was still needed, but the *Presto* had been put together and memorized and was ready for polishing.

STAGE 5: POLISHING

Preparing for the First Performance (Sessions 18–24)

There were two new features of practice at this time: the use of slow practice and playing for practice audiences. Slow practice checks and strengthens conceptual memory by lessening the contribution of motor memory. Practice audiences provide an opportunity to check the operation of performance cues under conditions closer to those of the recital hall.

These activities point to one of the main goals of polishing—the selection of expressive cues to attend to during performance. Expressive cues were avoided as stopping places—a form of practice in context—at the same time that almost every other dimension was receiving attention. Slow practice was part of this process of reorganization too, allowing time to think about both the higher level expressive cues and the lower level cues and features at the same time, forging links between them. Two of the dimensions reworked as part of this process were fingering, which had not been worked on since the end of Period 1 and bars containing more familiar patterns, which had not been worked on since Sessions 1 to 6. It seems likely, however, that the reorganization of the retrieval hierarchy was not completed in time for the first performance. One indication of this is that Gabriela felt it necessary to have the score open during the performance. Another is that the description of the piece at the end of Session 24 focused mostly on interpretation rather than on expression suggesting that during the first performance Gabriela was attending more to interpretive than expressive performance cues.

Another aspect of polishing is refining the interpretation, which was going on at the same time. Part of this is checking and adjusting the overall shape of the piece, making sure that the different sections are in balance with one another. This was reflected in the attention to interpretive and expressive cues already mentioned, but also in attention to the formal structure. The latter is apparent in the renewed work on the beginnings of sections—another thing that had not happened since Period 1. Another part of refining the interpretation was revisiting established interpretive features and adding new ones. There was work on phrasings for the first time since Session 13, and dynamics and pedaling both received practice in context. The addition of new interpretive refinements is evident in the comments, for example, about a polyphonic theme: "It's kind of fun to bring out . . . really scrumptious."

A final goal of polishing is building up confidence for trouble spots. For this reason, technical difficulties were not reworked, but avoided as much as possible. This spared Gabriela's injured hand and avoided unnecessary mistakes, which the injury might have introduced at this critical stage. Despite her confidence-building tactics, Gabriela was not at all sure that the piece was really ready. She decided to perform with the score open as insurance in case things went drastically wrong—something she rarely does. Yet the chance to try out the *Italian Concerto* in concert was too good to miss. The setting was informal, the audience small, and the injury to her hand required something less punishing than the *Bach/Busoni Chaconne* originally programmed. The performance went off uneventfully.

Repolishing (Sessions 26–30)

The polishing of the *Presto* began again after a 2-month interval with the beginning of the third learning period. First, the basic dimensions needed review. There was work on fingerings, and runs started at technical difficulties. This relearning was completed in Sessions 26 to 27 and these effects did not reappear. Another thing that needed reviving in Sessions 26 to 27 were the memory cues. Runs were interrupted to repeat basic and interpretive performance cues, and there was attention to the beginnings of sections and switches. Practice of memory cues continued in Sessions 28 to 30 with practice in context for basic performance cues and more work on section beginnings and switches as the switches continued to interrupt runs.

Practice did not immediately return to the long runs and practice performances of Sessions 20 to 24. The length of runs dropped sharply at the beginning of Period 3 and only returned to its former level in Sessions 31 to 44. In the intervening sessions, runs were shorter as practice focused on the further honing of interpretation. Gabriela was, ". . . making some more musical decisions. . . . There are a few themes I want to bring up." She wanted it to be, "exciting and very full of stuff"—a "stereo effect" here, "bring out the left hand" there. These goals are reflected in the practice of all four interpretive dimensions in Sessions 26 to 27—the first time this had happened. Work on phrasing, dynamics, and pedaling developed the motor skills needed to bring out the themes and voices, while practice in context of dynamic and tempo features during runs integrated the new skills with their surrounding context.

As she put the final touches on her interpretation in Sessions 28 to 30, Gabriela continued to distil a set of expressive cues from the larger set of interpretive cues. This was reflected in the repetition of expressive performance cues during runs, which provided opportunities to evaluate expressive goals and link them to the interpretive performance cues on which they were based. Evidence that this process of distillation and reorganization was completed by the end of the learning process came from recall of the piece more than 2 years later. At this time, expressive cues, along with section boundaries, organized the piece in Gabriela's memory. It seems likely that the expressive cues were in place by the end of Session 31 because it was here that Gabriela reported the expressive cues for Section C.

Increasing the Tempo (Sessions 31–44)

The learning process might have concluded at this point, but Gabriela was still not satisfied. The piece still needed more excitement, more energy. At the beginning of Session 31, she announced the intention to play it "even faster." The new tempo created a "wild chitter-chatter. A different music, like a hidden polyphony, that if you play a bit slower you don't hear." To bring out voices and syncopations, new dynamic features and pedalings were added, both requiring practice in context.

First, Gabriela let it "adjust by itself." Yet for some passages, notably the fugue in Section D, this was not enough. Movements had to be simplified and the number of performance cues reduced. This was done with the help of the metronome and slow practice. Repeatedly the tempo was slowed and then systematically speeded up, a step at a time, until the new target tempo was surpassed. During this process, runs were interrupted at fingerings, and renewed work was needed on technical difficulties, both types of practice not seen for a long time. The simplification of movements had reduced the automaticity of motor memory so that renewed practice was needed to reinstate the patterns. To reduce the number of retrieval cues, increasing reliance was placed on beginnings of sections and interpretive performance cues, which both needed work as a result. Retrieval from long-term memory was still often not fast enough, resulting in the disruption of runs at these locations and at switches, the other type of retrieval cue whose operation was critical.

STAGE 6: MAINTENANCE (SESSIONS 45–57)

The long task of increasing the tempo was finally completed in Session 44. From now on, it was a matter of "just basically [running] once or twice through everything." In the 2 weeks remaining before the recording session, the piece was honed by regular run throughs. To avoid getting stale from overpractice, however, these runs were limited to once or twice through the piece.

ELEVEN

CODA

Roger Chaffin, Mary Crawford, and Gabriela Imreh

T he three of us started this project with different goals. Gabriela wanted to gain understanding of her memorization process—to know in a more systematic way what works for her—to make her practice more efficient and rewarding. She also wanted to use our results to help other pianists, both students and professional concert artists. Roger hoped to extend the scientific literature on expert memory to a new and interesting domain and identify characteristics of expert practice. Mary shared their goals and also hoped to examine the process of interdisciplinary collaboration by using Gabriela's and Roger's research as a case study. In this concluding chapter, we assess how well we met all these goals. We first address Gabriela's and Roger's goals by summarizing what we learned about memory, performance, and piano practice. We then address the lessons learned from our attempt to work together despite differences in epistemological viewpoints, domains of expertise, and social positions. Finally, each of us speaks briefly about how we were changed by participating in this research.

WHAT DID WE LEARN ABOUT MEMORY
AND PERFORMANCE?

When we began, our goal was to see whether principles of expert memory developed through the study of other kinds of expertise would apply to the memorization of a concert pianist. Because these principles were developed in domains like chess, in which motor memory and aesthetic considerations are minimal, we did not know how well they would apply to piano performance. Our conclusion is that they do apply extremely well. They also provide the key to the second question we wanted to answer: What does a pianist think about while performing? Our answers to these two questions turn out to be closely related. During a performance, Gabriela thinks about memory cues that have been carefully selected to enhance her expressive goals. She trains herself so that the cues she needs are available rapidly and reliably. Some of the retrieval cues represent the structure of the music, and others are performance cues representing decisions about how the piece should be performed. The hierarchical structure of the music organizes these cues, with section boundaries, switches, and performance cues making up the lower levels of the retrieval hierarchy.

With a fast piece like the *Presto*, prolonged practice is needed to make the operation of retrieval cues rapid enough to keep up with the pace of performance. Like other expert memorists (Ericsson & Kintsch, 1995), this pianist engaged in extended practice to make retrieval fully automatic.[1] Use of a retrieval organization allows the performer to recall the piece to mind and hand as the performance unfolds and to keep track of the current location in the overall structure of the music. The performer's conceptual representation of the piece provides reassurance that recovery is possible if a wrong turn is taken at a switch or if there is some other major disruption to the performance. It also makes possible spontaneous, improvisational adjustments during the course of a performance without destroying the carefully balanced relationships among the various sections of the piece. By keeping the overall structure clearly in mind, a change in one section can be carried through to similar sections or balanced by appropriate changes in contrasting sections.

The Formal Structure Acts as a Memory-Retrieval Scheme

Expert pianists use the formal structure of the music to divide it into sections for practice. During the practice-by-sections stage, Gabriela worked through the piece a few sections at a time, dividing it into sections on the basis of the formal structure. Boundaries in the formal structure were used as starting places for practice segments. Starting repeatedly at a particular spot establishes it as a retrieval cue so that later the pianist is able to start playing at that spot simply by summoning it to mind. We were able to see the effects of this when Gabriela recalled the score two years later. Because the beginnings of sections were used as retrieval cues, they were remembered better.

Gabriela's attention to the formal structure was also evident in comments that identified boundaries between sections—for example, "[I] probably hit another repeat of the main theme" (Session 2). She also noted the need to make a deliberate point of not starting at section boundaries. "Eventually I do break away from [starting at boundaries . . . . in order] not to have cuts in my memory..." (Session 12).

Do other expert pianists use the formal structure to organize practice in the same way? Clearly they do. The pianist studied by Miklaszewski (1989) divided up the piece for practice into sections that were reportedly based on the formal structure, as did the student pianists studied by Aaron Williamon (1999; Williamon & Valentine, 2000, 2002). Direct observational evidence from the practice of other concert pianists is lacking, but several of the pianists in chapter 3 mentioned using the musical structure to memorize. Alicia de Larrocha finds memory more reliable for the form than for the rhythm; Edwin Hughes recommends memorizing the form right from the start; Benno Moiseiwitsch and Olga Samaroff recommend memorizing by sections. Moriz Rosenthal recommends understanding the structure first away from the piano. Maurice Dumesnil appears to be referring to what we have called switches when he says that he memorizes "a few flag-posts" that include "the variance between repeats one and two in the classical sonata." With a little reading between the lines, several others who do not explicitly mention structure can be added to the list. Surely the mental practice recommended by John Browning and Walter Gieseking involves attention to structure and, likewise, the memorizing of musical progressions that Vladimir Ashkenazy prefers.

What of those whose accounts seem to suggest that conceptual memory plays no part—who, like Jorge Bolet and Rudolf Firkusny, claim that their memories are "almost one hundred percent aural" or who, like Ernest Hutcheson and Mitja Nikisch, trust "unconscious memory"? We believe that if these pianists had been asked whether they could describe the formal structure of the pieces they were playing, they would reply, "Of course!" This is what Rita Aiello (2000a) found when she interviewed seven concert pianists about how they memorized.[2] Williamon (1999) reached a similar conclusion when he asked two professional pianists to learn two pieces and then describe the aspects they focused on while performing. Just because some of the pianists in chapter 3 did not mention memorizing form does not mean that they do not do so. Many reported studying the formal structure of pieces they were learning, but appeared not to think of this as memorization. Others, like Abbey Simon, simply preferred not to think about how they memorize.

The Performer Thinks About Performance Cues

What an artist thinks about affects the aesthetic impact of the performance on the audience. Ideally, the performer wants to be thinking about expressive goals for the piece. To focus attention on expression, the performer needs to practice thinking about these goals during practice so that they spring readily to mind during the performance. Not to prepare in this way is to risk the possibility that distractions will intrude. With the adrenaline induced hyperalertness that generally occurs on stage, there are too many opportunities for distraction: coughs and rustles in the audience, idiosyncrasies of the instrument, anticipation of problems and difficulties in the music.

Even when an artist plans to rely on the inspiration of the moment—as Gabriela did to a large extent with the other piece whose practice we recorded, *Clair de Lune*—spontaneity must be prepared. The mind must be trained to attend to the performance cues that elicit the looked-for inspiration. Some degree of improvisation is important even in a piece as highly prepared as the *Presto*. It rapidly becomes boring to perform a piece in exactly the same way every time, so the artist adds little subtleties to make each performance more interesting and original. For these nuances of interpretation to enhance the expressive impact of the piece, the performer has to have its expressive shape clearly in mind. This requires that expressive performance cues come to mind automatically and reliably.

The idea of performance cues developed gradually. The germ of the idea came from Gabriela's conversation with her teacher, Harald Wagner, about how to prepare for her debut in the United States (chap. 3). They talked of the weeks immediately before an important performance as a time to remap thinking, reworking every detail to focus on the artistic and inspirational elements of the music so as to enter a trancelike state in which worries and details could be put in the background and the performance could be governed by artistic goals. Later, when Roger came to talk to Gabriela's students about the psychology of memory, his description of retrieval cues and how they could be organized into hierarchies to improve recall connected with these earlier ideas (chap. 2). We started to talk about the process as one of rechunking—overlaying lower level retrieval cues used in the earlier stages of practice with new, higher level cues. As she learned the *Presto*, Gabriela described the retrieval cues she was using on three occasions (Sessions 12, 17, and 24). The next step came when Gabriela sat down and put this information onto a copy of the score (after Session 31). She divided her retrieval cues into three performance dimensions, giving tangible shape to ideas that she had been mulling over for a long time. From there it was a simple step to identifying performance cues with the psychological concept of retrieval cues and the remapping of Harald Wagner's prescription with the extended practice of retrieval cues used by other kinds of expert memorists.

According to Gabriela, performance cues are selected and practiced during the polishing stage. So it was with some surprise and consternation that Roger discovered, as he ran the regression analyses on the initial practice sessions, that the performance cues had been singled out for special attention right from the start. As reported in chapter 8, Gabriela was delighted because it suggested that her interpretation had begun with the overall musical shape of the piece rather than evolving in a more piecemeal fashion. True, but it also suggested that Gabriela was wrong when she said that she rechunked things, training herself to use different, higher level retrieval cues in performance than she did in practice. Was she wrong when she said that "the artistic, inspirational elements" of a piece were emphasized in the final weeks before a performance? If Gabriela started focusing on performance cues much earlier, what is to be made of this claim? It took us a long time to reconcile the apparent conflict between the pianist's account of what she did and what we were able to extract from the practice records.

As Gabriela recognized with such delight when she first heard about the regression results, the effects of performance cues in the early practice sessions show that the detailed, practical decisions about fingering, dynamics, phrasing, and pedaling were being determined by larger musical goals that later became performance cues. But this early identification of performance cues was necessarily tentative. The operation of performance cues is a delicate and complicated process that cannot be fully anticipated even by an expert. Cues must be tested at performance tempo and in the context of the whole piece to see what works and what does not. Some of the features identified early on as likely problems for performance turn out not to be problems after all and are not needed as performance cues. Others must be rechunked and subsumed under a higher level feature to reduce performance cues to a manageable number.

Sometimes rechunking is simply a matter of "wrapping" a lower level, basic feature inside an interpretive or expressive cue. By giving an expressive gloss to a difficulty the pianist is able to prevent the problem from interrupting the emotional flow of the music. The lower level detail is rechunked, becoming part of an interpretive or expressive goal. This is what was happening during polishing for the first performance. In these sessions, the renewed effects of the basic and interpretive dimensions bear witness that the remapping process involved "reworking every detail." At the same time, effects of structure, interpretive performance cues, and expressive cues support the idea that the lower level features were being linked to these higher level cues in the retrieval hierarchy.

On other occasions, rechunking is needed to eliminate cues. This happened after the decision to increase the tempo in Session 31 required a major reorganization of cues for the fugue (Section D). First Gabriela tried to let it "adjust by itself," simply dropping or merging adjacent cues, but this was not enough. A more radical realignment was needed. Gabriela described it as "miserable work" as she started at slow speeds, playing the same sections over and over at steadily increasing tempi to establish a new set of performance cues.

Although use of performance cues begins early on, rechunking does not become a major focus of practice until the pianist is ready to polish the piece. It is this winnowing, in the final approach to a performance, that Gabriela had in mind when she said that polishing involved practicing performance cues. This is when the expressive performance cues must be practiced repeatedly until they automatically elicit all the other, lower level cues. Letting go of the lower level cues allows the artist to achieve the trancelike state of focused attention associated with optimal performance. At the same time, the lower level cues must still be available in case something goes wrong. In this case, the expressive cue may not be sufficient and a basic or interpretive performance cue is needed to keep things on track.

When a piece is first memorized, its performance is controlled primarily through the basic performance cues. As performance becomes more polished, these become wrapped in and subsumed by interpretive performance cues. Finally, control is transferred to expressive cues. We can see this process in the three successive descriptions that Gabriela gave of what she was paying attention to as she played. The "map of the piece" given at the end of Session 17 was primarily a list of basic cues and switches. By the time the piece was ready for performance at the end of Session 24, the much longer and more detailed description of "what I am working on" consisted primarily of interpretive performance cues. However, it is significant that almost no expressive cues were mentioned. The piece was not quite ready. Although Gabriela was going to perform it for the first time the next day, the final step of distilling a small set of expressive cues out of the larger mass of interpretive performance cues was not yet complete. This is not to say that the first performance was not expressive. A lot of expression was built into the basic and interpretive cues and the motor memories they controlled. But expression was not yet at the top level of the retrieval hierarchy. It was not the focus of Gabriela's attention as she performed.

What she was surely thinking about during that first performance were the cues that she had listed the day before in Session 24. Here they are for Section C.

> I'm trying to bring out, in 77 [start of Ca], the C's and F in left hand at the beginning of each bar. And I'm still trying to do a fairly aggressive [ending to the Ca sections . . . PLAYS], just in left hand. And then I return to very lightly pianissimo [at the beginning of the second Ca section]. And again, just the left hand B-flat (accented), and then I return to pianissimo [in bar 85, the beginning of Cb]. . . . And that gives me again room for a nice crescendo in 86 and on.

There is little mention of expression here. Even *aggressive* seems to be more about the technicality of ending a phrase with an emphasis than about expressing aggression.

The expressive goals behind these interpretive effects were not articulated until six practice sessions later, after session 31, when Gabriela listed the expressive cues she was using for Section C. In this report, the "C's and F in the left hand at the beginning of each bar" are transmuted into "Light but mysterious." The "fairly aggressive ending" becomes "Surprise." The "return to very lightly pianissimo" becomes "Hold back." The "return to pianissimo [giving] room for a nice crescendo" becomes "Start building crescendo" followed by "No holding back." We see here, in the pianist's own words, the process of rechunking. Between Sessions 17 and 24, basic performance cues were folded into interpretive performance cues. Between Sessions 24 and 32, interpretive performance cues were subsumed under expressive cues.

When a piece is fully polished, the pianist plays with expressive cues in the spotlight, getting the full focus of attention every time. During final polishing, rechunking establishes expressive cues at the top of the tangled hierarchy of retrieval cues. Activating the conceptual memory for a cue like, *surprise* or *hold back* in working memory elicits an echo of the corresponding feelings in the pianist, as well as the full set of motor responses required to put it into effect. At the same time, the levels of the hierarchy immediately above (the sections and switches of the formal structure) and below (the interpretive performance cues) form a penumbra on the fringes of awareness ready to be called on when needed. For example, if the expressive cue *surprise* in Section C of the *Presto* is not sufficient, then thinking of the dynamic emphasis on the A, which introduces this passage, should accomplish the same end. In an ideal performance, only the top levels are called on, but ideal performances are not the norm, and the pianist is preparing for the worst. Even on a bad day, when the pianist has to struggle with the piece, if the basic and interpretive performance cues are doing their job, the notes are there and the audience has no inkling of the struggle that lies behind it. This is the art and skill of performance.

So the answer to our first question about how a concert pianist memorizes is that she practices using performance cues as retrieval cues until they function rapidly and reliably. Their operation must be so sure that they not only guarantee note-perfect performance, but also permit recovery from distractions and mistakes. The answer to our second question is the same. What the pianist thinks about during performance is carefully selected and practiced retrieval cues that produce a reliable and expressive performance.

We hope that by drawing attention to this aspect of the preparation for performance and describing in detail how it works, we can help pianists improve their own playing for audiences. For our readers who are pianists, we suggest that you reflect on your own use of performance cues. Every musician uses them. It is just a matter of whether the selection is more or less deliberate and more or less well prepared. By describing and naming them, we hope to help pianists attend to their importance and help teachers better convey to their students the steps needed to prepare fully for playing in public.

WHAT ARE THE CHARACTERISTICS OF EFFECTIVE PRACTICE?

Are some forms of practice more effective than others? It seems likely that high levels of ability in any field are due, at least in part, to the use of strategies that make the most of time spent in practice. Observing the practice of an accomplished artist provided an opportunity to identify characteristics that might have contributed to her high level of skill. We observed the same characteristics of expert practice found in earlier studies of experienced pianists (chap. 5) and identified others that were not so evident in earlier studies. We begin with the latter.

The "Rage to Master"

One feature of Gabriela's practice that undoubtedly contributed to its effectiveness was the concentration with which she worked. On the videotapes, she appears to be totally absorbed in what she is doing. The pace is unrelenting. One practice segment follows another without pause. The only breaks that occur with any regularity are to talk to the camera, and often she scarcely stops for that. In the early sessions, the fast tempo creates an impression of frenzied activity. Practice segments are continually interrupted to correct fingerings with such speed that we did not even try to record these rapid-fire corrections, adopting instead the stutter-rule (chap. 6) to exclude them from our practice records. When asked why she had played so fast in these early sessions, Gabriela responded,

> I probably played faster than I should have. I am impatient and I probably make it harder for myself, but when I start on a new piece, I have such an appetite to take hold of it and make it mine.

This is what Ellen Winner (1996b) called the *rage to master*.[3] It produces a concentrated absorption in the learning process that has been characterized as *flow* by Csikszentmihalyi and Csikszentmihalyi (1988). Flow is characteristic of creative engagement, generally occurring when people are working, like Gabriela, on challenging, self-assigned tasks that they are highly motivated to accomplish (Custodero, 2000). This "appetite to take hold" is behind many features of Gabriela's practice: intensity of concentration, willingness to work long hours, focus on goals, continuous monitoring and evaluation of progress, varied use of practice strategies, and division of practice into work and runs. We say a little about each characteristic in turn.

Concentration

In an attempt to capture something of the focused intensity of Gabriela's practice, we measured the rate of practice and the ratio between this rate and the average tempo of the session, looking for a quantitative measure of the intensity of effort that was evident on the videotapes. Contrary to our initial expectations, we had to conclude that intense concentration was reflected in low rates of practice and low rate/tempo ratios rather than by high values (chap. 6). Intense problem solving requires a lot of thought, and thinking takes time. For the challenging *Presto*, the rate/tempo ratio was an astonishing one third. Gabriela spent most of her practice time playing below the target tempo of the moment. The slower tempi, pauses, and hesitations allowed time for her to think about and control what she was doing. Two thirds of practice time was taken up with this kind of thinking. Effortful indeed!

We cannot know for sure whether the low rate/practice ratios that we found for Gabriela's practice are a general characteristic of effective practice and high task involvement. We need a comparison with the practice of less skilled and less motivated musicians. One example is James Renwick and Gary McPherson's (2000) study of student practice. As part of a longitudinal study of musical development, nine students involved in a primary school band program videotaped their practice sessions periodically over several years. One young girl, a clarinetist, spent most of her practice on task, simply playing through one piece after another, not noticing mistakes and not stopping to repeat anything. This style of practice would be reflected in a high rate/practice ratio. Then one day during a lesson, her teacher played a jazz piece for her that caught her interest. The difference in the next practice session was dramatic. She struggled with the new piece, playing the same short passage over and over. In between repetitions, she sat staring at the music, trying to figure out how to reproduce the sounds she had heard. Far more time was taken up with thinking than with playing. The rate/tempo ratio for this session would have been even lower than Gabriela's. The student clarinetist—first dutiful but uninvolved, then actively engaged in her music making—shows us that stopping to think (and its resulting low rate/tempo ratios) might be a general characteristic of effortful, rage-to-master practice.

Adapting the rate/tempo ratio for use with student musicians is not straightforward. Most of McPherson and Renwick's students spent a considerable amount of time off task (McPherson & Renwick, 2000). In one sad instance, a trumpet student spent more time urging his mother that it was time to stop than he did practicing. In cases like this, higher rates of practice obviously reflect more effort, rather than less. Only when the student is on task, like the clarinetist, do lower rate/tempo ratios reflect greater effort. However, with suitable boundary conditions, the rate/tempo ratio should provide researchers with a useful measure of the effortfulness of practice and may provide a way to identify the rage to master and flow that appear to characterize effective practice.

Goal Setting

Approaching a new piece with an "appetite to take hold"of the music transforms a difficult and time-consuming chore into a triumphal progress to a beautiful, exciting, and perfect performance. Problems and difficulties become stepping stones to this goal rather than obstacles. Gabriela's learning of *Clair de Lune* in just 4 hours shows us how short the road to mastery can be, whereas the *Presto* shows us just how long it can be on other occasions.

Whether the road was long or short, the pianist remained on target, continually setting up subgoals that would bring her closer to where she wanted to be. "I am going to go back to the first page or two and get them really good" (Session 9). For example, the initial goals were to identify familiar patterns, decide on fingerings, solve technical difficulties, and map out the formal structure. These goals were reflected in many comments during the section-by-section stage (chap. 7) as well as the effects on practice in the regression analyses of same sessions (chap. 8).

"Just trying to see if the fingerings match together." (Session 1)

"It's really a logistic[al] problem here . . . the hands get too close." (Session 2)

"Tiny changes [in a theme] are sometimes the worst." (Session 2)

We might expect to see some decrease in problem solving during polishing. Surely the pianist could relax a little and enjoy her hard-earned accomplishment. This is not what seemed to happen. Instead, Gabriela kept looking for problems. "I'm running through my program, fixing little things . . ." (Session 43). Work continued to be a significant part of practice even during the final polishing, accounting for 5% of practice during Sessions 31 to 44. Only when polishing was finally completed did Gabriela stop looking for problems. Then she called it *maintenance*, not *practice*, and did not consider it worth recording for our study.

Evaluation

Just as important as setting goals is evaluating how well they are met. Gabriela did this continually, assessing every aspect of her playing as well as the effectiveness of the learning strategies she was using. Most of her comments about basic, interpretive, and performance issues involved evaluation on the dimension in question:

"This is a terribly big extension." (Session 2)

"My finger gets stuck. That part is so hard to hold those notes." (Session 13)

"I would say that's an excellent tempo." (Session 31)

Other evaluative comments were not directed at a particular dimension, but expressed a more general satisfaction or dissatisfaction.

"Not too bad. . . . " (Session 17)

"That's about a million times better. . . . " (Session 20)

These nonspecific evaluative comments were more frequent than any other single category, accounting for 38% of the total. Evaluation was all pervasive. To improve, one must know what needs to be changed, and Gabriela had no shortage of ideas.

Practice Strategies

Expert musicians have a wide range of practice strategies and use them flexibly (Chapter 5). This was certainly true of Gabriela's practice. She used a variety of strategies, dealing with everything from the selection of fingerings, to the scheduling of practice sessions, to the management of her own physical and mental state. Effective strategies make practice more efficient. The range and subtlety of the strategies Gabriela used in her practice were undoubtedly important in attaining the level of artistry evident in the CD performance of the *Presto*.

We already mentioned two important examples: the use of the formal structure to organize practice and practice of performance cues. Other strategies are evident in the effects of different types of complexity on practice. For example, early work on fingering was the result of the general strategy of making these decisions at the outset: "I have to find a good fingering" (Session 1).

The care taken with fingerings was part of a larger strategy of never doing anything that would interfere with later learning or that would have to be unlearned. For example, whenever she used the wrong fingering, Gabriela would immediately correct it. A second example was Gabriela's unwillingness to play the *Presto* from memory when she was asked to do so 2 years later. She knew that the wrong notes she would inevitably play would interfere when she came to relearn the piece.

Other strategies minimized the amount of playing required to achieve a goal. For example, memory retrieval was sometimes practiced by running up to a retrieval cue and stopping. Gabriela also described using a kind of "Reader's Digest" review before a performance, running through the piece starting at each retrieval cue and playing just a few notes (chap. 9).

The most direct and detailed evidence of the use of strategies comes from comments made during practice. Strategies of many different sorts lay behind the many decisions about basic and interpretive features and performance cues (chaps. 7 and 9). The comments often mentioned the strategy involved in making these decisions. Other strategies involved the fine-grained division of the music into segments for practice and identification of goals for each practice session.

Scheduling Practice

Gabriela's scheduling strategies began with the decision to start learning the *Presto* 10 months before the targeted performance date, allowing time to relearn it twice. (In contrast, practice of the much easier *Claire de Lune* began only 6 weeks before the targeted performance date.) The spacing of practice sessions changed over the course of the learning process. In scheduling sessions during Periods 1 and 2, Gabriela tried hard to practice on consecutive days to minimize the opportunity for forgetting between sessions and bemoaned the demands on her time that made it impossible to do so. During the third period, in contrast, sessions were more spread out and the learning period was longer.

Monitoring Energy Levels

The concentrated attention required for effective practice takes a lot of energy. Monitoring energy levels and stopping when efficiency decreases may be another characteristic of expert practice. Gabriela was careful to see that she had the energy she needed. When she got too tired, she stopped even if it was not convenient. For example, in Session 4, she stopped reluctantly, loathe to give up on completing section-by-section work on the whole piece. After noting that she was too tired, she carried on for another 15 minutes, but eventually stopped without reaching her goal.

Work and Runs

Another feature of practice that stems from the desire to master the piece in the shortest possible time is its division into work (to solve a problem) followed by runs (to evaluate the effectiveness of the solution). Miklaszewski (1989) found this same pattern in the pianist he studied. The pianist identifies a problem and works on finding a solution. Then the solution is tested in a longer run. If it is satisfactory, the pianist moves on. If not, more work ensues. Repeating short segments allows the pianist to focus on the specific problem to be addressed with a minimum of distraction.

We initially distinguished between work and runs because Gabriela felt that was how she organized her practice. The record bears this out, showing practice organized into blocks of work separated by runs. The fact that this pattern continued throughout the learning process strengthens the idea that it is essential. Even during final polishing, when the average run segment covered a quarter or more of the entire piece, the length of work segments remained remarkably constant at 3 to 5 bars in length. Work segments lengthened slightly only in sessions where the focus was on playing from memory, when the average length increased to 6 to 9 bars.

Do other pianists organize their practice into work and runs in the same way? Again, we suspect so. We already mentioned that Miklaszewski (1989, 1995) found this type of organization in the experienced pianists he studied. Even relatively inexperienced pianists appear to organize their practice in this way (Williamon, 1999, Appendix C).[4] It seems that this aspect of effective practice is learned early on. The ability to focus work on specific problems may, however, continue to develop with experience.

Use of the Formal Structure

Use of the formal structure may be another characteristic of effective practice. We have already discussed Gabriela's reliance on this structure as a retrieval scheme. Using structural boundaries as starting places is an essential part of this strategy because it establishes structural features as retrieval cues.

Students are taught to use the formal structure to divide up a piece for practice, and they appear to master this fairly early. Aaron Williamon found that students at all levels of training used this strategy, although their divisions did not always correspond exactly with the formal structure of the piece (Williamon, 1999; Williamon & Valentine, 2002). If using structural boundaries as starting points is effective, then students who do it more should perform better than those who do it less. This is exactly what Williamon and Valentine found. Students who used this strategy gave better performances. Why? Because starting at boundaries established them as retrieval cues to be attended to during performance. Because the composers' expressive intentions are encoded in the musical structure, directing attention to structural features makes the performance more expressive. This is the idea behind the concept of performance cues—that it matters what a pianist thinks about during performance.

Anticipation of Future Goals

Experts have the ability to anticipate future developments. Chess masters playing lightning chess anticipate developments much later in the game even though they cannot be thinking more than a few moves ahead (Gobet & Simon, 1996b). Previous experience allows them to recognize the similarity of the current situation to previous games, and to make good choices on this basis without explicitly thinking through the consequences. Similarly, when a musician encounters a new piece of music, experience with similar pieces provides a useful guide to interpretation and expression even though initial decisions cannot be fully evaluated until later.

The ability to anticipate future decisions is particularly important in selecting fingerings because relearning a fingering is so much more difficult than learning it in the first place. This is why fingerings for students are dictated by editors and teachers. Experienced pianists, however, typically make their own decisions, choosing fingerings suited to the physical characteristics of their own hands and training.

More than other features of expert practice, anticipation of interpretive decisions may be a strategy that students cannot adopt deliberately. Most students have more than enough to do when they first encounter a piece just identifying familiar patterns, selecting fingerings, and coping with technical difficulties (Hallam, 1997b). The ability to anticipate aesthetic goals depends on prior experience. There may be no substitute for long years of exposure to the repertoire.

WHAT DID WE LEARN ABOUT INTERDISCIPLINARY COLLABORATION?

As described in chapter 2, there were many differences among the participants in this project. We differed in the weight we were prepared to give to scientific explanations, in our views of the importance of talent versus practice in artistic expertise, in the vested interests we brought to the research, and even in our basic epistemological assumptions. We all expected that these differences would affect our collaboration, creating difficulties and misunderstandings, but we could not foresee exactly how these problems would arise.

The difference we were perhaps most aware of was that the norms of psychological research positioned Gabriela as a subject rather than an active agent in the research. We all worked hard throughout the project to minimize the implicit power hierarchy brought about by Roger and Mary's status as psychologists and experts on behavior. We wanted Gabriela's own understanding of her expertise to have equal weight with our outsiders' account. To that end, we determined the order of authorship on this book at the start, and we attempted to integrate the first-person accounts of Gabriela and the other pianists in chapter 3 with the third-person account provided by Roger. Yet even after nearly a decade of working together, the differing social positions of the three collaborators sometimes affected the project and our relationships with each other.

An example occurred when Roger applied for an internal grant from his university to extend the research. He and Gabriela agreed that the budget would include a small fee to be paid to Gabriela as an expert subject. The fee seemed a suitable way to mark the difference in the potential rewards that spending time on the research might bring to each of them. As described in chapter 2, for Roger the rewards include publications, increased professional status, and grants. In contrast, time involved in research for Gabriela is time away from the activities that will increase her professional status—performing and marketing her skills. When the grant was received, however, Gabriela decided that on further reflection selling her practice in this way was demeaning and declined the fee. During this process, there was considerable misunderstanding of each other's positions, and Mary's attempts to mediate were largely unsuccessful. Looking back on it, we believe that this conflict came about because our project did not fit the norms for psychological research, with their clear hierarchy between the expert experimenter and the compliant, naive subject. We had no normative way to represent in the structure of our project the equal collaboration we all desired.

In contrast, the differing epistemological perspectives brought to the project by Roger and Mary did not become cause for conflict. Throughout the project, empiricism reigned, as Roger developed his quantitative analyses of Gabriela's practice and uncovered the various relationships between them. Mary's social constructionist perspective had some impact, as Gabriela and Roger were encouraged to reflect on their involvement in the project, what it meant to each of them, and how it changed them. The project—and this book—are no doubt a great deal more self-reflexive than they would have been without this influence. However, there remain important aspects of the social and historical framework of this research project that have been kept in the background. What will be the fate of playing serious music from memory—indeed of playing it at all—in a digital and synthesized era when classical music makes up less than 2% of music sales? Are we studying a dying art? Are the loss of privacy and artistic mystique for the performer, described by Gabriela in chapter 3, related to this decline? Questions like these form part of the social context of our research, but have not been integrated into our analysis.

One effect of our interdisciplinary collaboration has been to problematize the idea of musical genius. By showing in greater detail than ever before just how an outstanding musical performance is created, we have opened up the construct of talent for a new kind of examination. The view that extraordinary musical abilities only depend on some special, inborn genius is harder to maintain when we see just how much work goes into the preparation and honing of those skills, even for someone whose talents have been recognized since childhood and who has been developing her skills ever since. On the one hand, Gabriela performed *Clair de Lune* from memory after less than 5 hours of practice—the kind of feat that seems to support the idea of musical skill as a God-given gift that arises spontaneously without effort. On the other hand, it took 33 hours to bring the *Presto* to the perfection of the recorded performance. At 11 hours of practice for each minute of performance, this is work by any reckoning. Practice is essential, even for the very talented, even after a lifetime devoted to practice and playing.

Of course, this does not mean that talent is unimportant. We are divided on the issue. Gabriela, the musician, is convinced from her own experience as a pianist and teacher that talent is essential. When she meets a new student for the first time, she feels that she can usually tell the student's potential very quickly. Hard work, good teaching, and determination are necessary, to be sure, but the student's musical abilities determine the outcome of all the effort. Without the necessary gifts, student and teacher will labor in vain. The mixture is different for each individual, Gabriela maintains. Some have more talent, others more capacity for hard work. The rare individual has both. The two psychologists, Roger and Mary, are less convinced. Clearly the notion of talent is part of an important ideology, shaping people's choices and actions. Its role as a causal factor is less clear. The enormous importance of practice and training leave a lot less for talent to explain than is commonly supposed. To Roger and Mary, it seems more interesting to see how far differences in talent can be explained in terms of differences in motivation and practice skills. Can the effectiveness of a person's practice be modified through the use of better techniques? We do not yet know, but we all believe that we have taken some exciting and useful steps toward answering this question.

Our message is an optimistic one. Gabriela's performance of the *Presto* was not simply the product of unreproducable and unattainable ingredients—talent, genius, and inspiration. It was the product of long hours of hard work, focus on each problem to be solved, and effective use of sophisticated practice strategies. This is good news for those who are not born musicians. Although we may never match Gabriela's technical ability, dexterity, and individuality of interpretation, we can emulate the process by which they were created in improving our own skills.

If we are right in our belief that we have identified some of the general characteristics of expert practice, then future research may find them in the practice of other pianists who perform at the same level as Gabriela and, more generally, in the work of those who achieve eminence in any field. Also, student pianists whose practice has more of these characteristics will be found to progress faster and perform better than students whose practice has fewer of them. Finally, and most important, the same should be true of student pianists who are taught to practice in these ways. We have not demonstrated any of these things here, of course, having just identified key characteristics in the practice of one performer. We describe a program for our own and others' research that may lead to ways of improving the performance of others.

We set out to make the tools of cognitive psychology available to the artist to ask her own questions about how she learned and memorized rather than starting with a set of hypotheses to be tested using the performer as subject. This approach has proved fruitful for us, and we hope it provides a useful model for others. Collaborations between artists and researchers seem to represent a natural alliance (Davidson & Eiholzer, in press). The performers get the opportunity to learn more about what they are doing in practice, developing the metacognitive knowledge that is such a critical part of expertise. The researchers get to study important skills in their natural settings. Each of us feels that we gained something important from the collaboration.

REFLECTIONS: WHAT DID WE LEARN ABOUT OURSELVES?

The Cognitive Psychologist

When we started this research, I had no idea what I was getting into—Gabriela's invitation just seemed like too good an opportunity to ignore. However, the research rapidly took on a life of its own. Colleagues and students alike responded with extraordinary enthusiasm. It seems that everyone relates to the experience of going on stage and performing from memory before an audience. In the meantime, my main line of research on semantic memory has become secondary in the time I devote to it. My amateur but enjoyable practice of playing the flute has been another casualty. I have not played for several years now. However, as this book goes to press, I hope to pick up the flute again. When I do, I will approach it differently. The biggest change is my appreciation of the importance of a good teacher. When I took up the flute about 5 years before starting this research, I felt that any teacher who knew more than I did would be good enough. After seeing Gabriela at work, both as a musician and a teacher, I now see it differently. The teacher is vital. There are many routes from where you, the student, are to where you want to get, but they are not all the same length. Also there are dead ends to be avoided. The better the teacher, the better the chance of reaching the destination and the shorter the route.

More generally, doing this research has made me aware of the difference between practice and play. I am an avid white-water kayaker, paddling the rivers of the Northeastern United States with small groups of other experienced paddlers. Running a white-water river has much in common with musical performance. One must know the danger spots and tricky switches beforehand. Once on the river, moves must often be made rapidly within narrow time windows that grow smaller as the speed of the water increases. In both domains, feedback about a decision is immediate and forceful. A pianist who has lost her place in Rachmaninoff's Third while an entire orchestra roars behind her probably feels a lot like the paddler who has just missed his line [route] in a Class V rapid and is heading down the drop into heaven knows what, improvising and hoping for the best. These days when I am on a river, I notice when I am working (building skills) and when I am just playing around. Mostly, I play, but I have gained an increased appreciation for the importance of practice. Going in and out of a Class III hole a hundred times or rehearsing the Eskimo roll until it is performed automatically despite the adrenaline shock of being upside down in turbulent water are ways of ensuring the reliability of a motor skill for the day when the unexpected happens in performance.

The Social Psychologist

Although my part in this project was relatively small, it has affected my thinking both as a psychologist and an amateur musician. I have long been interested in innovative methods for psychological research (Crawford & Kimmel, 1999; Crawford & Marecek, 1989). Observing Roger and Gabriela develop original ways of conceptualizing their work, obtaining data, and analyzing results has been a unique experience for me. Of course, I have known for a long time that the process of scientific research is much more human, subtle and individualized than textbook accounts would suggest. Still it was fascinating to watch and record an instance of creative collaboration in the production of knowledge by two such different individuals. It is a tribute to both of them that after nearly a decade of working together across differences, our mutual friendship is intact.

As a music lover, I believe that being part of this project has made it easier for me to feel comfortable with my own skill level at the piano. Instead of thinking of myself as stupid or completely untalented when I stumble through a simple piece of music, I remember the thousands of hours of practice required for the development of expertise. I know I will never put in those hours—indeed, like Roger, I virtually stopped playing music as we wrote this book—but I am comforted by the thought that *IF* I decided to put in those thousands of hours and *IF* I developed effective practice strategies, I could probably play pretty well. In a strange way, this allows me to bumble on happily when I do have the rare opportunity to sit down at the piano.

I have also gained increased respect and admiration for the skills—and the temerity—of concert artists who continue to perform live in an electronic era. Because people who listen to classical music now hear most of it in recorded form, technically perfect performances are the norm. This increases the pressure for perfection in live performances. Despite the pressure or perhaps because of it, live performances can have an incomparable excitement. As we were in the last stages of writing this book, I turned on the kitchen radio one morning and recognized the first movement of Rachmaninoff's Piano Concerto #3 in progress. I knew almost immediately that this must be a live performance. There was a vitality—an electric charge of excitement—that could only come from the high-wire act of performing this difficult work in real time, with palpable reactions from an audience. I stopped what I was doing and gave the performance my full attention.[5] When the pianist, Arcadi Volodos, sounded the last notes, the roar of applause was instantaneous. Reflecting on what I had learned from our research project, I felt an increased appreciation of the music and the artist's expertise.

The Pianist

I started this project totally unaware of the ramifications, complexities, and sheer amount of time and work that would be involved. I constantly had to fight the impulse to limit work that took me away from the piano and practice. Once I switched gears and got away from my music, I was excited and stimulated by the beauty of the intellectual challenges and by the possibility of opening new doors and making discoveries (or at least understanding old ideas better). The ideas in this book are the result of endless hours of discussion, brainstorming, somehow converging from the two sides—music and psychology—hopefully getting the best from each.

In the process, I learned to appreciate a different kind of dedication: the serious, meticulous, and sometimes tedious work of setting up an experiment and analyzing data. I was amazed at how much patient work went into those wonderful, long charts of pure, dry data. Beyond all this, the most lasting discovery has been that studying, analyzing, and deciphering data are ultimately just as creative and passionate as music making. It seems to take the same imagination, dedication, and courage.

To my knowledge, this project is the first to examine a professional artist's preparation for performance using methods so scientific and esoteric. Yet it is certainly not the first time that psychology has been used by musicians to help enhance their performance. In the first decade of the 20th century, Sergei Rachmaninoff made the courageous decision to undergo psychotherapy to treat his deep depression, and by all accounts the treatment was successful. Since then, musicians have looked to psychology for help in dealing with anxiety, and the study of performance anxiety has now revolutionized our approach to this dark side of preparing for performance. I hope that our work opens the door to a similar revolution in musicians' approach to memorization and preparation for performance.

Without a doubt, this research helped demystify a complex and touchy subject for me. At times, however, I still have the same reaction that I suspect most musicians would have if they had to constantly face their worst fears: I just want to turn around and run! There is definitely a problem in switching back from theory to practice. For a long time, Roger and I had a standard rule—that we could not talk about the research too close to a performance. I knew that this could interfere with my confidence and focus. Generally this has been a thrilling ride—a wonderful opportunity to learn, discover, and work with such extraordinary scholars and friends.

I do not think our research has changed my playing, but knowing myself better does help. Perhaps it has made me more efficient in practice and more focused. Probably the biggest thing I have learned is that memory is not voodoo. It gives me great confidence to know that there is a scientific basis for what I do. It has helped me develop better strategies and memorize faster. When we began our research, I used to follow the standard path, beginning with motor memory and getting the music into the fingers first. As our research progressed, I noticed that I was pushing the deliberate development of other forms of memory earlier and earlier. I cultivated this, and now I start memory work right away, with the first reading of a new piece. Spending that extra time on all of its different aspects improves and solidifies the memory overall.

I have also developed better ways to test memory. I could see this on a recent tour when I was performing Liszt's *Malediction* for the first time. This is one of the most difficult works written for the piano. It is technically difficult, and the relentless pace makes it hard to memorize. First perform-ances are difficult at the best of times, and this time we had changed the program so that I was playing it 2 months earlier than originally planned. Then I was unable to practice much for over a week because of traveling and the orchestra's rehearsal schedule. Finally, I got terribly sick in the days before the performance. The rehearsal before the performance was a nightmare, with hundreds of waiters running all over the place making a horrendous din, setting up for a banquet. The only thing that got me through that first performance was my preparation. I was so well pre-pared; I could start anywhere in that piece. Any bar! Either hand!

Ten years ago, I could not have done that. I remember reading about Janina Fialkowska's habit of intense mental practice, going through the whole piece the night before. The thought of doing that made me so nervous it gave me the creeps. What if I did not know a note? What if I could not remember it? It would freak me out and completely blast the performance. I did mental practice of course, but just at the level of performance cues, not all the details. Now I can do the details as well. My memory is so secure, I do not have to worry, and I know how to test it, with frequent interruptions—each hand coming in as fast as possible afterward. Sometimes I go through a piece in my mind, getting inside every bar, sometimes with both hands, sometimes with one. I do memory practices before performances where I sit down and look at one hand. Ten years ago, this would have been inconceivable. I would not have dared to try. Now I can do it if I need to for my sense of security, and I do it well.

But I don't do it right before a performance. I still think there is a certain emotional flow that might suffer. In fact, it is possible to overdo the kind of conceptual preparation that we focus on in this book. In preparing the *Malediction* right now, I am avoiding intensive testing of conceptual memory and relying more on motor memory and the flow of the music. I want to see what happens when I take a simpler, more naive approach. I am continually looking for the limits as well as the applications of the knowledge we have compiled.

Together, the three of us hope that our research is a source of increased knowledge and appreciation of music for others. We believe that our account of performance cues, the intimate link between memorization and performance, and the process of interdisciplinary research will be of value not only to researchers, but to performers and pedagogues, and that it will apply not only to pianists, but to other kinds of skilled performers. It is truly collaborative knowledge that could only have come from uniting the insights of an artist about performance with those of a cognitive psycholo-gist about the mechanisms of expert memory. In combining our perspec-tives on performing from memory, we hope to provide a model for others who would like to integrate the experience of musicians with the scientific study of music and the mind.

ENDNOTES

1. Gabriela's learning of *Clair de Lune*, in contrast, gave a somewhat different picture. Because its slower tempo allowed retrieval to occur at a more leisurely pace, the learning process was much briefer and retrieval difficulties disappeared after only two memory runs.

2. However, it may be possible to give a credible performance without being able to articulate the formal structure of a piece. Aiello (2000b) suggested that this was the case for two of the six students she interviewed who could report little about the structure or features of a piece they had learned although they were able to perform it musically.

3. Ellen Winner (1996b) used the term *rage to master* to describe the intense, obsessive involvement of gifted children in the activities in which they show precocity. By extending the term to adult behavior, we are suggesting that the motivational and attentional processes that produce this kind of behavior in children persist in later life.

4. Rather than dividing segments into runs and work, Williamon (1999) used a measure of dispersion that reflects the extent to which the length of practice segments are randomly dispersed around a mean. Greater deviation from a pattern of random dispersion indicates that a pianist is deliberately playing shorter and longer segments. When a pianist is organizing practice into work and runs, higher dispersion values indicate a more marked separation in the length of work and run segments. The dispersion measure may prove to be a useful tool for comparing the practice of different pianists. A limitation of dispersion as a measure of work and runs is, however, that it does not distinguish short practice segments that are part of a run from those that are part of an episode of work.

5. Volodos, Arcadi (2000). *Rachmaninoff: Piano concerto No. 3 + solo piano works*. New York City, Sony Classical, SK 64384.

Appendix 1

Discography for Gabriela Imreh (pianist)

J. S. Bach. New York: Connoisseur Society, CD 4207.

Hungarian Fantasy for Piano and Orchestra. In *Bizet-Shchedrin—Carmen Ballet and Liszt-Spalding—Hungarian Fantasy.* New York: Connoisseur Society, CD 4213.

Soirées de Vienne: Liszt. New York: Connoisseur Society, CD 4225.

Appendix 2

Score of the Italian Concerto (Presto)

C.F. Peters Corporation (1937). *J.S. Bach: Klavierübung II. Teil, Italienishches Konzert, Urtext.* K. Soldan (Ed.), Edition Peters Nr. 4464. Reprinted by permission of C.F. Peters Corporation.

Il Fine

References

Adams, N. (1996). *Piano lessons: Music, love, and true adventure.* New York: Delacourt.

Aiello, R. (1999). Strategies for memorizing piano music: Pedagogical implications. Poster presented at the Eastern Division of the Music Educators National Conference, New York.

Aiello, R. (2000a). Memorizing two piano pieces: The recommendations of concert pianists. In C. Woods, G. Luck, R. Brochard, F. Seddon, & J. A. Sloboda (Eds.), *Proceedings of the sixth international conference on music perception and cognition* [CD]. Keele, UK: Keele University, Department of Psychology.

Aiello, R. (2000b). Playing the piano by heart: From behavior to cognition. Poster presented at the Biological Foundations of Music Conference, The Rockefeller University, NY.

Allard, F., & Starkes, J. L. (1991). Motor-skill experts in sports, dance, and other domains. In K. A. Ericsson & J. Smith (Eds.), *Toward a general theory of expertise: Prospects and limits* (pp. 126–152). Cambridge: Cambridge University Press.

Anderson, J. R. (1983). *The architecture of cognition.* Cambridge, MA: Harvard University Press.

Baars, B. J. (1988). *A cognitive theory of consciousness.* Cambridge: Cambridge University Press.

Baddeley, A. D., Thomson, N., & Buchanan, M. (1975). Word length and the structure of short-term memory. *Journal of Verbal Learning and Verbal Behavior, 14,* 575–589.

Berman, B. (2000). *Notes from the pianist's bench*. New Haven: Yale University Press.

Bernstein, S. (1981). *With your own two hands: Self-discovery through music*. New York: Schirmer.

Bousfield, W. D. (1953). The occurrence of clustering in the recall of randomly arranged associates. *Journal of General Psychology, 49*, 229–240.

Broadbent, D. E., Cooper, P. J., & Broadbent, M. H. (1978). A comparison of hierarchical matrix retrieval schemes in recall. *Journal of Experimental Psychology: Human Learning and Memory, 4*, 486–497.

Bronfenbrenner, U., & Ceci, S. J. (1994). Nature-nurture reconceptualized in developmental perspective: A bioecological model. *Psychological Review, 101*, 568–586.

Brower, H. (1926). *Modern masters of the keyboard*. New York: Frederick A. Stokes Company.

Bryan, W. L., & Harter, N. (1899). Studies on the telegraphic language: The acquisition of a hierarchy of habits. *Psychological Review, 6*, 345–375.

Chaffin, R., & Imreh, G. (1994). Memorizing for piano performance: A case study of a concert pianist. Paper presented at the 3rd Practical Aspects of Memory Conference, University of Maryland, College Park.

Chaffin, R., & Imreh, G. (1996). Effects of musical complexity on expert practice : A case study of a concert pianist. Poster presented at the meeting of the Psychonomic Society, Chicago.

Chaffin, R., & Imreh, G. (1997). "Pulling teeth and torture": Musical memory and problem solving. *Thinking & Reasoning, 3*, 315–336.

Chaffin, R., & Imreh, G. (2001). A comparison of practice and self-report as sources of information about the goals of expert practice. *Psychology of Music, 29*, 39–69.

Chaffin, R., & Imreh, G. (in press). Practicing perfection: Piano performance as expert memory. *Psychological Science*.

Chaffin, R., Imreh, G., de Vries, H., & Taylor, S. (1999). Memory retrieval in a concert pianist. Poster presented at the meeting of the American Psychological Association, Boston, MA.

Chase, W. G., & Ericsson, K. A. (1981). Skilled memory. In J. R. Anderson (Ed.), *Cognitive skills and their acquisition* (pp. 141–180). Hillsdale, NJ: Lawrence Erlbaum Associates.

Chase, W. G., & Ericsson, K. A. (1982). Skilled and working memory. In G. H. Bower (Ed.), *The psychology of learning and motivation* (Vol. 16, pp. 1–58). New York: Academic Press.

Chase, W. G., & Simon, H. A. (1973). Perception in chess. *Cognitive Psychology, 4*, 55–81.

Clarke, E. F. (1988). Generative principles in music performance. In J. A. Sloboda (Ed.), *Generative processes in music* (pp. 1–26). Oxford: Clarendon Press.

Clarke, E. (1995). Expression in performance: Generativity, perception and semiosis. In J. Rink (Ed.), *The practice of performance: Studies in musical interpretation* (pp. 21–54). Cambridge: Cambridge University Press.

Cooke, J. F. (1948). *How to memorize music*. Bryn Mawr, PA: Theodore Presser.

Cooke, J. F. (1999). *Great pianists on piano playing: Godowsky, Hofmann, Lhévinne, Paderewski and 24 other legendary performers.* Toronto: Dover. (originally published 1913, expanded edition published 1917)

Coon, H., & Carey, G. (1989). Genetic and environmental determinants of musical ability in twins. *Behavior Genetics, 19,* 183–193.

Crawford, M., & Chaffin, R. (1997). Cognition in social and cultural context. In P. J. Caplan, M. Crawford, J. S. Hyde, & J. Richardson, *Gender differences in cognition* (pp. 81–130). Oxford: Oxford University Press.

Crawford, M., & Kimmel, E. (1999). Promoting methodological diversity in feminist research. *Psychology of Women Quarterly, 23,* 1–6.

Crawford, M., & Marecek, J. (1989). Psychology reconstructs the female. *Psychology of Women Quarterly, 16,* 83–89.

Csikszentmihalyi, M., & Csikszentmihalyi, I. S. (1988). *Optimal experience: Psychological studies of flow in consciousness.* New York: Cambridge University Press.

Custodero, L. A. (2000). Engagement and experience: A model for the study of children's musical cognition. In C. Woods, G. Luck. R. Brochard, F. Seddon, & J. A. Sloboda (Eds.), *Proceedings of the sixth international conference on music perception and cognition* [CD]. Keele, UK: Keele University, Department of Psychology.

Davidson, J., & Eiholzer, H. (Eds.) (in press). *The music practioner: Exploring practices and research in the development of the expert music performer, teacher and listener.* London: Ashgate.

Dubal, D. (1997). *Reflections from the keyboard: The world of the concert pianist* (2nd ed.). New York: Schirmer.

Elder, D. (1986). *Pianists at play: Interviews, master lessons, and technical regimes.* London: Kahn & Averill.

Ericsson, K. A. (1985). Memory skill. *Canadian Journal of Psychology, 39,* 188–231.

Ericsson, K. A. (1997). Deliberate practice and the acquisition of expert performance: An overview. In H. Jorgensen & A. C. Lehmann (Eds.), *Does practice make perfect? Current theory and research on instrumental music practice* (pp. 89–108). Oslo, Norway: Norges Musikkoskole.

Ericsson, K. A. (1996). *The road to expert performance: Empirical evidence from the arts, sciences, sports, and games.* Mahwah, NJ: Lawrence Erlbaum Associates.

Ericsson, K. A., & Charness, N. (1994). Expert performance: Its structure and acquisition. *American Psychologist, 49,* 725–747.

Ericsson, K. A., & Faivre, I. A. (1988). What's exceptional about exceptional abilities? In L. K. Obler & D. Fein (Eds.), *The exceptional brain: Neuropsychology of talent and special abilities* (pp. 127–155). New York: Guilford Press.

Ericsson, K. A., & Kintsch, W. (1995). Long-term working memory. *Psychological Review, 102,* 211–245.

Ericsson, K. A., & Lehmann, A. (1996). Expert and exceptional performance: Evidence of maximal adaptation to task constraints. *Annual Review of Psychology, 47,* 273–305.

Ericsson, K. A., & Oliver, W. (1988). Methodology for laboratory research on thinking: Task selection, collection of observation and data analysis. In R. J.

Sternberg & E. E. Smith (Eds.), *The psychology of human thought* (pp. 392–428). Cambridge: Cambridge University Press.

Ericsson, K. A., & Oliver, W. L. (1989). A methodology for assessing the detailed structure of memory skills. In A. M. Colley & J. R. Beech (Eds.), *Acquisition and performance of cognitive skills* (pp. 193–215). Chichester: Wiley.

Ericsson, K. A., & Polson, P. G. (1988). An experimental analysis of a memory skill for dinner orders. *Journal of Experimental Psychology: Learning, Memory, & Cognition, 14,* 305–316.

Ericsson, K. A., & Simon, M. A. (1980). Verbal reports as data. *Psychological Review, 87,* 215–249.

Ericsson, K. A., & Smith, J. (1991). Prospects and limits of the empirical study of expertise: An introduction. In K. A. Ericsson & J. Smith (Eds.), *Toward a general theory of expertise: Prospects and limits* (pp. 1–37). Cambridge: Cambridge University Press.

Ericsson, K. A., Krampe, R. T., & Tesch-Römer, C. (1993). The role of deliberate practice in the acquisition of expert performance. *Psychological Review, 100,* 363–406.

Ewick, P. (1994). Integrating feminist epistemology in undergraduate research methods. *Gender & Society, 8,* 92–108.

Faurot, A. (1974). *Concerto Piano Repertoire: A manual of solo literature for artists and performers.* Metuchen, NJ: Scarecrow Press.

Fine, M., & Gordon, S. M. (1989). Feminist transformations of/despite psychology. In M. Crawford & M. Gentry (Eds.),*Gender and thought: Psychological perspectives* (pp. 146–174). New York: Springer Verlag.

Fischler, I., Rundus, D., & Atkinson, R. C. (1970). Effects of overt rehearsal procedures on free recall. *Psychonomic Science, 19,* 249–250.

Galton, F. (1979). *Hereditary genius: An inquiry into its laws and consequences.* London: Julian Friedman. (original work published 1869)

Gergen, K. J. (1985). The social constructionist movement in modern psychology. *American Psychologist, 40,* 266–275.

Gieseking, W., & Leimer, K. (1972). *Piano technique: Consisting of two complete books, "The shortest way to piano perfection" and "Rhythmics, dynamics, pedal and other problems of piano playing."* New York: Dover.

Gobet, F., & Simon, H. A. (1996a). Templates in chess memory: A mechanism for recalling several boards. *Cognitive Psychology, 31,* 1–40.

Gobet, F., & Simon, H. A. (1996b). The roles of recognition processes and look-ahead search in time-constrained expert problem solving: Evidence from grand-master-level chess. *Psychological Science, 7,* 52–55.

Green, B., & with Gallwey, T. (1986). *The inner game of music.* Garden City, NY: Anchor Press/Doubleday.

Gruson, L. M. (1988). Rehearsal skill and musical competence: Does practice make perfect? In J. A. Sloboda (Ed.), *Generative processes in music: Psychology, improvisation, and composition* (pp. 91–112). Oxford: Clarendon Press.

Hallam, S. (1994). Novice musicians' approaches to practice and performance. *Newsletter of the European Society for Cognitive Sciences of Music, 6,* 2–10.

Hallam, S. (1995a). Professional musicians' approaches to the learning and inter-pretation of music. *Psychology of Music, 23,* 111–128.

Hallam, S. (1995b). Professional musicians' orientation to practice: Implications for teaching. *British Journal of Music Education, 12,* 3–19.

Hallam, S. (1997a). Approaches to instrumental music practice of experts and novices: Implications for education. In H. Jorgensen & A. C. Lehmann (Eds.), *Does practice make perfect? Current theory and research on instrumental music practice* (pp. 89–109). Oslo, Norway: Norges Musikkoskole.

Hallam, S. (1997b). What do we know about practicing? Toward a model synthesiz-ing the research literature. In H. Jorgensen & A. C. Lehmann (Eds.), *Does practice make perfect? Current theory and research on instrumental music practice* (pp. 179–231). Oslo, Norway: Norges Musikkoskole.

Halpern, A. R., & Bower, G., H. (1982). Musical expertise and melodic structure in memory for musical notation. *American Journal of Psychology, 95,* 31–50.

Harding, S. (1991). *Whose science? Whose knowledge? Thinking from women's lives.* Ithaca: Cornell University Press.

Hayes, J. R. (1981). *The complete problem solver.* Philadelphia: Franklin Institute Press.

Hinson, M. (1987). *Guide to the pianist's repertoire* (2nd ed.). Bloomington: Indiana University Press.

Howe, M. J. A. (1990). *The origins of exceptional abilities.* Oxford: Blackwell.

Howe, M. J. A. (1996). The childhoods and early lives of geniuses: Combining psychological and biographical evidence. In K. A. Ericsson (Ed.), *The road to excellence: The acquisition of expert performance in the arts and sciences, sports, and games.* Mahwah, NJ: Lawrence Erlbaum Associates.

Howe, M. J. A., Davidson, J. W., & Sloboda, J. A. (1998). Innate talent: Reality or myth? *Behavioral and Brain Sciences, 21,* 399–442.

Hughes, E. (1915). Musical memory in piano playing and piano study. *Musical Quarterly, 1,* 592–603.

Imreh, G. (Pianist). (1996). *J.S. Bach* [CD]. New York: Connoisseur Society.

Imreh, G., & Chaffin, R. (1996/97). Understanding and developing musical mem-ory: The views of a concert pianist and a cognitive psychologist. *American Music Teacher, 46*(3), 20–24,67.

Kihlstrom, J. F. (1987). The cognitive unconscious. *Science, 237,* 1445–1452.

Kimmel, E., & Crawford, M. (Eds.). (1999). *Innovations in feminist psychological research.* Cambridge: Cambridge University Press.

Krampe, R. T. (1997). Age-related changes in practice activities and their relation to musical performance skills. In H. Jorgensen & A. C. Lehmann (Eds.), *Does practice make perfect? Current theory and research on instrumental music practice* (pp. 165–178). Oslo, Norway: Norges Musikkoskole.

Krampe, R. T., & Ericsson, K. A. (1996). Maintaining excellence: Deliberate practice and elite performance in young and older pianists. *Journal of Experimental Psychology: General, 25,* 331–359.

Landauer, T. K., & Dumais, S. T. (1997). A solution to Plato's problem: The latent semantic analysis theory of acquisition, induction, and representation of knowledge. *Psychological Review, 104,* 211–240.

Lehmann, A. C., & Ericsson, K. A. (1998). Preparation of a public piano performance: The relation between practice and performance. *Musicae Scientiae, 2*, 69–94.

Lehrer, P. A. (1988). Memorizing. *Artistry Journal, 1*, 29–33.

Mach, E. (1991). *Great contemporary pianists speak for themselves.* New York: Dover. (originally published in two volumes, 1980 and 1988)

Mandler, G., & Pearlstone, Z. (1966). Free and constrained concept learning and subsequent recall. *Journal of Verbal Learning and Verbal Behavior, 5*, 126–131.

Matthay, T. (1926). *On memorizing and playing from memory and on the laws of practice generally.* Oxford: Oxford University Press.

McHugh, M. D., Koeske, R. D., & Frieze, I. H. (1986). Issues to consider in conducting nonsexist psychological research: A guide for researchers. *American Psychologist, 41*, 879–890.

McPherson, G. E., & Renwick, J. (2000). Self-regulation and musical practice: A longitudinal study. In C. Woods, G. Luck, R. Brochard, F. Seddon, & J. A. Sloboda (Eds.), *Proceedings of the sixth international conference on music perception and cognition* [CD]. Keele, UK: Keele University, Department of Psychology.

Miklaszewski, K. (1989). A case study of a pianist preparing a musical performance. *Psychology of Music, 17*, 95–109.

Miklaszewski, K. (1995). Individual differences in preparing a musical composition for public performance. In *Psychology of music today: Proceedings of the international seminar of researchers and lecturers in the psychology of music* (pp. 138–147). Warsaw: Fryderyk Chopin Academy of Music.

Miller, G. A. (1956). The magical number seven, plus or minus two: Some limits on our capacity for processing information. *Psychological Review, 63*, 81–97.

Miller, G. A., Galanter, E., & Pribram, K. H. (1960). *Plans and the structure of behavior.* New York: Holt, Rinehart, Winston.

Murdock, B. J. (1960). The distinctiveness of stimuli. *Psychological Review, 67*, 16–31.

Neisser, U. (1976). *Cognition and reality.* San Francisco: Freeman.

Neisser, U. (1982). John Dean's memory: A case study. In U. Neisser (Ed.), *Memory observed: Remembering in natural contexts* (pp. 139–159). San Francisco: W.H. Freeman.

Nersessian, N. (1992). How do scientists think? Capturing the dynamics of conceptual change in science. In R. Giere (Ed.), *Cognitive models of science* (pp. 3–44). Minneapolis: University of Minnesota Press.

Nielsen, S. G. (1997). A case study of a church organ student preparing a musical work for performance. In H. Jorgensen & A. C. Lehmann (Eds.), *Does practice make perfect? Current theory and research on instrumental music practice* (pp. 109–122). Oslo, Norway: Norges Musikkoskole.

Nielsen, S. G. (2000). Self-regulated use of learning strategies in instrumental practice. In C. Woods, G. Luck, R. Brochard, F. Seddon, & J. A. Sloboda (Eds.), *Proceedings of the sixth international conference on music perception and cognition* [CD]. Keele, UK: Keele University, Department of Psychology.

Nisbett, R. E., & Wilson T. D. (1977). Telling more than we can know: Verbal reports on mental processes. *Psychological Review, 84*, 231–259.

Noice, H. (1991). The role of explanations and plan recognition in the learning of theatrical scripts. *Cognitive Science, 15*, 425–460.

Noice, H. (1992). Elaborative memory strategies of professional actors. *Applied Cognitive Psychology, 6,* 417–427.

Noice, H., & Noice, T. (1993). The effects of segmentation on the recall of theatrical material. *Poetics, 22,* 51–67.

Noyle, L. J. (Ed.). (1987). *Pianists on piano playing: Interviews with twelve concert pianists.* Metuchen, NJ: Scarecrow.

Peplau, L. A., & Conrad, E. (1989). Beyond non-sexist research: The perils of feminist methods in psychology. *Psychology of Women Quarterly, 13,* 379–400.

Portugheis, A. (1993). Who's who of pianists: Martha Argerich talks to Alberto Portugheis. *Piano Journal, 14*(40), 5, 9–11.

Portugheis, A. (1996). Who's who of pianists: Lazar Berman talks to Alberto Portugheis. *Piano Journal, 17*(50), 11–13.

Potter, J. (1996). Discourse analysis and constructionist approaches: Theoretical background. In J.T.E. Richardson (Ed.), *Handbook of qualitative research methods for psychology and the social sciences.* Leicester: British Psychological Society.

Reisberg, D. (1997). *Cognition: Exploring the science of the mind.* New York: Norton.

Renwick, J., & McPherson, G. E. (2000). "I've got to do my scale first!": A case study of a novice's clarinet practice. In C. Woods, G. Luck, R. Brochard, F. Seddon, & J. A. Sloboda (Eds.), *Proceedings of the sixth international conference on music perception and cognition*[CD]. Keele, UK: Keele University, Department of Psychology.

Repp, B. H. (1992). Diversity and commonality in music performance: An analysis of timing microstructure in Schumann's *Träumerei. Journal of the Acoustical Society of America, 92,* 2546–2568.

Repp, B. H. (1998). A microcosm of musical expression: I. Quantitative analysis of pianists' timing in the initial measures of Chopin's Etude in E major. *Journal of the Acoustical Society of America, 104,* 1085–1100.

Roediger, H. L. III., & Crowder, R. C. (1976). A serial position effect in recall of United States Presidents. *Bulletin of the Psychonomic Society, 8,* 275–278.

Rubinstein, B. (1950). *The pianist's approach to sight-reading and memorizing.* New York: Carl Fisher Inc.

Rundus, D. (1971). Analysis of rehearsal processes in free recall. *Journal of Experimental Psychology, 89,* 63–77.

Salmon, P. G., & Meyer, R. G. (1992). *Notes from the green room: Coping with stress and anxiety in musical performance.* New York: Lexington Books.

Sandor, G. (1981). *On piano playing: Motion, sound, expression.* New York: Schirmer.

Searleman, A., & Herrmann, D. (1994). *Memory from a broader perspective.* New York: McGraw-Hill.

Sears, D. O. (1986). College sophomores in the laboratory: Influences of a narrow data base on social psychology. *Journal of Personality and Social Psychology, 51,* 515–530.

Shaffer, L. H. (1976). Intention and performance. *Psychological Review, 83,* 375–393.

Shaffer, L. H. (1981). Performances of Chopin, Bach and Bartok: Studies in motor programming. *Cognitive Psychology, 13,* 327–376.

Shaffer, L. H. (1996). Musical performance as interpretation. *Psychology of Music, 23,* 17–38.

Shockley, R. (1986). A new approach to memorization. *Clavier, July-August,* 20–23.

Simonton, D. K. (1991). Emergence and realization of genius: The lives and works of 120 classical composers. *Journal of Personality and Social Psychology, 61,* 829–840.

Simonton, D. K. (1999). Talent and its development: An emergenic and epigentic model. *Psychological Review, 106,* 435–457.

Simonton, D. K. (2001). Talent development as a multidimensional, multiplicative, and dynamic process. *Current Directions in Psychological Science, 10,* 39–43.

Sloboda, J. A. (1985). *The musical mind.* Oxford: Clarendon.

Sloboda, J. A. (1996). The acquisition of musical performance expertise: Deconstructing the "talent" account of individual differences in musical expressivity. In K. A. Ericsson (Ed.), *The road to excellence: The acquisition of expert performance in the arts and sciences, sports, and games.* Mahwah, NJ: Lawrence Erlbaum Associates.

Sloboda, J. A., Clarke, E. F., Parncutt, R., & Raekallio, M. (1998). Determinants of finger choice in piano sight-reading. *Journal of Experimental Psychology: Human Perception and Performance, 24,* 185–203.

Sloboda, J. A., Davidson, J. W., Howe, M. J. A., & Moore, D. G. (1996). The role of practice in the development of performing musicians. *British Journal of Psychology, 87,* 287–309.

Sloboda, J. A., Hermelin, B., & O'Connor, N. (1985). An exceptional musical memory. *Music Perception, 3,* 155–170.

Snyder, B. (2000). *Music and memory: An introduction.* Cambridge MA: MIT Press.

Soldan, K. (Ed.). (1937). Italienisches Konzert. In *J.S. Bach, Klavierubung II. Teil, Nr. 4464* (pp. 12–18). New York: C.F. Peters Corporation.

Sosniak, L. A. (1985). Learning to be a concert pianist. In B. S. Bloom (Ed.), *Developing talent in young people* (pp. 18–67). New York: Ballantine.

Staszewski, J. J. (1988). Skilled memory and expert calculation. In M. T. H. Chi, R. Glaser, & M. J. Farr (Eds.), *The nature of expertise.* Hillsdale, NJ: Lawrence Erlbaum Associates.

Thompson, C. P., Cowan, T. M., & Frieman, J. (1993). *Memory search by a memorist.* Hillsdale, NJ: Lawrence Erlbaum Associates.

Tulving, E. (1962). Subjective organization in free recall of "unrelated" words. *Psychological Review, 69,* 344–354.

Wegner, D. M., & Vallacher, R. R. (1986). Action identification. In R. M. Sorrentino & T. E. Higgins (Eds.), *Handbook of motivation and cognition: Foundations of social behavior* (pp. 550–582). New York: Guilford.

Williamon, A. (1999). *Preparing for performance: An examination of musical practice as a function of expertise.* Unpublished Dissertation, University of London.

Williamon, A. (2002). Memorizing music. In J. Rink (Ed.), *Musical performance: A guide to study and practice.* Cambridge: Cambridge University Press.

Williamon, A., & Valentine, E. (2000). Quantity and quality of musical practice as predictors of performance quality. *British Journal of Psychology, 91,* 353–376.

Williamon, A., & Valentine, E. (2002). The role of retrieval structures in memorizing music. *Cognitive Psychology, 44,* 1–32.

Winner, E. (1996a). *Gifted children: Myths and realities.* New York: Basic Books.

Winner, E. (1996b). The rage to master: The decisive role of talent in the visual arts. In K. A. Ericsson (Ed.), *The road to excellence: The acquisition of expert performance in the arts and sciences, sports, and games*. Mahwah, NJ: Lawrence Erlbaum Associates.

Zilberquit, M. (1983). *Russia's great pianists*. Neptune, NJ: TFH Publications.

Author Index

Subject Index